The Universal Translator

Everything you need to know about
139 languages that don't really exist

YENS WAHLGREN

This English language edition first published 2021

First published in Swedish by Volante Förlag in 2015
This edition published by agreement with the Kontext Agency
The cost of this translation was defrayed by a subsidy from the Swedish Arts Council,
gratefully acknowledged

The History Press
97 St George's Place, Cheltenham,
Gloucestershire, GL50 3QB
www.thehistorypress.co.uk

British Library Cataloguing in Publication Data.
A catalogue record for this book is available from the British Library.

ISBN 978 0 7509 9320 3

Typesetting and origination by The History Press
Printed and bound in Great Britain by TJ Books Limited, Padstow, Cornwall

Trees for LYfe

Contents

Introduction

It begins on the changing table. '**Da-da, goo-goo**' – a little baby looks with curiosity and delight at the new world revealed to them after nine months of darkness and tries to name everything using their own invented language. This is not unlike Adam in the Bible, who names all living things with his own made-up language, the Adamic language, which many people throughout history have regarded as a divine protolanguage conveying the true name and essence of all things. But really, the first invented language probably wasn't much more advanced than a curious '**da-da**' and '**goo-goo**'.

Just as a baby soon applies systems and structure to their language – incomprehensible though it may be for anyone other than the child and their closest family – it didn't take long for the first humans to become more systematic in their communication. It is very possible that language originated among a small group of individuals early on in human history and then spread throughout the world with human migration.

After the baby babble stage, many of us continue to concoct our own languages. I remember talking and singing in made-up English when I was little. Before I could read for real, I remember reading aloud in my own secret language and pretending to write before I could write. In primary school, my friends and I were fascinated by the Smurfs and spoke to each other in Smurf language. I remember to this day how thrilled we were when we actually managed to understand each other. I also remember the frustration of being unable to crack the code of the Robber Language (think a Swedish equivalent to Pig Latin, invented by the author Astrid Lindgren) that the girls in our class seemed able to converse in fluently.

After primary school came middle and high schools, and I made new linguistic acquaintances: the language of the great apes in *Tarzan*, Elvish in J.R.R. Tolkien's books, and the alien languages in *Star Wars* and *Dune*; the secret runic alphabet I developed during a two-week holiday in Sicily but never used; and of course the Latin used by the pirates in the *Asterix* comics, which is still all the Latin I know.

Other than Latin, the languages that fascinated me most in childhood were invented. Languages that had no purpose beyond adding flavour and depth to literature and films. Languages that could hardly be used for communication. Languages you couldn't study at a language school in Brighton in the summer holidays.

My interest in artificial languages continued into adulthood and I began to study them more systematically. This book is the result. My interest has also given rise to a number of articles and academic essays on the extraterrestrial language Klingon; I like to say I have a BA in Klingon.

I have also discovered that I am far from alone in my fascination with artificial languages. People have always invented languages, for their own amusement, for political, religious, social or aesthetic reasons. Many have sought the 'perfect language' and tried to construct a means of communication that is more precise, logical or beautiful – in other words, better – than natural languages. English, Swedish, French – indeed, most of the nearly 7,000 living languages we know of – have evolved over millennia and are not consistent, logical or regular. What's more, change tends to evoke strong feelings in most people.

Just take the word 'they', to mean a singular person of undefined gender. Is this new use of the word a grammatical abomination or a natural solution to fill a gap in the English language? I would imagine that my readers' opinions differ on this subject. But it is precisely this type of change that has been the driving force behind many people's attempts to create 'better' languages. That is, the creator's subjective idea of what makes a language 'better'. Most of the hundreds of supposedly perfect, world-enhancing languages invented have been ideal according to their creators alone, and have never actually reached a larger audience. But that's good enough, isn't it? A handful have reached a wider audience – the most noteworthy example being Esperanto.

The name Esperanto means 'hope' and the language was created with the intention of spreading peace and international understanding. Inventor Ludwig Zamenhof fantasised that one day everyone in the world would have Esperanto as a second language, and therefore be able to communicate via a neutral language that was not native to anyone in particular. Nowadays, there actually are native speakers. It is estimated that around 1,000 people were raised speaking Esperanto, and so in practice it has become a natural language. It is also estimated that 200,000–300,000 people speak Esperanto fluently and up to 2 million speak it to a reasonable degree.

There has been similar development in two other constructed languages: Hebrew and Norwegian. Yes, you read that correctly. Both modern Hebrew and Norwegian are constructed languages.

Modern Hebrew originated in Palestine in the 1890s when Jewish immigrants decided to revive Hebrew as an oral language. For many centuries, Hebrew had not been spoken day to day and was used only in ritual. The initiator of this endeavour was Eliezer Ben-Yehuda, who raised his children speaking Hebrew. In order for the ancient Hebrew of the Torah to be used as a spoken language, a lot had to be added and changed in terms of vocabulary, grammar and pronunciation – essentially constructing a language.

In the 1840s, the father of Nynorsk, or New Norwegian, Ivar Aasen, constructed the modern tongue from medieval Norwegian, with a review and systematisation of the western Norwegian dialects and the introduction of a new standard of written language. Naturally, if Norway was going to be a nation, it needed a proper language of its own.

This sort of development is taking place continually in most languages, although to a lesser degree. Existing languages go through overhauls with spelling reforms, the addition of loan words or the creation of new words, such as 'selfie' or 'mansplain'. Incorporating loan words, new words or slang into the standard lexicon can cause some people, often older generations, to protest loudly. But what some consider to be the downfall and degeneration of language is simply natural development.

International auxiliary languages, logically perfect languages, pidgin and other semi-planned, semi-natural languages are all fascinating, but these are not the constructed languages that this book is about. This book is about the fantastical languages we encounter in popular culture: languages created for artistic reasons, or sometimes simply as background props. They are often called artlangs, short for 'artistic languages', a term that originated in the conlang movement. Similarly, conlang is simply shorthand for 'constructed languages'. People who count language creation as a hobby, whatever the purpose of the language might be, are thus called conlangers.

Over 100 languages are mentioned in this book and, unsurprisingly, most originate from the genres commonly known as science fiction or fantasy – that is, stories that take place in alien worlds and different epochs. Just as a newborn infant and the biblical Adam feel an unstoppable urge to name all the new things they see in the world, an author must name everything in the strange world that emerges through their story. What do you call the blue sea creature with wings, a beak and moose antlers? How do people speak in the future? How has language changed in 40,000 years? How do two-headed Martians think and speak? Is centaur language neigh-based? Won't cinema-goers find it strange if the protagonist lands on an extraterrestrial planet and its inhabitants start speaking English?

Most authors solve these issues simply by describing the phenomena in their native language, but sometimes the more linguistically inclined prefer not to take these shortcuts. In Anthony Burgess' *A Clockwork Orange*, readers pick up the slang as they go along. George Orwell's Newspeak in *1984* has coined new words – not least the word 'Newspeak' itself. In the novel, the language represents an attempt to deprive people of any words to express critical thought. In her books, Suzette Haden Elgin has explored how a feminist-constructed language, Láadan, would differ from the languages of our reality. The difference between extraterrestrial and human languages is an issue many writers and filmmakers have had to contend with.

Sci-fi literature is the ideal testing ground for the linguistic relativity principle, or Sapir–Whorf hypothesis, which states that the grammar and vocabulary of each language contains an in-built world view that defines the way its speakers think. This hypothesis, named after linguists Edward Sapir and Benjamin Lee Whorf, is somewhat outdated today and controversial in linguistic circles, to put it mildly. However, most people can recognise the often embarrassing mistakes that occur when people speak a second language but continue to think in their mother tongue. But within science fiction and fantasy this hypothesis continues to be useful because they are genres with the capacity for more complex examples than reality allows: intelligent space insects – how do they think and speak? Can they make themselves understood to humans at all?

So, it doesn't take a great deal of imagination to understand why writers and filmmakers strive to make their stories and worlds more credible through the construction of languages. But why do so many people spend their time exploring and studying the languages of these extraterrestrial and fantastical creatures? Indeed, many people learn to read, write and speak them.

If you are going to study a language, why not learn one you can actually use like Chinese, Arabic or French? Many would posit that even Latin, Ancient Greek, Sanskrit, Ancient Egyptian or any other classical dead language would be better, which is to say more useful. Because although these classical languages are extinct and not easily used for communication, many claim that they have intrinsic value. A certain lofty beauty and refinement is attributed to these major ancient languages, endowing anyone who masters them with an air of culture and intelligence. The same cannot be said for artificial alien languages.

It also makes sense to study Latin, Ancient Greek and Sanskrit, for example, because a great deal of vocabulary in our modern languages originates from these classical tongues. The study of artlangs cannot compare in this respect either, although many of them are rooted in both modern and classical languages and thus display similarities.

But perhaps the most important argument for studying the languages of sophisticated ancient societies is that they give access to the history and folklore of bygone cultures. By learning their language and studying their texts, we can gain insight into the way of thinking of a particular writer who lived 3,000 years ago. Mastering a language can give access to the world view of a remote culture.

To a lesser degree, we can say the same of fictitious languages in popular culture. They allow us to tune into an author's mindset as well as into a strange alien culture. The extraterrestrial languages of *Star Trek*, *Avatar*, *Dune* and *Stargate* are by no means just random sounds thrown together; they are carefully developed to reveal aspects of the beings that speak them.

The *Star Trek* language Klingon was specifically created to correspond to the portrayal of the fictional extraterrestrial Klingon race in the TV series. Its grammar and range of sounds give a deeper insight into the culture and outlook of these fictional beings. The language contains elements and combinations not found in any existing terrestrial language, therefore giving its speakers a glimpse into an 'alien' way of thinking.

Are Tolkien's books meaningful if the reader has no understanding of the various Elvish tongues? Can they be understood without this knowledge? Syldavian and Arumbaya in *The Adventures of Tintin* say a lot about their author, Hergé, and add another dimension to the exploits of the eternally youthful Belgian journalist. What can be read between the lines by knowing the origin of the languages spoken in *Dune* or the Disney movie *Atlantis*?

To some extent, the answer to the question of why people study artificial languages is simply because it provides a deeper insight into the literary or cinematic works that birthed them. It is the quest to know everything about one's passion. Perhaps a similarity can be drawn between conlang enthusiasts and people who are not content to simply admire the beauty of their favourite artist's work, but instead choose to study the progression of brush strokes or colour palettes throughout their career, or experts interested in whether or not the nails and padding in a Gustavian chair are original. It gives added value to simple statements about the chair being attractive to look at and comfortable to sit on.

If you think about it, asking someone *why* they study an artificial language is about as arbitrary as asking someone why they enjoy poetry or music. Or, for that matter, to ask someone why they read fiction when there is such a thing as non-fiction. And why do people watch football anyway?

I cannot deny that artificial languages are something of a nerdy niche. Not everyone feels the urge to write poetry in

Quenya or Huttese, or make an animation with Lego figures performing *Fiddler on the Roof* in Klingon (search for lurDech on YouTube – you won't regret it!). But when it comes down to it, language is an interest we all share and that affects us all, adults and children alike, from the moment you first define the world around you with your own invented language as an infant.

Foreign languages – dead, alive or constructed – open a window to something new. This book is not a grammar guide or a dictionary, but a journey of discovery through worlds and universes created by the imagination. In order to understand these worlds and universes, we need to understand their languages. The motto of the Klingon Language Institute (KLI) is '**qo'mey poSmoH Hol**' – 'Language opens worlds'. This is exactly what I hope *The Universal Translator* will do: deepen our understanding of supposedly familiar literary worlds, and open up new worlds, unknown and waiting to be discovered.

Artificial Languages Throughout History

STARTING WITH THE ANCIENT GREEKS – OBVIOUSLY

Goídelc, Lingua Ignota, Balaibalan, Enochian, Utopian, Ringuam Albaras, Moonspeak, Lilliputian, Houyhnhnm, Nazarian, Quamite, Volapük, Esperanto, Solresol

---

'**I artamane Xarxas apiaona satra**' is the first known phrase of an artificial language in literature. It was the opening line from the King of Persia's minister, Pseudartabas, in what was supposed to be made-up Persian in Aristophanes' comedy *The Acharnians*, from 425 BCE. The response to the aforementioned line was, 'Does anyone understand what he is saying?' Fortunately, someone present does understand Pseudartabas and lets us know that this introductory sentence means – 'The great King is going to send you gold.'

Aristophanes understood the subtle art of using an artificial language to give the audience a sense of foreignness. Some years later in his comedies *The Birds* and *The Frogs*, he uses both a bird language and a frog language. Of the forty comedies he wrote, only eleven have been preserved, so who knows how many artificial languages may have been lost? Several well-known phrases are also attributed to Aristophanes, such as, 'These impossible women! How they do get around us! The poet was right: We cannot live with them, and we cannot live without them.'

No more examples of constructed languages have survived from antiquity, but naturally the great thinkers of Ancient Greece mused upon linguistic–philosophical questions. In the dialogue *Cratylus*, Plato ponders the connection between things and their names – is it arbitrary, or is there a natural, essential relationship? Is there a natural connection between a word and what it signifies?

Another Greek author, Athenaeus, who was active in the third century CE, approached the phenomenon of artificial languages in his mammoth work, *Deipnosophistae*. He tells the story of a man from Sicily, Dionysius, who invents his own words for invariably Greek concepts.

English	Greek	Neologism
Virgin	*parthenos*	**menandros** (*menei* – wait; *andra* – husband)
Spear	*akontion*	**ballantion** (*balletai enantion* – 'to throw at someone')

These examples of neologisms – new words – are probably not a rigorous attempt to build a new language, but rather a playful demonstration that alternatives to familiar words are possible.

The first mention of the concept of an artificial language appears in the Old Irish manuscript, *Auraicept na n-Éces*, written mainly in the 1300s but with some sections estimated to date as far back as the seventh century. It tells of the learned Scythian King Fénius Farsaid, great-grandson of Noak, who came to the Tower of Babel to study the great language confusion shortly after it arose. He brought with him seventy-two scholars whom he sent out on a mission to study how the only language previously spoken had been divided into different languages. The scholars scattered in all directions, while Fénius established a headquarters at Nimrod's tower to co-ordinate the work. For ten years, Fénius and the seventy-two scholars studied and compiled an artificial language, Bérla tóbaide – 'the selected language' – based on the best parts of each of the confused tongues. Fénius named his conlang Goídelc (Gaelic). A particular kind of Irish hubris, perhaps, that the legendary Fénius took on the godlike task of creating a language, as well as supposedly joining together what God had divided!

According to legend, Fénius also created, or possibly discovered, the perfect script for his new perfect language. He named the twenty-five letters after the twenty-five prime scholars of the seventy-two he had brought with him. However, Ogham is an alphabet from the early Middle Ages, mainly used in the Irish-language area. Its origins are not entirely clear, but it is unlikely to have been created by Fénius. Ogham is also called the Celtic tree alphabet because the letters are named after types of trees, and not after twenty-five scholars, as the legend would have it.

Fénius' grandson, Goídel Glas (who composed Goídelc, according to some versions of the legend) then married Scota, a pharaoh's daughter. After the pharaoh and his army were drowned by Moses in the Red Sea, the lovers fled and ended up in Spain. From a tower in Spain, Goídel Glas saw a beautiful green island, which turned out to be Ireland, where they eventually settled.

Lingua Ignota

In the twelfth century, we see clearer evidence of, and more than just individual sentences from, an artificial language. Hildegard of Bingen (1098–1179) could be the patron saint of conlangs. Canonised in 2012, she is also known as Saint Hildegard. Her constructed language, Lingua Ignota, was not the reason behind her canonisation; that was her life's work as a nun, abbess, philosopher, mystic and physician.

Why Hildegard invented her own language and what she planned to do with it is a mystery. Since she was an abbess at a monastery in Rupertsberg, it seems fair to speculate that it was a mystical language for religious use. Or a secret language for her diary?

She described parts of the language in *Lingua Ignota per simplicem hominem Hildegardem prolata*, which has been preserved in two manuscripts. This document lists 1,011 words of her artificial language with explanations in Latin and sometimes German. It seems that these words are used with grammar borrowed from Latin. The only snippet that has been preserved is a Latin sentence interspersed with words in Lingua Ignota:

> *O* **orzchis** Ecclesia, armis divinis praecincta, et hyacinto ornata, *tu es* **caldemia** *stigmatum* **loifolum** *et urbs scienciarum. O, o tu es etiam* **crizanta** *in alto sono, et es* **chorzta** gemma.

> Oh **orzchis** church, girded with divine arms, and adorned with hyacinth, you are **caldemias** of **loifolum** wounds, and the city of the sciences. Oh, oh, you are **crizanta** in loud noise, and you are **chorzta** the jewel.

Unfortunately, only one of the words, **loifol** – 'people', appears in the glossary, which originally was probably more extensive than the 1,011 words that have been preserved. The glossary is arranged hierarchically, starting with the divine, then moving on to humans and animals and, lastly, things:

aigonz – God
aieganz – angel
diueliz – devil
inimois – human
jur – man

vanix – woman
peueriz – father
maiz – mother
limzkil – child
luschia – duck
sizia – beetroot
libizamanz – book

The Voynich Manuscript

The history of artificial languages doesn't get much more intriguing than the case of a fifteenth-century manuscript discovered by a bookseller in 1912. It was written in an unknown language with an unknown script by an unknown author. The 240 pages of the manuscript depict unidentified constellations, mysterious plants, bathing women, astrological tables and long pieces of beautiful but incomprehensible text. Absolutely incomprehensible. Linguists and code crackers have been trying in vain to solve the mystery for over a century.

The first to try to solve the riddle was bookseller Wilfrid Voynich, who had dedicated his life to the search for unusual literature. In Villa Mondragone, Italy – one of the many mansions of the Jesuit order – in a chest packed with ancient, dusty volumes, he made the greatest discovery of his life with the eponymous manuscript. Voynich bought it from the Jesuit monks and devoted the rest of his life to trying to interpret the text. When he died in 1930, he had still not been able to decipher a single word.

Since then, linguists, cryptologists, occultists and various wannabe geniuses have tried to solve the mystery. Theories differ: a fifteenth-century prank; fake magic intended to impress people; or indeed some kind of written language. Voynich was also suspected of forging the manuscript himself as a cry for attention (or being deceived by a forger), but all sorts of expertise has gone into analysis of the book, including carbon dating, which placed its origin somewhere between 1404 and 1438. The book is genuine.

The document is written on vellum (calfskin) and consists of 240 pages containing 170,000 characters. A letter dated 1666 came with the manuscript, from Jan Marek Marci of Kronland, Rector of the Charles University in Prague at the time, to Jesuit scholar Athanasius Kircher of Rome. When asked to decipher the manuscript, Kircher discovered that it was once purchased by Emperor Rudolf II of Bohemia (1552–1612) for 600 gold ducats in the belief that it was an undiscovered work by the English Franciscan friar Roger Bacon, the genius polymath who predicted the invention of guns, aircraft, the telescope and the microscope. Could this be Bacon's great encyclopedia of the sum of all knowledge?

There has also been speculation as to whether it is simply a conlang – an artificial language – perhaps for no other reason than to satisfy the author's aesthetic taste for linguistics. William F. Friedman, one of the world's foremost cryptologists who cracked the Japanese code during the Second World War, concluded that it was an artificial language after he and a group of cryptoanalysts failed to interpret the document. It must have been the only code that Friedman didn't manage to crack.

But the most common theory is that it is a cipher. The language/script has been analysed in every conceivable way, and it does appear to be structured like a real language, not just random scrawls of decorative characters. The words are, on average, four to five characters long, which is consistent with many European languages. However, there are almost no character sequences with fewer than three or more than ten characters, which does not correspond to Western languages.

When experts examined the frequency of different characters, they saw that they follow a pattern comparable to those of natural languages, but some are arranged in an unnatural way within the words. Different pages in the manuscript are devoted to different subject areas and, quite logically, specific words appear more frequently on these pages than others. On the other hand, there are oddities, such as a specific sequence being repeated three, four or five times in a row on other pages.

Many literary works have been inspired by the enigma of the Voynich manuscript: thriller novels such as *Codex* by Lev Grossman; an orchestral piece by Hanspeter Kyburz; and the computer game *Assassin's Creed IV: Black Flag*, where players have to gather pages from it. In the game, the manuscript originated from an alien race that created humankind before becoming extinct.

A modern-day successor, Luigi Serafini, published *Codex Seraphinianus* in the 1970s – a mammoth work in two volumes containing strange drawings of flora and fauna, written in an unknown language with an unknown script …

Balaibalan

Another language whose origin and function is as mysterious as the Lingua Ignota is Balaibalan from the sixteenth century. It was likely created by a Turkish gentleman by the name of Muhyî-i Gülşenî (1528–1605). He was a member of a Sufi order founded by the Kurdish Sheikh Pir Ibrâhim Gülşenî, which has given rise to speculation that the language has mystical, spiritual undertones. It has also been hypothesised that several people were involved in its creation and the vocabulary may have been developed as a collective effort.

Another theory posits that it was an early attempt at an international auxiliary language for the Muslim world. Balaibalan features aspects of the three major Islamic languages of the time: Turkish, Persian and Arabic, belonging to the Altaic, Indo-European and Semitic language families, respectively. However, the case against the theory of Balaibalan being intended as an auxiliary language is that it was largely incomprehensible to speakers of all three languages.

It is an a priori language, meaning most of the vocabulary is not based on any existing lexicon. Some of the 4,000 words show similarities with Arabic or other languages, while some words seem to originate from metaphors used in Persian and Turkish poetry.

The numerals **ad**, **baz**, **jal**, **dom** and **han** were chosen so that the first letter corresponds to the original Arabic alphabet (a, b, j, d, h). Perhaps the language was used specifically for poetry.

Two copies of the Balaibalan dictionary (Dātayvakšāv aḥātaybakšā) have been preserved, one in Paris and one at Princeton University in the United States. There was a third copy in Baghdad, but it has been lost. No significant corpora have been preserved, so the spread of the language has been limited. Balaibalan was written in a variation on the Arabic script used in the Ottoman Empire, which also included letters from Turkish and Persian. Grammatically, Balaibalan resembles Arabic, but word formation is agglutinative – prefixes and suffixes are added to a short root word, as in Turkish.

The name of the language is itself a good example – **bāl-a-ibal-an**: **bāl** – 'language'; **a** – 'of'; **I** – (definite article); **bal** – 'bring to life'; **an** – (participle). So: 'the language of that which gives life' – 'God's language'.

Let's take another example using the verb 'to know':

> **bar** – knows
> **baram** – to know
> **baras** – he knew
> **barar** – he knows

Add the prefix **ki-**, which marks a place name, to **bar** ('knows'), and it becomes **kibar** – 'school', or 'place for knowledge'. Adding **-nak** to the end of a word indicates that something is 'in abundance', so **barnak** is a 'wise old man or woman' – someone with an abundance of knowledge.

Balaibalan is also interesting because, unlike most well-known artlangs, it originated outside Western culture. Assuming that Muhyî-i Gülşenî was the creator of the language, this dates its origin to the 1580s or thereabouts. There is a note in one of the manuscripts that suggests this is the case, plus the language came about at the same time as another language with mysterious, magical purposes. The language of the angels themselves …

Enochian

In the 1580s, British mathematician, astronomer, astrologer and court magician (to name but a few professional titles) John Dee began a project with spirit medium Edward Kelley in which they attempted to establish continuous contact with angels. Through this work, Dee learned Angelical, or Enochian. This is the language that God used when he created the world and that Adam and Eve spoke before the Fall. When they were banished from paradise, they forgot most of it and began to speak a watered-down version of Enochian, which became a kind of proto-Hebrew. Proto-Hebrew was then the spoken language until the great language confusion caused by the Tower of Babel.

Ever since Adam was banished from the Garden of Eden, the Patriarch Enoch was the only person to learn Angelical until 26 March 1583, when John Dee and Edward Kelley began receiving lessons in the language – via mirrors and crystal balls. First, Kelley had a vision of the special twenty-one-letter alphabet, written from right to left, which allowed the angel Nalvage to bash out the first text a few days later, backwards, in Enochian (the English translation was found on pieces of paper that came out of the angel's mouth):

Ol sonf vors g, goho Iad Balt, lonsh calz vonpho; sobra zol ror I ta nazps od graa ta malprg; ds holq qaa nothoa zimz, od commah ta nobloh zien; soba thil gnonp …

This is from the introduction of an invocation believed to have been used for magical purposes. In the nineteenth century, Samuel Liddell MacGregor Mathers and Aleister Crowley, in the occult society the Hermetic Order of the Golden Dawn, took up the baton and developed a system of magic that they named after Enoch and in which Enochian was used as the magical language.

Some are unimpressed by the Angelical language and believe that Enochian is either simply speaking in tongues with no significance, or some sort of code for English. John Dee and his spiritualist colleague Edward Kelley, who was a well-known forger, were also suspected of being behind the Voynich manuscript. Dee was the foremost Bacon expert of his time, and Dee and Kelley sold the manuscript to Emperor Rudolf II, King of Bohemia, on a visit to Prague in the 1580s, convincing him that it was the work of Roger Bacon. However, their possible involvement with the Voynich manuscript is mostly based on circumstantial evidence and speculation.

Utopian

Thomas More's 1516 dialogue *Utopia* belongs to the great classics of Renaissance literature. Perhaps More wasn't the first to write about ideal states and utopian societies, but his work gave rise to the concept of utopian – and, indirectly, dystopian – literature. In fact, the word 'utopia' is derived from Greek and means 'nowhere'.

Utopia parodies contemporary travelogues and harks back to Plato's *Republic*, but also depicts a radical social utopia, foretelling the idealistic egalitarianism of socialism and communism in the distant future. The land of Utopia is an island republic where all property is common. The inhabitants, called Utopians, have a six-hour working day. Utopia enforces a labour rotation, whereby every urban resident must work in agriculture for two years of their lifetime. But a lot of the heavy labour requires slaves and prisoners of war …

Thomas More also gives examples of the language spoken in Utopia and, with the help of his friend Peter Giles, he created a new alphabet consisting of geometric figures. The only longer text that exists in the language is a four-line poem, from which it is clear that Utopian was grammatically similar to Latin.

Raphael Hythlodaeus, the protagonist who narrates his stay in Utopia, believes that the language is related to Greek because the inhabitants seem to pick up Greek easily, but also thinks that many root words originate from Persian. The poem begins:

Vtopos ha Boccas peu la chama polta chamaan. Bargol he maglomi baccan ſoma gymnoſophaon.

Vtopos – Utopos (the legendary founder of the country)
boccas – leader
chama – island
bargol – the only
baccan – of all
gymnoſophaon – philosophy

François Rabelais picked up the artlang baton with *The Life of Gargantua and of Pantagruel*, the most famous work of the French Renaissance. Rabelais wrote the first of the five books in 1534. They are a collection of gathered references and quotes, sardonic satire, and coarse, crude jokes. Rabelais' aptitude for storytelling is boundless. It is no wonder that he gives examples of no fewer than three artificial languages in his books, one of which is a nod to Thomas More's *Utopia*, including one sentence actually in the Utopian language:

Agonou dont oussys vous desdagnez algorou: nou den farou zamist vous mariston ulbrou.

This foreign language is uttered when one of the main characters, the giant Pantagruel, meets the polyglot Panugre, who alternates between German, Italian, Scottish, Dutch, Spanish, Danish, Hebrew, Greek and Latin, not to mention French and three invented languages. Pantagruel can also identify the language of the exotic Antipodean people:

Albarildim gotfano dechmin brin alabo dordio falbroth ringuam albaras.

This is a language so difficult that 'the devil himself couldn't get his teeth into it'. **Ringuam albaras** may be an anagram of *linguam arabas* – 'the Arabic language'. Perhaps the Antipodean language is Rabelais' version of a pseudo-Arabic? I wouldn't like to speculate as to whether Harry Potter's creator, J.K. Rowling, has read Rabelais, but a certain Antipodean word brings to mind a character in her universe: **voldemoth**.

The Seventeenth-Century Languages of Logic

The seventeenth century saw the first major wave of artificial languages. But whereas previous creations had been of a religious, mystical or artistic nature, this new wave was more philosophical. These were languages based on the classification of ideas, some even attempting to encompass the sum of all human knowledge.

In the 1600s, after serving as the international language (lingua franca) for educated men in Europe for 1,000 years, Latin went into decline. Mathematics, philosophy and natural sciences, however, were on the rise. Thanks to the development of the printing press, books started being published in national languages, calling into question the prevalence of Latin, which was so irregular and difficult to learn. With the decline of Latin, international communication became more difficult.

What was needed was, quite simply, a better language. A more precise language. Maybe an artificial language could herald a return to the time before the Tower of Babel and the great confusion of tongues? Prior to the Fall, Adam had named all the animals, and a natural relationship was assumed to exist between the animals themselves and their given names. Surely, if academics put their minds to it, they should be able to recreate such a language.

During this time there was also great interest in the West for Chinese characters. The philosopher Francis Bacon considered these characters to be 'authentic' because they represent pure ideas as opposed to words or sounds. He noted that, for example, speakers of Mandarin and Cantonese who do not understand each other's spoken language do understand each other's written language. This gave rise to the hope that it might be possible to construct a language that, like the Adamic language, reveals the true name and essence of things. Seventeenth-century thinkers were generally of the opinion that languages simply stood in the way of the things themselves.

A very early science-fiction novel, Francis Godwin's *The Man in the Moone* from 1638, tells the story of how protagonist Gonsales flies to the moon with the help of swans. On the moon, giants live in a utopian society where a universal moon language is used and understood by everyone. Inspired by a travelogue about China and its description of the Chinese languages, Godwin created a musical lunar language consisting of both words and tones. The vocabulary seems limited to Gonsales, but a variety of tones help to make different words.

Cyrano de Bergerac exhumes the melodic moon language in *A Voyage to the Moon* (1657). The hero of de Bergerac's sci-fi novel, *Dyrcona*, even meets Godwin's main character Gonsales.

As well as their spoken language, the lunar people of Godwin's novel have another form of expression consisting entirely of gestures and body language. Dyrcona later encounters the perfect language spoken on the sun and comes to a forest where the trees speak Greek, which they learned on Earth.

These and similar stories provided intellectual fodder for the objectives of the universal language project: the need for international communication and a precise, logical language.

Francis Lodwick was the first of at least sixteen thinkers with his common writing in the 1600s. There then followed, among others, Thomas Urquhart's Logopandecteision, Cave Beck's Universal Character, Joakim Becher's Linguarum Universali, George Dalgarno's Ars Signorum, Isaac Newton's Universal Language, Gottfried Leibniz's Clavis Universalis, and then it all culminated, so to speak, with John Wilkins' mammoth Philosophical Language.

Many took mathematical principles as their starting point so sentences could be built up like formulae. New writing systems were devised that could better, more logically, express true principles. Above all, they tried to organise the world and classify everything into strict hierarchies.

Just such a philosophical language was very extensively presented by John Wilkins in 1668 in a 600-page work. Wilkins divided all knowledge into forty major categories and many more subcategories denoted by various arbitrary syllables: for example, **da** – 'world', **de** – 'element', and **di** – 'stone'. A syllable can then be expanded to form subgroups for these basic concepts, such as **deb** – 'fire', and **debi** – 'lightning'. The word 'light' is not associated with fire or lightning but belongs to another category and is denoted by **bag**.

Any word beginning with 'z' signifies an animal. **Zi** identifies the genus (e.g. mammal), **zit** clarifies that it is a 'dog-like predator' and **zita** denotes the species 'dog'. And so on and so forth.

Wilkins classified the whole world according to his own logic. Everything is part of a hierarchy and you have to know the category to which a word belongs in order to translate it. Wilkins' a priori words don't *represent* a concept, they *define* the concept. The letters and syllables indicate the category and subcategory to which the word belongs. The word for 'salmon' – **zana** – tells us that it is a 'scaly river fish, with pinkish flesh'. The written language is based on the same principle: the characters are constructed with a similarly logical system, where dashes on letters denote the subcategories relating to the concept.

Most linguistic philosophers of the time made similar classifications, building up a lexicon of concepts and trying to find universal semantic categories in the world's languages. Wilkins' life work is undoubtedly impressive, but as was the case with other philosophical languages, it was very hard to learn and next to impossible to speak fluently.

The idea behind artlangs in the 1600s was to invent an international auxiliary language, but in practice it became mainly language for its own sake – early conlangs, published in a book somewhere and expressing little more than the author's views on logic and the world. Each one represented a linguistic utopia of its own, and none came close to surviving contact with reality.

Gulliver's Travels

Linguistic philosophers were probably mocked in their day, and Jonathan Swift's *Gulliver's Travels* (1726) certainly made fun of the attempts of scholarly gentlemen to create the perfect language. Lemuel Gulliver visits Lagado, capital of the flying island of Laputa, where he meets three professors at the university's Faculty of Languages who are eagerly discussing how to improve the native language. Their proposal is to condense speech by turning polysyllabic words monosyllabic, and omitting all verbs and particles because everything one can think of is, in fact, a noun. Another suggestion is to abolish words altogether in an effort to shorten conversations, which would be kinder on the lungs, among other things. Since words are really just the names of objects, it would be more appropriate for everyone to simply carry the items in question around with them instead of using words. If a person wants to say something, they need only show the object in question. The downside is that everyone would have to carry around a large pack of objects in order to have a conversation.

This sterling idea would surely have become a reality, 'If the women, in conjunction with the vulgar and illiterate, had not threatened to raise a rebellion, unless they might be allowed the liberty to speak with their tongues, after the manner of their forefathers; such constant irreconcilable enemies to science are the common people'.

On his travels to fantastical places, Gulliver encounters more strange languages which Swift exemplifies with a few phrases here and there. The Lilliputians in Lilliput (the word 'Lilliputian' comes from Swift's invented land) call Gulliver **quinbus flestrin** – 'the big human mountain', and 'britches' are called **ranfu-lo**. Just as Gulliver wakes up and finds himself captured by the Lilliputians, Swift highlights Gulliver's strange experience on hearing several (untranslated) exotic phrases – **tolgo phonac, hekina degul, langro dehul san, borach mevolah, peplom salan**. Gulliver also describes some measurements of length, such as **drurr** and **glumguff**, and titles such as **nardac, clumglum** and **hurgon**. The written language is unusual; instead of from right to left or left to right, from top to bottom or bottom to top, the Lilliputians write diagonally from one corner to the other.

There is no evidence to suggest that Jonathan Swift invented a language to any great extent. The phrases and words that appear in the book were probably created separately and intended only to give the reader a sense of exotic otherness.

Lilliput has two political factions, the **Tramecksan** and the **Slamecksan**, meaning 'high heels' and 'low heels', respectively, which is an important point of political contention, as are religious disputes over the interpretation of sacred texts or indeed the best way to peel eggs.

The giants in the land of Brobdingnag have their own language as well, of course. There they call Gulliver **grildrig**, which means 'small/Lilliputian', and he is likened to the animal **splacknock** and described as **relplum scalcatch** – 'freak of nature'.

On his travels, Gulliver also encounters a race of talking horse people, the Houyhnhnms, whose tongue consists of nasal and throat sounds which Gulliver thinks resembles German but more beautiful and expressive. The most interesting thing about the Houyhnhnms' language is that Swift thinks in terms similar to the Sapir–Whorf hypothesis. Gulliver notices that it is extremely difficult to discuss certain concepts with the Houyhnhnms. Since they have few 'needs and desires', their language is poor. They have no words for doubt, mistrust, lies and false promises, and therefore find these concepts very difficult to understand when Gulliver talks about them. There are also no words for power, government, war, law, punishment, money, theft, bribery, flattery, astrology, sainthood, free thinking or 'thousands of other concepts', making it almost impossible for Gulliver to give his Houyhnhnm master a notion of the society he comes from.

In the world of the Houyhnhnms, horses are masters, and a vile, unintelligent, humanlike race, the Yahoos, is by and large the only thing that disturbs the peace. **Yahoo** is also the Houyhnhmns' word for all that is bad: 'the folly of a servant, an omission of a child, a stone that cuts their feet, a continuance of foul or unseasonable weather' is defined by adding the epithet **yahoo**.

Some examples of the Houyhnhnms' language:

shnuwnh – to retire to one's first mother

hnhloayn – request
hlunnh – oats
nnuhnoh – a rabbit-like animal
gnnayh – a kind of bird of prey

The Journey of Niels Klim to the World Underground

Scandinavia's first bestseller was Ludvig Holberg's *The Journey of Niels Klim to the World Underground* (1741), or as it was originally called, *Nicolaï Klimii Iter Subterraneum*, because the Danish–Norwegian author originally wrote the book in Latin and published it in Germany, suggesting that he was predicting an international success. It has appeared in four English translations in 1742, 1828, 1845 and 1960.

Protagonist Niels Klim from Bergen returns home after graduating in philosophy and theology at the University of Copenhagen. In the city of his birth, Klim is eager to get involved in a project and decides to descend into a legendary cave in order to investigate it scientifically. The descent becomes a headlong fall and Klim suddenly finds himself in the underworld, where he lands on the planet Nazar, in the principality of Potu, populated by intelligent, speaking trees. Klim is taken for a monkey (**pikel emi**), put on a vegetarian diet, appointed as a courier on account of his quick legs and is also taught in the underground (**Nazar**) language.

Niels Klim mainly refers to different titles in the underground language:

Kadok – lord chancellor
Smirian – high treasurer
Madik – philosophy teacher
Masbatti – fighter, disputer
Kabalki – the one who incites the disputer
Karrati – supervisor

Klim also reproduces a piece of legislation: '**Spik, antri, Flak, skak mak, Tabu mihalat Silak**', as it says in the fourth book of law (**Skibal**), third chapter (**Kibal**), on slanderers. No translation of the legal text is given; however, Klim also mentions some book titles that are translated. **Sebolac tacsi** – *The True Characteristics of a God-Fearing Tree* – and **Mahalda Libab Helil** – *The State Oarsman*.

These titles and legal texts are apt because Ludvig Holberg used Niels Klim's journey to another planet and underground kingdoms as a means for writing social criticism disguised as satire. Of course, it is no coincidence that the principality of Potu is Utop(ia) spelled backwards, and in many respects perhaps Holberg's work has more similarities with Thomas More's *Utopia* than Jonathan Swift's *Gulliver's Travels*, published only twenty years before.

Like Gulliver, Niels travels from kingdom to kingdom, each of which highlights different tendencies that Holberg sees in society. Niels Klim spends ten years underground and meets a wide range of creatures in strange countries. The kingdom of Mardak is populated exclusively by cypress trees divided into eight tribes according to the number and shape of their eyes. The most numerous tribe are the Nagirians, who also constitute the kingdom's elite. They have oblong eyes and therefore perceive all objects as oblong. In order to become something in the cypress kingdom, one has to swear an oath in honour of the sun, which is the longest continuous text found in the underground language:

Kaki manaska qvihompu miriac jakku mesimbrii caphani crukkia manaskar qvebriaz krusundora.

I swear, that the holy table of the sun seems oblong to me, and I promise to remain in this opinion until my last breath.

As the inhabitants of the various countries Klim visits adopt more humanlike forms, the utopia gradually becomes a dystopia, from the towering trees of Potu with developed moral and sophisticated spiritual lives, through the less-developed tree kingdoms, to the realms populated by fantastical animals and creatures. Finally he gets to the realm of Quama – completely humanlike beings.

The Quama society is steeped in and governed by selfishness, vanity and absolute power. Most of the kingdoms in the Nazar world speak the same language, but the Quamites have their own language. **Jeru pikal salim** is Quamite and means 'show me the way'. Niels Klim comes to power in this kingdom and receives the titles **Pikil-su** ('messenger of the sun'), **Jakal** ('generalissimo') and finally **Casba** ('great emperor').

So Scandinavia's first bestseller contains a hefty dose of invented language and I can warmly recommend this entertaining satirical utopia to anyone interested in the linguistic history of imagined languages. If not the Latin original, then the modern English translation from 1960.

The Second Wave of Improved Languages

Interest in the perfect language gradually waned. French emerged as the lingua franca of culture and science, but nineteenth-century Europe changed dramatically through industrialisation as steamboats and trains allowed more people to travel greater distances. Telegraphs suddenly enabled communication with people much farther away. Maybe a common language was needed for the masses and not just the scientists?

The scientist, or rather engineer, archetype of Captain Nemo in Jules Verne's *Twenty Thousand Leagues Under the Sea* (1869) emerged amid the technological optimism of the nineteenth century. And it might be seen as a reflection of the zeitgeist that the crew of Captain Nemo's submarine *Nautilus* speaks an unknown, possibly invented, language. Professor Aronnax, the narrator of the novel, believes that *Nautilus'* crew is of mixed origin. The language they speak is unknown to the professor and his two colleagues, who between them speak French, English, German and Latin. There is only one untranslated sentence in the Nautilus language, when the second officer repeats a phrase to the submarine's control panel: '**Nautron respoc lorni virch**.'

The linguistic innovators of the nineteenth century did not use mathematics to build a better language, but comparative linguistics. In 1786, British linguist Sir William Jones presented the theory that Greek, Latin and Sanskrit all originated from an ancient proto-Indo-European language. This was the starting point for comparative linguistic research and gave rise to many a eureka moment in the study of European languages and how many similarities they share. Maybe someone could create a real lingua franca that everyone could understand?

Many people were called upon during the nineteenth century and hundreds of languages were developed and published, most of them with the ambition to become a new world language: an international auxiliary language that would be easy to learn and neutral to the extent that it was not anyone's native language. Many of the languages were based on the idea of an international vocabulary, borrowing words from several European languages, and tried to set out a simple and logical grammar without the irregularities and bizarre spellings that occur in natural languages.

New languages based on existing ones are called a posteriori languages. The names of these languages reveal their purpose: Langue Universelle (1836), Communicationssprache (1839), Lengua Universal (1852), Universalglot (1886), Weltsprache (1883), Néo-Latine (1884) and Neulatein (1884), to take but a few examples from the plethora.

Several of the proposed international auxiliary languages did manage to spread beyond their creator. In 1879, Volapük and, ten years later, Esperanto, both succeeded in this regard, and they were trendy to learn among certain circles. Esperanto is the great success among artificial languages and is still alive and well today. Volapük's success was shorter lived, and when Esperanto first appeared and began to gain momentum, some Volapükists jumped ship and opted for the Esperanto train instead.

International auxiliary languages are not the focus of this chapter, so I won't say much more about them, except to mention the strange Solresol language created by Jean-François Sudre in the 1830s. It was the first language of its type to gain any kind of success and be used. Solresol was also intended to serve as an international auxiliary language, but it fits comfortably within the concept of artlang – artistic languages.

Solresol is based on the notes of the musical scale using combinations of the syllables **do**, **re**, **mi**, **fa**, **sol**, **la** and **si**. It is therefore a language that can be spoken, whistled, semaphored, or any combination thereof; or communicated via sign language or colours. The platitude of music as a universal language finally came true with Solresol. In its own language, the word Solresol simply means 'language' or 'linguistics'.

The idea of a musical language existed before in the lunar tongues of Godwin's and Bergerac's novels. Like the seventeenth-century language philosophers, Sudre constructed an a priori language; that is, one in which the vocabulary is completely new, whereas the fashion of the nineteenth century was a posteriori language. Sudre also created a classification system reminiscent of the none-too-successful attempts at logical categories made by his predecessors. For example, if a word starts with **re**, the word refers to home or family:

> **redorefa** – shirt
> **redomido** – wash oneself
> **redosifa** – wedding ring
> **resiresol** – son, daughter

Body parts and food fall into the same class that starts with **do**:

dosifasol – coffee
dosisoldo – chocolate
dorelasol – buttocks
dolasolsi – ham
doremire – eyes
doremisol – mouth

The seven basic syllables were allocated to basic words:

do – no
re – and
mi – or
fa – to
sol – about
la – denotes definite form
si – yes

Everyday words have fewer syllables than words of a more specialised use. One word can have a maximum of five syllables which, interestingly, makes it possible to calculate the upper limit of the language's vocabulary: 11,732.

A word's opposite can be created by reversing the order of the syllables: **misol** – 'good'; **solmi** – 'bad'.

In 1833, François Sudre was invited to a press conference where he presented Solresol for the first time, then played his violin and had his students translate the melody into French. Rumours of this fascinating musical language and the 'prophet of sound' quickly spread, and François Sudre became a welcome guest at many a salon in Belgium and France where he performed to show off the merits of his language. He promoted Solresol as a language for the deaf and blind, performing blindfolded and getting his audience to write down words or sentences. One of his students came up to Sudre and pressed different points on his hand to silently convey a message which Sudre then announced to the astonished audience. To Sudre's disappointment, he was regarded primarily as an entertainer and few were genuinely interested in learning Solresol. Now it looks like the internet might enable Solresol to undergo a renaissance. The smattering of enthusiasts have found each other and made resources for learning Solresol available online.

Of course, linguistic history includes more artificial languages than the ones I have listed here. My intention has mainly been to give an overview of some historical works containing artlangs and conlangs to show that the phenomenon of artificial languages in popular culture, or as a hobby in themselves, is nothing new. Klingon and Na'vi are just a couple of the more recent relatives of Lingua Ignota and Godwin's musical moon language and belong to the same tradition as Aristophanes.

Grammelot

PRESENT AND FUTURE DIALECTS

Line Language, Pinguish, Simlish, Huttese, Jawaese, Ewokese, Kanjiklub

---

Grammelot is an international language dating back to the sixteenth century, a language that works in all contexts and for any audience. Now, you may be wondering why you've never heard, or heard of, this magical language. However, you would be mistaken, because you probably have heard it. If you are a little older, you may have heard it in the animated series *Lineman* and if you are a little younger, you probably grew up with grammelot in *Pingu* and *The Sims* life simulation game. In Charlie Chaplin's film *The Great Dictator* there is a well-known scene in which dictator Anton Hynkel delivers a fire-and-brimstone speech in a German-esque grammelot.

It would be generous to describe grammelot as a language in its own right. It can perhaps be better defined as a technique for producing a nonsense language that nevertheless conveys both meaning and emotion – a bit like spoken body language. Nobel Laureate Dario Fo addressed the phenomenon in his winner's speech and attributed the language's creation to Renaissance author Angelo 'Il Ruzzante' Beolco:

Ruzzante, the true father of the Commedia dell'Arte, also constructed a language of his own, a language of and for the theatre, based on a variety of tongues: the dialects of the Po Valley; expressions in Latin, Spanish, even German; all mixed with onomatopoeic sounds of his own invention. It is from him, from Beolco Ruzzante, that I've learned to free myself from conventional literary writing and to express myself with words that you can chew, with unusual sounds, with various techniques of rhythm and breathing, even with the rambling nonsense-speech of the grammelot.

Dario Fo uses the technique in *Mistero Buffo*, in which he developed an Italian grammelot from an old dialect, as well as French and American versions of grammelot.

The technique is old, but the term 'grammelot' is much younger. Believed to be of French origin, its name was likely coined in the French theatre scene, inspired by *commedia dell'arte* at the beginning of the twentieth century, and stems from the French word *grommeler*, which means 'to mumble' or 'mutter'.

Travelling jesters have used the method since ancient times to communicate with audiences of different native tongues – and for comic effect, of course. Grammelot was also an important tool for satire and for getting around censorship. After all, it could never be proven that a jester had actually said anything against the State or Church, because they could claim it was all just meaningless gibberish.

This is the important distinction between grammelot and gibberish – although these words are often used synonymously, which is misleading. Gibberish is entirely incomprehensible, while grammelot endeavours to convey a general sense and emotion even though the individual words are incomprehensible. And unlike gibberish, grammelot is a difficult skill to hone; developing your own grammelot dialect takes time.

Try it for yourself. Improvise a made-up language for a few minutes. It is extremely difficult to make it sound credible as a proper language. After a few phrases, you typically start repeating yourself, forgetting which words you have already used, and which ought to be repeated as common words. The tendency is to come out with gobbledygook. In most cases, the result simply doesn't sound credible. It sounds made up. Gibberish.

Grammelot speakers often refer to and mimic the melody of a real language or language family. To do this, they create a limited vocabulary that can be used for common words or recurring set phrases in a particular performance. These words may be directly related to terms within the mimicked language or belong to some kind of 'international vocabulary'. Or the phrases might be completely invented but have an onomatopoeic connection to the object or phenomenon the word denotes. Thus grammelot, unlike gibberish, is thought out and well rehearsed. Seeing as it emerged from comedy and theatre, it is also closely associated with expressive body language.

In the 1970s *Star Wars* films, sound designer Ben Burtt worked with student Larry Ward, who had an incredible ability to believably mimic any language he heard. Larry improvised Huttese, an example of a grammelot, by listening to recordings of the South American language Quechua. Other languages in *Star Wars* also seem to be modern forms of grammelot, although Burtt technologically modified many of the languages in his studio, speeding up recordings, adding effects, or splicing sounds and sentences together with animal noises.

Line Language

For those of us who grew up in the 1970s and 1980s, the appearance of *Lineman* on mainstream television was a big event. It was a rare cartoon featured regularly on one of the few TV channels available at the time that didn't forsake all humour in the pursuit of pedagogical worthiness.

La Linea, as it is called in the original Italian, is about Mr Linea, an outline of a large-nosed, often angry man walking along a line. He encounters various problems, like when the line he is walking on comes to an end. He then typically gets angry and barks at the cartoonist, who is represented by a hand who draws what Mr Linea wants, or more often, something completely different. The first eight episodes of the 1969 series were actually commercials for white goods from the Lagostina brand, and Mr Linea was called Agostino Lagostina, but the series subsequently moved away from appliance advertisement.

The bad-tempered, fast-talking Mr Linea was voiced by actor Carlo Bonomi as a parody of the Italian Milanese dialect. Bonomi has worked extensively in radio drama and dubbed various characters in imported TV series, as well as voicing a variety of cartoon characters, such as Fred Flintstone and Mickey Mouse. In interviews, Bonomi has explained that the language he used for Mr Linea is indeed grammelot and harks back to a long tradition of jesters and clowns in France and Italy who have used this abstract language to express themselves.

Mr Linea may not be much more than an advanced stick figure, but his emotional register is shown in big gestures. He is often angry, but also has characteristic sounds and tones of voice to represent satisfaction or joy. It is obvious to the audience that Mr Linea is speaking some variation on Italian. I remember many debates and speculations in my childhood home about whether Mr Linea really was speaking Italian, or some made-up, Italian-sounding language.

The cartoon's use of grammelot turned out to be a stroke of luck. *Lineman* has been shown in a number of countries, and no dubbing or subtitling is required to understand Mr Linea and his emotional register.

Pinguish

Just as *Lineman* gained international success with its communicative grammelot, the Swiss clay penguin Pingu also conquered the world. And Carlo Bonomi is the man behind the grammelot of both *Lineman* and *Pingu*. Pingu also sounds as if he is speaking Italian but with unique linguistic titbits such as the honking '**Noot-noot!**' that signals Pingu is upset, annoyed, or simply, 'I'm here!'

Pingu didn't need to be dubbed in any of the 150 countries where the series was shown because all children in all countries understand Pinguish. The first batch of *Pingu* included 105 episodes, after which a British company bought the rights to the series and produced new episodes. Initially, they continued using Carlo Bonomi's grammelot talent, but his lack of English soon became a problem and he was replaced by Marcello Magni and David Sant, an Italian and Spaniard respectively, who both lived in London and were familiar with grammelot.

In order for the spoken language to be understandable, the clay animations needed an expressive body language, which is arguably an intrinsic part of grammelot. The easily identifiable recurring words or sounds represent a mood rather than a precise meaning. '**Noot-noot!**' is used when Pingu is angry (and his beak becomes a trumpet), a wicked chuckle, '**hoo-hoo-hoo**', with a wing over his beak, means Pingu is about to get up to mischief, and '**mm-hmm**' is used along with a nodding head to signal agreement. Viewers have tried to distinguish individual words such as '**caa-caa**' for 'poop', '**mok-mo**', which is used by Pingu to refer to an eel, and '**cee-leef**' for a flatfish, etc. But it is probably not worth trying to decipher Pinguish via the meaning of individual words or a unified grammar. That's not how grammelot works.

Simlish

When Will Wright created his landmark life simulation computer game *The Sims*, he realised early on that the residents
of SimNation needed a language. His mind first turned to the
famous story of the US Army using the Navajo Indians to send
coded messages during the Second World War. The Japanese
failed to crack the code because they could not identify the language behind it. Navajo was entirely unrecognisable to them.

Initially, Will Wright and a linguist named Marc Gimbel
experimented with Navajo as a language for *The Sims* games
but realised it wouldn't work. Instead, they decided to create
Simlish, based on a plethora of languages, including Ukrainian,
Tagalog, Finnish, Latin and English. The idea was to create a
language that sounded familiar to a wide range of players with
a variety of mother tongues.

It is hard to say whether any features of these original languages survived in what was to become Simlish because actors
Stephen Kerin and Gerri Lawlor ended up improvising the dialogue that laid the foundation for the language. In other words,
they used grammelot.

Simlish is used to express emotions and provide an atmospheric background noise in *The Sims* games. It should not be
construed as made-up English or Italian (as with *Pingu* and
Lineman) but as a neutral language of its own. Vowels 'a', 'e', 'i',
'o', and 'u' are frequently used because it allows for a certain
perception of universality, with sounds that are recognisable
to a wide variety of people. But since many of the actors who
provide the voices for the characters are from the United States,
there is something very American about Simlish; it sounds like
Americans speaking a foreign language with a strong accent,
or a non-anglophone speaking an American-style grammelot.

Simlish was first used in the game *SimCopter* in 1996, but
really had its breakthrough in *The Sims* around the turn of the
millennium. Many new versions have developed over the years

and the language has been used in numerous translations of popular songs by international artists. Since *The Sims* simulates real life, it requires a wide range of voices from all sorts of characters in different situations and states of mind: retirees, teenagers, police officers, labourers, politicians, babies, bus drivers, nurses, professors, and so on. Soon, nine more actors were employed to help Stephen Kerin and Gerri Lawlor portray the various characters, and even more actors joined the ranks in later versions.

Voiceover artists provide the dialogue by reading or improvising Simlish while in character and in various emotional states. The actors are given certain words and sentences with an established meaning. Then, their voices end up in a database to be retrieved when a particular character has to say something in a given situation. So, when a new *Sims* game is made, a large bank of Simlish is available for all conceivable situations in the game.

Gradually, the language has transformed from pure grammelot into something that might be developing into a real language. The key to this evolution, as is so often the case, is the fans. Of all the millions of *Sims* players, a significant number of people have become curious about the language and begun to recognise recurring words. Others have looked up the Simlish version of their favourite pop song and analysed the translation. So, bit by bit, Simlish vocabulary lists have begun to emerge, some of a more official nature, and some personal glossaries gleaned from translating song lyrics. In a forum devoted to the game, a dedicated thread emerged that gathered the fans' analyses in *The Big Simlish Dictionary*.

One of the best-known words in Simlish is **nooboo** ('baby'), one of the standardised words that crops up frequently with a definite meaning, as well as **lalo** ('milk'), **chum cha** ('pizza'), **sul sul** ('hello'), and the Scandinavian-sounding **dag dag** ('goodbye' or 'OK').

Because there are words with a defined and analysable meaning, unlike Pinguish for example, the fans know that behind the seemingly incomprehensible babble there is in fact a language that can be understood and spoken. Key words in *The Big Simlish Dictionary* are analysed as follows:

Word – **cuh-teek-a-loo**
Used by – teenager
Used when? – To greet someone
Possible meaning – 'Hey, how's it going?'

Thus, the language is interpreted phrase by phrase, expanding Simlish vocabulary as it goes along. Some fans have pointed out to Simlish enthusiasts that it is not a real language, just nonsensical gibberish, and that they've heard the same words used for different things in different contexts. Their point is that there is no use in trying to analyse the language. Obviously, this doesn't discourage the enthusiasts.

In *The Sims* 2 and 3, a number of well-known musicians were invited to participate in the game with their own songs translated into Simlish. The artists wrote their own Simlish versions, using nonsense words to their own taste and liking. But since the original texts are available, some fans have translated the lyrics word for word and added the new Simlish words to their glossary.

Pop singer Katy Perry's song 'Hot 'n' Cold' has been translated into Simlish, and the first lines go like this:

vous, chikanip	You, change your mind
laka gurl, chika claps	like a girl, changes clothes

Not particularly hard to decipher, but since these translated texts are not consistent and mostly composed of plausible nonsense words, it makes it more difficult to make sense of Simlish as a whole. As it happens, Katy Perry has recorded a couple of songs in Simlish. After recording her first song, she was asked on MTV if she was a Simlish expert now, to which Katy replied that she was not: 'It is difficult to sing in Simlish. I have a cheat sheet when I sing and I follow it to the letter. It sounds kind of like talking in tongues, which I grew up with, by the way, so I feel I have a small advantage.'

Simlish also exists in an older form, namely Old Simlish, which is spoken in *The Sims Medieval*. It is the same basic *Sims* concept but in a medieval world. Here, efforts have been made to make Simlish sound a little more formal and 'medieval'. In reality, this means it sounds a bit more French; when a Sim kneels in front of a king on his throne, the king might say '**deboo**' (French: *débout* – 'rise'). But Old Simlish is not a French variant of Simlish, rather it is intended as a precursor to modern Simlish. One assumes there must be fans out there somewhere trying to figure out how the medieval form evolved into the modern lexicon.

There is also a written language used for Simlish. It is not really known exactly how the writing system works, but it looks very exotic, and consists of a wide variety of characters. The game-makers sometimes use symbols specially created for Simlish, the Wingdings font, or sometimes simply Simlish words written in the Greek alphabet.

Among the established expressions, many are exotic and bear no resemblance to English, but there are also many words that are similar to their English counterparts. Could they be English loanwords in a Simlish format?

kik – kiss
mik up – make out
sperk – speak
checkmar – checkmate
laka – like a
zo hungwah – so hungry

kat – cat
claps – clothes

Meanwhile, other common phrases are less closely related to the English language:

'**wabadebadoo!**' – 'I'm on fire!'
'**zep tor maboo!**' – 'help, fire!'
'**dis wompf es fredesche.**' – 'this food is delicious.'

Of the numerals, only the first three are known: **mik**, **mak** and **maka**. The question is, which direction will Simlish take in the future? Will the language continue to be an improvised grammelot, or will the increasing number of defined words and phrases eventually give Simlish the status of a real language, with grammar, glossaries and synonyms? It is not unlikely that Simlish will develop in several different directions; the game may continue to produce grammelot while the fans standardise a version of Simlish that fulfils their desires to write their own lyrics or use the language among themselves.

Glossolalia

So, back to Katy Perry and her religious upbringing in which people spoke in tongues. Katy referred to her experience of speaking in tongues as an advantage for singing in Simlish. And that certainly makes sense. Speaking in tongues, or glossolalia (from the Greek words *glossa*, meaning 'tongue' or 'language', and *laleo*, meaning 'speak') bears a lot of similarities to grammelot. They are both speech-like word streams, the difference being that grammelot is used to communicate, while speaking in tongues has no communicative purpose.

Glossolalia is a religious phenomenon in various Christian movements, such as Pentecostalism, and can be described as automatic speech consisting of mostly incomprehensible words. In the various charismatic church movements, speaking in tongues is explained as the language of divine prayer that somehow allows its speakers direct contact with the Holy Spirit. True glossolalia occurs in a trance-like state when the worshipper speaks in tongues 'automatically' and without knowing what they are saying. Of course, the speech is also incomprehensible to the audience, but it can be perceived as a real language. Inevitably, there are also those who fake speaking in tongues to gain status among their congregation, in which case the glossolalia is naturally not automatic or spontaneous. But in the past, the word streams produced by people in a trance state were considered a divine language. Could this be the pure language spoken by the angels?

When the phenomenon is studied scientifically, it shows that glossolalia seems to mimic real language and reflect the speaker's mother tongue. So English speakers, for example, would not speak a Chinese-sounding glossolalia, but one made up of the same building blocks as English.

Huttese

The corner of outer space that sets the stage for Anakin Skywalker's journey towards ruin, the dark side, and a shiny Darth Vader helmet is also home to a plethora of extraterrestrial languages. *Star Wars* provides us with a variety of languages and several significant characters who speak exclusively in alienese. To name but a few, the Wookiee Chewbacca consistently yelps in Shyriiwook, the cute little Ewoks speak no English (Galactic Basic) at all, and have to be interpreted by C3PO, and Jabba the Hutt roars in Huttese, naturally, to name but a few. In every nook and cranny of the *Star Wars* universe there is a strange language to be heard.

But if you compare *Star Wars* with *Star Trek* or the stories of Tolkien's world, which have given rise to real working languages, it is clear that George Lucas' team chose another path. In *Star Wars*, the languages are really just adornments or sound effects. In most cases, the languages are only meant to *sound* like real languages. Sound designer Ben Burtt was given responsibility for making them sound authentic.

Huttese is originally the language of the Hutts but has since spread and is now also spoken by other species. It serves as a trading language and lingua franca for many, especially among the more obscure and criminal inhabitants of the galaxy. But Huttese is also spoken in the corridors of power – Sheev Palpatine (speaking of lowlifes) speaks Huttese when a Rodian secretary presents a delegation in Huttese in *Episode II*.

Huttese is the most developed language in *Star Wars*. It first appeared in the original movie in the 1970s when Greedo confronts Han Solo in the seedy bar of the Mos Eisley cantina with the infamous phrase, '**Koona t'chuta, Solo**?' – 'Going somewhere, Solo?'

When Ben Burtt set out to create Huttese, his intention was to find a real language that could pass for alienese. He realised that if he just sat down and made up his own space language, it would be much too coloured by English and American pronunciation. The advantage of using an existing language is that it has the built-in credibility of a coherent tongue that has developed over time. For decades, rumours have been flying between *Star Wars* fans about which real-world languages are used by the aliens in the movies – there are some who claim that you can even hear Finnish phrases. In *Episode II*, Watto sounds like he is speaking Finnish when he says '**Kiitos**' ('Thank you') to Sebulba for the pod journey and he answers, '**Ole hyvä**' ('You're welcome'). In fact, this is Huttese. Although it has its basis in an earthly language, namely Quechua, Huttese is a language of its own that no native earthling can understand without intensive study.

Burtt came across a recording of the South American language Quechua and thought it sounded unusual and a little comical.

It had 'strange' sounds and a tendency to rhyme that Burtt found entertaining. Burtt gathered recordings of Quechua and sought out someone who could speak the language. He didn't find a Quechua speaker, however, but a student of linguistics named Larry Ward who had studied eleven other languages. Most importantly, he had the ability to imitate languages even if he couldn't speak them. He could listen to Quechua and start mimicking it as if he spoke it fluently. Of course, he wasn't really fluent; what he spoke was a made-up Quechua, a kind of grammelot.

At most, there are only a handful of real Quechua words in Huttese, but with different meanings. For example *chawa* in Quechua means 'raw, uncooked', while **chawa** in Huttese means 'to compete'. But there are traces of other languages in Huttese, some of which are obvious loans from Galactic Basic (English), such as:

poodoo – poo/doodoo
sleemo – slimeball
blastoh – blaster

One Huttese sentence of unknown meaning, '**Toota mishka Jabba du Hutt**?', sounds suspiciously like the Polish, '*Tutaj mieszka Jabba du Hutt*?' – 'Does Jabba the Hutt live here?'

Together, Burtt and Ward wrote down the sounds of Quechua phonetically, then began to invent sounds and sentences that sounded vaguely Quechan. Once Burtt had put together a list of Huttese words that sounded good, he chose words that matched Greedo's mouth movements in the scene with Han Solo. Thus, Huttese was born. The audience gets another taste of Huttese when Jabba the Hutt seeks out Han Solo outside the *Millennium Falcon*, a deleted scene included in *Star Wars: Special Edition*.

In *The Empire Strikes Back*, the Huttese vocabulary is expanded only with the untranslatable put-down, '**e chu ta**', used by a robot to insult a shocked C3PO. The next stage of

Huttese development is in *Return of the Jedi*, where Jabba the Hutt rumbles on a great deal in his native language and poor C3PO (who has handily mastered 6 million forms of communication) has to translate.

George Lucas himself contributed two words to Huttese: **bo shueda** and **boska**. The former has never been explained or translated, much to the great annoyance of fans, while '**Boska!**' means 'Come on, let's go!'.

A third person who contributed to the development of Huttese was Annie Arbogast, who worked in the audio department during filming. She was also a singer in a local punk band and Ben Burtt hired her to voice Sy Snootles in the scene where the character sings at Jabba's court. Annie wrote the Huttese lyrics to Sy Snootles' song herself, under Burtt's supervision.

After that, the evolution of Huttese more or less came to a standstill for twenty years until George Lucas returned to *Star Wars* with *Episode I – The Phantom Menace* (2001). Huttese really came into its own with this film, mainly through dialogues between the young Anakin Skywalker, winged trader Watto and vicious racer Sebulba. All the Huttese dialogue in the film was written and recorded by Ben Burtt for the actors to listen to and practise. Classic phrases like Anakin's '**Mee tassa cho-passa** …' ('I was cleaning the fan switches …') or Sebulba's, '**Yoka to bantha poo-doo!**' ('You are bantha poo!') entered language history forever. In the second film of the second trilogy, *Attack of the Clones* (2002), when teenage Anakin returns to Mos Eisley to look for his mother, he visits his old employer/owner Watto and speaks a bit of Huttese. Initially, the scenes were intended to be in English but just as they were about to start shooting George Lucas intervened and asked actor Andrew Secombe (who does Watto's voice and also appeared in these scenes as an animated blue, flying Toydarian) if the scene wouldn't make more sense in Huttese. Secombe agreed, and he and George Lucas spent ten minutes improvising the Huttese dialogue that then appeared in the film. Among other things, it included the practical phrase: '**No bata no tutu**' – 'Whatever it was, I didn't do it.'

Huttese has since been used as a sound effect in a variety of *Star Wars*-related computer games, and in 2001 Ben Burtt published a small book, *Star Wars: Galactic Phrase Book & Travel Guide*, a playful travel guide with phrases and background information on the languages. The phrases in the book don't always correspond to the Huttese spoken in the films, but nevertheless it must be regarded as an official source as Ben Burtt is the one behind it.

Perhaps the most interesting thing we learn about Huttese in the travel guide is its counting system. Here's how to count to ten in Huttese:

Word	Huttese Value	Value in Galactic Basic (English)
Nobo	0	0
Bo	1	1
Dopa	2	2
Duba	3	3
Fwanna	4	4
k'wanna	5	5
Kita	6	6
Goba	7	7
Hunto	10	8
Biska	11	9
Boboba	12	10

The Hutts have only four fingers on each hand and have therefore developed base-8 arithmetic rather than base-10 like humans. When they came into contact with five-fingered creatures, the Hutts realised that they could gain an advantage by negotiating prices according to their own numbers, aggressively asserting their claim should the other party realise the discrepancy and protest. So, when a Hutt offers you twelve toffees, that's only ten according to our way of counting. In the travel guide, Burtt issues a wise warning about doing business with the Hutts.

Although the *Star Wars* languages are just used as sound effects to add flavour, they represent real languages within the *Star Wars* universe, which is why many fans choose to decipher them. Unsurprisingly, there are also people who have tried to analyse and systematise Huttese, but little can be gleaned about the grammar behind it, for obvious reasons. Although the phonology of Huttese was taken from Quechua, there are no other similarities between the languages. Grammatically, they differ greatly.

The general rule for sentence construction seems to be roughly the same as English, but word order is either flexible or follows a pattern as yet not found by linguists. Hungarian Huttese expert Andras Rajki proposed a theory that Huttese is a so-called analytical language – that is, a language that expresses grammatical relations primarily through word order rather than with inflections. Chinese, for example, is an analytical language. In Rajki's version of Huttese, he 'corrects' certain phrases from the films to make them fit into a more logical grammatical structure.

When Rajki applies the rules he thinks he has found in the language, Jabba's phrase from *Episode VI*, '**Chone manya weesh asha beecho**' ('I will enjoy watching you die') becomes '**Jor maja ix asha pee cho**' (**jor** – 'with'; **maja** – 'pleasure'; **ix** – 'I will'; **asha** – 'see'; **pee** – 'when'; and **cho** – 'die').

An unusual feature of Huttese is that there are three different words for 'with' – **foo, gee** and **con**. Whether they are completely synonymous or used in different contexts is as yet unknown. It had decidedly extraterrestrial traits, but there is probably no thought behind this; rather, it is something that has arisen through improvised Huttese-sounding phrases.

Huttese has just over 300 words in its vocabulary, plus some yet to be translated. This is enough to allow fans to put together simple sentences and write poetry, often using English word order or trying to emulate the word order of a Huttese example sentence.

For many years, the most influential source of Huttese data has been the website 'The Complete Wermo's Guide to Huttese' (**wermo** – 'idiot'), where careful efforts have been made to expand the Huttese vocabulary by creating new words. In order to do this, enthusiasts have referred back to Quechuan to find new root words. So *lakilla*, which means 'sorry' in Quechuan, has become **lakeela**, with the same meaning in Huttese. The word for 'mouth' in Huttese, **bocha**, comes from French *bouche* and Spanish/Portuguese *boca*.

The Wermo's Guide is careful to make a distinction between canonical Huttese terms derived from official sources, and newly created words. But new words are also key words, which are necessary to allow Huttese to move further away from its beginnings as a mere sound effect and closer to becoming a real language.

One of the enthusiasts behind The Wermo's Guide popped up in a *Star Wars* talent contest with a newly written poem in Huttese and won. Here are some lines from the poem:

Che mwa panwa sa gocola, yocola mwa pateesa,	For my love is wine, drink my friend,
An mwa blutpum sa do, magi sunniullis makacheesa,	And my heart is yours, like starlight's pay-off,
Ateema jah grandio boska je katinka joppay,	When I consider this time the glorious search,
Tchuta nenoleeya soong nobata peetch alay,	Somewhere out there, it's not too late,
Hees naga foo je,	He needs to be with me,
Jee naga foo meekta,	I need to be with him,
Noleeya locktulla mwa yuna hees panwa jee jeeska.	In the vault of my soul, his love I keep.

So, it has already come a long way from its original status as sonic embellishment. Given that well-crafted constructed languages in TV shows and movies have become more common – and more important – in recent years, it is not unlikely that *Star Wars* producers and screenwriters will look at the developments that fans have made and begin to use Huttese more systematically and consistently in the future.

Jawaese

On the planet Tatooine in the *Star Wars* galaxy, there are at least two indigenous humanoid life forms: Jawas and Tusken Raiders (or Sand People). They are two very different races with a common ancestor – the Kumumgah – but they evolved in contrasting directions to become the tall, violent Tuskens and the small Jawas.

So, the languages of the Sand People and the Jawas must also have a common origin somewhere down the line, although it is difficult to see how they might be related to each other, particularly because of how Burtt created the languages. Just as in the case of Huttese, Burtt modelled Jawaese (unrelated to the real language Javanese) on a pre-existing language. This time, he looked to South Africa and the Zulu language.

Burtt asked a number of Zulu speakers to tell folk tales and other stories and express different feelings in order to build a soundbank of expressions in a range of emotional states. Burtt said that he tried to get a Zulu-speaking man to pretend to be scared, but he refused, asserting that he was a Zulu warrior and knew nothing of fear. Burtt has suggested this may have had a bearing on the fearless nature of the Jawas.

Based on the recorded material, Burtt picked out sounds he liked and combined them to fit his perception of the essence of Zulu. He then used these words and phrases to write new nonsense lines to be read by voice actors. He often recorded the actors outdoors to get echoes to match the shoot location in the Tunisian mountains. Burtt and a friend ran around for a whole day among the rocks screaming, '**Utinni**!' until they were hoarse.

Made-up Zulu phrases were also run through Burtt's sound devices and sped up to give the voices a higher pitch and, hey presto, Jawaese was born. In the second season of *The Mandalorian* we got some more Jawaese, and suddenly the Jawas sound – and behave! – more like Minions from *Despicable Me*. Interestingly enough, the Minions were inspired by both Willy Wonka's Oompa Loompas and Jawas, so it seems that the people behind the Mandalorian have 'borrowed back' from the Minions and found some new inspiration for the development of Jawaese.

It even turns out that the protagonist actually can speak some Jawaese, to their great amusement: 'You speak terrible Jawaese. You sound like a Wookie.'

The language of the Sand People also came to Burtt from mountain echoes. When the crew were filming in Tunisia, they used pack donkeys to transport film equipment. Sometimes the donkeys began to bray during filming, meaning scenes had to be refilmed. When the donkey brays echoed in the mountains, it created a sound that the film crew found eerie and strange, so they recorded it thinking it might pass for a Tusken language. When Burtt returned to the USA, he complemented these recordings with other sounds of the animals breathing and hissing, then mixed it all together and turned the sounds into the language of the Sand People.

It was not until 2020 that we came to view Tatooine's desert nomads in a new light. In *The Mandalorian*, the protagonist encounters Sand People a couple of times and gives us a glimpse of their culture; they are not 'savages' in rags that bray like donkeys.

We also get a deeper insight into their alien tongue, which seems to have a great element of sign language. To develop this

Tusken Sign Language (TSL), the team hired deaf actor Troy Kotsur to play one of the Sand People. Kotsur also taught the actor Pedro Pascal (the Mandalorian himself) to communicate in this alien sign language:

> I did research on the culture and environment of Tusken Raiders. My goal was to avoid [American Sign Language]. I made sure it became Tusken Sign Language based on their culture and environment.

This development of the Sand People's language was immediately embraced by fans, who set up a Facebook page to decipher and research TSL. So after forty years, we finally know a lot more about the Tuskens' 'braying' and have a chance to understand them. Time brings everything to those who wait.

Ewokese

Ewoks are small, hairy, teddy-bear-like creatures that live on the moon of Endor. They are just over a metre tall and live in harmony with nature, Stone Age-style, in cool tree houses. They enter into the action of *Star Wars* because the evil Galactic Empire has built a base on the moon where they live, and the rebels come to disengage the energy shield around the Death Star.

Originally, this part of the adventure was supposed to take place on the home planet of the Wookiees, but as Chewbacca and the Wookiees ended up with sophisticated technology including laser crossbows and the like, George Lucas invented a new breed. If Wookiees were big bears, Ewoks could be little bears. The Ewoks' name was inspired by the Miwok, indigenous people of the redwood forest where the scenes were filmed.

And, of course, the Ewoks speak exclusively in their own language. They don't seem to have mastered other common space languages, which is not all that unexpected for a Stone

Age population, but thankfully C3PO speaks Ewokese and can interpret. One might wonder why C3PO has mastered an isolated Stone Age moon language, but it could be because Ewokese seems closely related to Tibetan.

The general consensus on Ewokese is that it is an invented language that mimics Tibetan, Nepali and Kalmyk in the same way that Huttese imitated Quechua. In other words, it is a non-sense language. However, back in 1980, the same year the film came out, the magazine *Tibetan Review* commented on the strange language spoken by the Ewoks, as it contained many Tibetan words and sentences.

Anthropologist Maria S. Calkowski, who speaks Tibetan herself, later went through the dialogue, which turns out to contain many direct Tibetan sentences. These include, 'I'm a quiet person. Best to leave me alone' and 'There's plenty of money here!' When the Ewoks encounter the shiny gold robot C3PO and take him for a god, they begin to recite a prayer from *The Tibetan Book of the Dead*, which in a way is rather fitting. When C3PO levitates (with the help of Luke Skywalker and the Force) to prove his divinity, it is somewhat reminiscent of the stereotypical image of Tibetan Buddhist monks levitating during meditation.

Like most other languages in *Star Wars*, Ben Burtt is the sound designer behind Ewokese. At first, Burtt tested various Native American languages for Ewokese but didn't think any sounded right for the hairy little creatures. Then Burtt heard Tibetan in a BBC documentary and thought it sounded extraterrestrial. He managed to find some Tibetans and even an 80-year-old Kalmyk woman, whom he recorded speaking. He got them to say everyday phrases and tell folk tales but was not satisfied. The Tibetans were asked to read from a script and give various commands to try to get the right tone, but Burtt thought the older woman worked best – apparently, she told very intriguing Kalmyk folk tales after a couple of glasses of vodka.

Burtt discovered that older women worked best for extra-terrestrial voices – recording children or older men just made the aliens sound like human children or older men, whereas mature female voices made it harder to identify gender and age. When he played these recordings faster and a little distorted, he found his Ewokese. Thus, some recordings of the 80-year-old Kalmyk lady made their way into the Ewokese vocabulary, along with Tibetan phrases and Kalmyk-sounding grammelot recorded by voice actors.

According to Burtt, the Tibetan lines don't match the content, but Maria S. Calkowski notes that they suit their contexts very well. Burtt also says he doesn't know the origin of the reference to money but believes that the line may have come from one of the Tibetan ladies who were very impressed with the technical equipment of the Lucasfilm studio.

The Ewokese spoken by C3PO, on the other hand, is not Tibetan and was improvised by actor Anthony Daniels with the help of Ben Burtt, based on the Tibetan and Kalmyk recordings:

'… **ee mann ma-chu Vader con yum-num**.'

'… and he struck at Vader with a laser sword.'

Ben Burtt also wrote the Ewokese lyrics to the song that the Ewoks sing at the end of the film as they celebrate their victory. The English text was written by Joseph Williams, the son of John Williams, the legendary composer who scored the films. The song's first stanzas go like this:

Yub nub, eee chop yub nub;	Freedom, we got freedom;
ah toe meet toe peechee keene,	and now that we can be free,
g'noop dock fling oh ah.	come on and celebrate.

Later, Burtt increased our knowledge of Ewokese in *Star Wars: Galactic Phrase Book & Travel Guide*. This taught us that **yub nub** means 'freedom', as in the song above, but outside of this, it is difficult to find the song's lyrics contained in the lexicon. For example, 'free' is defined in the lexicon as **che**, 'now' is **sta**, and 'we' is **ees**, none of which are included in the text. Then again, we know very little about the grammar and synonyms of Ewokese.

Other useful phrases that give a picture of Ewokese include:

'**chiotto bat flingo lah**?' – 'Can I have something to drink?'
'**chiotto g yeesha ah-ah**?' – 'Please, can I have some water?'
'**chi ita lungee**.' – 'I'm lost'.
'**noroway bi toto ka sunee re fopa**?' – 'In which direction is the sun rising?'

The meaning of the sentences is known, but not all the words are yet identified. However, Ewokese experts are currently aware of the following:

'**chiotto …**' – 'can I have …'
g yeesha – please
ah-ah – water
lungee – lost
noroway – which
bi toto – direction
sunee – sun

Maybe we can also, with a little imagination, see an English influence on the language. 'I like it' is **yun yum** and 'It is very good/tasty' is the English-sounding '**yun yum it goot**'.

Kanjiklub

In the later *Star Wars* films, like *Episode VII, VIII, IX* and other various spin-offs, there is a melange of phrases in extraterrestrial languages, but so far little is known about their background – with one notable exception. In *Star Wars: The Force Awakens* (2015), Finnish YouTube phenomenon Sara Forsberg, from Jakobstad, took up Ben Burtt's mantle as the language effect creator. The film's director, J.J. Abrams, had relaunched *Star Trek* with three new films between 2009 and 2016, in which he used Klingon and hired Ben Burtt as sound engineer, so it is not surprising that he hired a language expert for *Star Wars* as well.

Sara Forsberg initially became famous for a YouTube video in which she performed grammelot versions of about twenty different languages. In other words, she produced incomprehensible speech that sounded recognisable as various languages. The clip went viral, and Sara Forsberg became well known, appearing in media around the world, including on Ellen DeGeneres' talk show in the USA.

J.J. Abrams contacted Sara and asked her to develop an extraterrestrial language for the film. The name of the language is not known, but we can call it Kanjiklub after its speakers in the film, who belong to the hard-boiled criminal gang Kanjiklub that tracks down Han Solo for his unpaid debts.

The gang's leader Tasu Leech accounts for most of the extraterrestrial speech and, since the actor Yayan Ruhian comes from Indonesia, many have mistakenly assumed that he is speaking Indonesian or his mother tongue, Sundanese. Director J.J. Abrams was delighted when he first discovered Ruhian and two other actors, Iko Uwais and Cecep Arif Rahman, in an Indonesian action movie called *The Raid*. He wanted them to speak an alien form of Indonesian in *Star Wars*.

This was how these actors' native languages became the initial inspiration for Sara Forsberg. Sara listened to Indonesian, Sundanese and other Asian languages as the basis for Kanjiklub.

In order not to sound like gibberish, she created words and scripted sentences for the actors, who then listened and practised with a dialect coach before recording. Yayan Ruhian said that he liked the Kanjiklub's proximity to Sundanese, as well as its traces of Indian and Thai languages.

The film used only a few of the phrases conceived by Sara Forsberg. Then they assigned subtitles to the edited audio tracks seemingly at random.

> '**sicikadiga madiam**.' – 'It's over for you.' (The same phrase also seems to mean 'twice'.)
> '**kadiam**.' – 'Search the cargo ship.'

Thus, in the *Star Wars* galaxy, the characters continue to speak alienese, but their creators haven't adopted the trend of investing in the creation of real languages that fans can learn. They simply remain faithful to their grammelot heritage.

A Posteriori

LANGUAGES WITH THEIR ROOTS ON EARTH

Proto-Indo-European, Old Norse, Old English, Ancient French, Ulam, Beama, Atlantaen, Goa'uld, Fremen, Galach, Chakobsa, Sullustan, Dog Latin, Latatian, Macaronic, Europanto, Minionese, Cityspeak, Syldavian, Bordurian, Arumbaya, Wakandan, Hen Linge

---

One important distinction to be made in the field of artificial languages is between that of a priori and a posteriori. An a priori conlang, as we have seen, is a language in which the constructed vocabulary is not based on any pre-existing language, such as Na'vi, Klingon, Dothraki or Valyrian. In these cases, the creator of the language has invented every word from scratch. It follows that an a posteriori conlang is one based on existing vocabulary or roots, such as Hergé's Syldavian, Burgess' Nadsat or Orwell's Newspeak, as well as better-known languages such as contemporary Hebrew and New Norwegian.

Constructed languages are not exclusive to literary fiction and sci-fi films; many languages that have grown organically for millennia are also constructed to some extent. Most languages have undergone a process of standardisation wherein people come to agreements on formalities such as spelling and grammar. Languages with no written form that go on to develop a writing system have to consider which characters to use. A pidgin language, which is when two languages are mixed, becomes a creole language when children grow up with it as their mother tongue and, eventually, a full language evolves over generations that requires formalisation. One timely example of the conscious creation of a new word in Swedish is that of *hen*, a gender-neutral alternative to *han/hon* ('he'/'she') that was literally thought up by someone sitting at a desk trying to figure out what the language and its speakers needed.

Artificial languages like Esperanto and Interlingua, which were intended as neutral world languages, are a posteriori art-langs whose vocabulary was derived from existing languages. In the case of Interlingua, this was done very systematically, the idea being that it should include the common international vocabulary that has crept into many (Western, at least) languages as loanwords. In practice, it might be considered a modern Latin, easily understood by anyone who reads French, Spanish or Italian. Brits and Scandinavians can also get a good grasp of it, especially if they have studied a little French at school. Interlingua was launched in 1951 by the International Auxiliary Language Association and is one of the most widely used international auxiliary languages around today, second only to Esperanto.

A posteriori language is useful in literature and popular culture when portraying ancient civilisations through the use of historical language forms or trying to extrapolate languages into the future. The Galach language, from the desert planet of Arrakis in Frank Herbert's *Dune* novels, is described as Anglo-Slavic and reflects the time when it was written – the Cold War, during which the United States and Soviet Union grappled for world domination.

Nadsat in *A Clockwork Orange* is also a product of the same period, so it is no wonder that its teen slang is made up of words borrowed from Russian. In *1984*, Orwell starts from English, then constricts the scope of vocabulary to demonstrate the suppression of rebellious thoughts. In the acclaimed TV series *Vikings*, the actors mainly speak English, but sometimes they break into Old Norse or other language variants of the times.

So, should these be counted as artlangs, revived languages or genuine Old Norse dialects?

In any case, artificial languages are taken seriously in film and TV these days, and the *Vikings* team were no different, putting a lot of thought into how their characters would speak and employing an expert. Kate Wiles, PhD candidate in Old English at the University of Leeds, was given the task of developing some Old English dialogue for when Ragnar Lothbrok and his Viking friends go on a plundering mission to England. Wiles said it was a real challenge to convert Old English into a spoken language, adding that the translation of the script's dialogue was hard work. One unexpected problem she encountered was coming up with a word for 'fur', of which there is no record in Old English. Other challenges included finding synonyms for 'go away' and 'get lost' when the frightened monks in Lindisfarne are attacked by the Vikings.

For the Old Norse, Kate Wiles contacted her colleague, Erika Sigurdsson, an Icelandic doctoral student. The biggest head-scratcher was how to translate the script's lewd insults into Old Norse.

> '**maðrstroðinn!**' – 'Fucker!'
> '**færðu at moga kellingu sjúka!**' – 'Go bang a sick old lady!'
> '**Þú berjast sem kellingr!**' – 'You fight like an old woman!'

For the Vikings' travels to tenth-century Paris, the series needed dialogue in Ancient French, which was created by Dr James Simpson at the University of Glasgow. The lines were relatively easy to translate into Ancient French and Simpson found most of what he needed in *The Song of Roland* from the 1100s. Fortunately, it contains some texts that are rich in colourful language and insults, which certainly came in handy in the TV series. A greater challenge was writing lines in Ancient Low French, a West German language influenced by Ancient French and Ancient German, for which Simpson had to fill the linguistic gaps with loanwords from other ancient Germanic languages.

The show also features some dialogue in Classical Arabic and old East Slavic, occurrences of Latin, proto-Samic and Medieval Greek, as well as battle cries in proto-Latvian. Kate Wiles enjoys it when the Vikings encounter other languages; she sees it as a unique way for a researcher such as herself to put her knowledge into practice and reach an audience of millions. Never before has spoken Old English been exposed to such a large number of people.

Another artificial language used in linguistic–historical contexts is proto-Indo-European, some form of which was probably spoken on the Pontic–Caspian steppe around 5,000–6,000 years ago. The language is a reconstruction – a kind of origin for the Indo-European language family, which makes up a hefty proportion of the languages used today, from Sanskrit and Persian to Irish and Swedish. It is estimated that over 400 Indo-European languages are currently spoken around the world.

This large language family was 'discovered' when people started drawing parallels between Sanskrit, Latin and Greek in the late 1700s and early 1800s, and noticed striking similarities between several seemingly disparate languages.

Swedish	German	English	Irish	Latin	Greek	Sanskrit	Persian
broder	*bruder*	brother	*bráthair*	*frater*	*phrater*	*bhratar*	*baradar*
namn	*name*	name	*anim*	*nomen*	*ónoma*	*naman*	Nam

Through comparing the phonetic divergence among the Indo-European languages, rules could be extrapolated on how these changes came about to track the languages' devolution, so to speak, back to proto-Indo-European – a kind of reconstructed protolanguage.

This idea certainly sparks the imagination, but proto-Indo-European, or PIE, is not a language that historical re-enactors speak in the woods on weekends when they're dressed up. In fact, PIE is never spoken and hardly ever written either. It is mostly a dry scientific hypothesis.

The best-known text in PIE is also the first – a fable from 1868. August Schleicher's text, *The Sheep and the Horses* – Avis Akvāsa's Ka – is just a few sentences long and the original version bears a great deal of similarity to Sanskrit. However, over the next 150 years, as research into PIE deepened, new versions of Schleicher's fable appeared. The first version of the fable goes like this:

Avis Akvāsas Ka

Avis, jasmin varnā na ā ast, dadarka akvams, tam, vāgham garum vaghantam, tam, bhāram magham, tam, manum āku bharantam. Avis akvabhjams ā vavakat: kard aghnutai mai vidanti manum akvams agantam.

Akvāsas ā vavakant: krudhi avai, kard aghnutai vividvant-svas: manus patis varnām avisāms karnauti svabhjam gharmam vastram avibhjams ka varnā na asti.

Tat kukruvants avis agram ā bhugat.

The Sheep and the Horses

A sheep that had no wool saw some horses, one pulling a heavy wagon, one carrying a great burden, one quickly carrying a human. The sheep said to the horses: 'It pains my heart to see a man riding horses.'

The horses said, 'Listen, sheep! It pains our heart to see this: Man, the master, making the sheep's wool into a warm garment and the sheep having no wool.'

On hearing this, the sheep ran away to the field.

In Ridley Scott's *Prometheus* (2012), a kind of prequel to *Alien*, the android David recites Schleicher's fable as he learns PIE in preparation for communicating with creatures that ostensibly visited Earth thousands of years ago. Later in the film, he gets to put his knowledge to use when he speaks a sort of PIE with an ancient space creature. Apparently, there was more of this spoken language developed by English linguist Anil Biltoo, but it was cut. In the film, PIE represents a language that came to humankind from extraterrestrial beings who visited Earth in prehistoric times.

Ulam

Jean-Jacques Annaud's fantasy film *Quest for Fire* (1981) doesn't contain a single word of English, nor of French for that matter, even though it is a French film. It is all in protolanguage.

The film takes place 80,000 years ago when several human species lived side by side. We follow the Ulam, a Neanderthal-like tribe who face catastrophe when they come under attack by another, more primitive, tribe of ape people. The ape people kill many of the Ulam tribe, but worse still, as a result of the fighting and flight from their caves, the Ulam lose their ever-burning source of fire. Fire is the cornerstone of their culture, but they do not possess the knowledge to make it. Three warriors are chosen to seek out new fire and bring it back to the tribe, and the audience follows them on their quest to steal fire back from the gods, or somebody else.

The Ulams' main method of communication is body language, which was created by zoologist Desmond Morris, author of *The Naked Monkey*. He taught the actors a body language based on that of the great apes. But the Ulam language also contains grunts and a few more articulated words. These building blocks of language were formulated by linguist and author Anthony Burgess, who had previously created the teen slang Nadsat in *A Clockwork Orange*.

Morris and Burgess agreed on wanting to move away from the previous stereotypes of Stone Age men beating their chests and grunting, with Desmond Morris believing it possible to reconstruct a credible body language based on our own and that of the great apes, as well as what we know about the environment our prehistoric ancestors inhabited.

When it was dark, or when there was no eye contact, there remained a need to be able to express oneself with something other than gestures and body language. Burgess thought that an early language would be agglutinative – that is, a language consisting of root words to which a prefix or suffix is added. For example, the Ulam tribe's word for 'fruit' is **bouaa**, but fruit hanging in a tree is **bouailt**, where -**ilt** indicates height.

It was the film producers' intention from the beginning to have the Ulam speak a form of proto-Indo-European, and Burgess reasoned that he could take inspiration from the Indo-European language family that would be spoken thousands of years later in the area where the film's action takes place. The first word uttered in the film is '**atr**' – 'fire'. He borrowed this from the Latin *ater/atris* which means 'black' (the French *âtre* means 'fireplace'). He chose this instead of using, for example, the Latin word for 'fire', *ignis*, because Burgess thought that in their world it would be taboo to name the life-giving fire directly, and so they refer instead to the blackened fireplace:

'**atra**.' – 'The fire sees me.'
'**atrom**.' – 'I see the fire.'
'**atrois**.' – 'I am surrounded by fires.'

The word for 'moon' is **buuuun**. Burgess chose this based on an observation that the word for 'moon' in many languages includes a sound that shapes the lips in such a way as to 'imitate the round shape of the moon': moon – *måne* (Swedish), *luna* (Spanish), *bulan* (Indonesian), *tsuki* (Japanese). Thus, Burgess assumed that a proto word for 'moon' should probably contain a long 'oo' or 'u' sound:

'**buuuunan**.' – 'I love the moon.'
'**buuuunu**.' – 'The moon loves me.'

Similarly, Burgess saw a connection between breasts and the 'u' sound. As an example, he mentions the Russian *grud* (which becomes **groodies** in Nadsat), Japanese *mune*, and 'boobs' in English. Therefore, the Ulam word for 'breasts' became **muuv**.

The word for 'animal' is **tir**, taken from the German *tier*, which is also related to the Swedish *djur*. An animal with horns is **tir dondra** ('tree animal'), thus **dondra** is 'tree'. Burgess borrowed this from the Greek *dendros*, which means 'tree'. **Tir hor ro** is a 'horse' and **tir meg** is a 'mammoth'.

aga – water (Latin – *aqua*)
vir – man (Latin – *vir*)
virku – woman
bratt – brother
otim – good
gais – hello
ahaman – peace
jalkan – to go, or move
kas – to give, hand over

The three fire-seekers of the Ulam encounter other tribes and one in particular, the Ivaka, seems to consist of Cro-Magnon people who are more advanced and can make fire. Their speech is largely made up of the Cree language spoken by indigenous people in northern Canada. However, the Cree words used in the film have no connection to the action, supposedly arousing great amusement among speakers of this small language group.

Beama

The film *Alpha* (2018) might be considered a modern version of *Quest for Fire*, with a protagonist on a journey away from his family and tribe, containing sparse dialogue that is a kind of protolanguage. In *Alpha,* however, the foreign dialogue is subtitled and the Stone Age language is at least as credible as Burgess' Ulam, having been created with even more knowledge of the protolanguage.

Dr Christine Schreyer, who teaches anthropological linguistics at the University of British Columbia in Canada, created the language Beama for the film. She based this on three protolanguages, which were an attempt to scientifically reconstruct three truly ancient languages, namely proto-Eurasiatic, proto-Dené-Caucasian and proto-Nostratic. These are hypothetical reconstructed common ancestors of large language families and are as close a representation as possible of language as it may have been 20,000 years ago when the film is set. Based on the phonology and common grammatical features of these protolanguages, Schreyer produced Beama, her version of Cro-Magnon language, with around 1,500 words. Then, she was given the film script and proceeded to translate all the dialogue into this Ice Age language.

So far, little is known about how words might be spelled, but 'son' is **sawa** and 'home' is **mana**. In an interview, Schreyer also gave an example sentence:

'**moa-ta-mi il-ti, nu**.' – 'Now you are my family.'

Christine Schreyer had previously created around 300 words of Kryptonian for the Superman film, *Man of Steel* (2013), where only the written language, inspired by Cree, made it to the silver screen (see the section on Kryptonian, p. 268). She also created the extraterrestrial language Eltarian for *Power Rangers* (2017), about which very little is known.

Atlantean

The idea of a protolanguage is an important part of the animated film *Atlantis: The Lost World* (2001), which saw Disney take part in the long-standing tradition of reimagining the sunken island of Atlantis, the mythological basis of which was taken from Plato's dialogues. Plato himself is said to have heard the legend from the poet Solon, who in turn heard it from an Egyptian priest. Since then, various scholars and amateurs have attempted to locate Atlantis and put forth bold theories about its existence.

One notable example is Swedish natural scientist Olof Rudbeck the Elder (1630–1702), who believed that Atlantis was in fact Sweden. Over centuries the myth has been built on, to the point where it has transformed into a kind of quasi-science in New Age circles, where the idea of unlocking the hidden wisdom of secret Atlantis masters is on a par with telepathic contact with dolphins.

Disney's version of the legend is, of course, just a background for an adventure-filled plot, which races ahead in classic *Indiana Jones* style, but still contributes something unique to the spectrum of Atlantis curiosity – a bona fide Atlantic language.

The film's protagonist, Milo Thatch, is unusual in the world of movie heroes in that he is a linguist. Linguist protagonists have been thin on the ground since Henry Higgins gave Eliza elocution lessons in *My Fair Lady*. Besides Milo Thatch, the most credible cinematic portrayals of linguists are Egyptologist/linguist Dr Daniel Jackson in *Stargate*, and Dr Louise Banks in *Arrival*. Then there is the *Native Tongue* trilogy (which has not been made into a film) where linguists have become a powerful upper class, if not quite heroes. These linguists and languages are discussed later in the book.

In Disney's film, it is 1914 and Milo works in a dusty museum but dreams of following in the footsteps of his explorer grandfather by solving the enigma of Atlantis once and for all. The key to the mystery is found in an old diary written in an unknown language with strange symbols, which Milo manages to decipher: Atlantean.

Disney called in Klingon creator Dr Marc Okrand to construct an 'ancient' language. The people at Disney thought that Atlantean should be the mother of all tongues, the language from which all others originate – a root language. Marc Okrand pointed out that, from a linguistic point of view, it is not a particularly well-grounded theory, but since it is what Milo believes in the film, Okrand constructed a language that could at least stand up to that hypothesis. Okrand, like many others, sought inspiration from proto-Indo-European, and used Indo-European roots as the basis for Atlantean words, unless they were too reminiscent of words in English or other modern languages.

If he couldn't find an appropriate Indo-European root, Okrand turned to other ancient languages such as proto-Tibetan, Hebrew, Arabic, the Native American family, Greek and Latin – or he simply invented one himself. But there is a certain overemphasis on Indo-European roots because, in the film, Atlantis is located in the North Atlantic. The reconstructed words of proto-Indo-European are marked with an asterisk:

ba – to speak (proto-Indo-European: *bha-)
badeg – to be kind (proto-Indo-European: *bhad – 'good', as in 'better')
mar – sea (Latin: *mare*)
mebel – flood (Hebrew: *mabul* 'great flood in the Bible')
ket – whale (Greek: *kētos*)
luk – six (Cantonese and related languages)
ya – eight (one of two Japanese pronunciations of the number *ya [ttsu]*; the more common is *hatchi*.)

As the last two examples show, Atlantean has obtained at least some of its numerals from non-Indo-European languages.

If we compare the words for the numbers one to ten in English, Atlantic and proto-Indo-European (PIE), we may be able to predict a certain relationship between some numbers, while others have their roots in other languages such as Cantonese and Japanese.

English	Atlantean	PIE
one	din	*oynos/*sem
two	dut	*duwo:
three	sey	*treyes
four	kut	*kwetwores
five	sha	*penkwe
six	luk	*sweks
seven	tos	*septm
eight	ya	*okto
nine	nit	*newn
ten	ehep	*dekm

To make ordinal numbers, one can simply add -(d)lag, so 'second' becomes **dutlag** and 'third' becomes **seydlag**. The 'd' is not included after obstruent or nasal consonants.

To write the figures, Okrand drew inspiration from an ancient high culture of Central America. The Atlantean numeral system is a variation on the Mayan numerals.

An Extraterrestrial Egyptian Dialect

The television series *Stargate* features a smattering of words spoken in the extraterrestrial language Goa'uld, which give the impression of being random phrases invented by the script-writers on the fly. Some words are recurring and have a defined meaning, such as:

chappa'ai – Stargate
tau'ri – Earth/Earthling
shol'va – traitor
kree – come/listen/go/be ready/aim/focus

Pretty much all the space creatures encountered by the main characters, Colonel Jack O'Neill and Egyptologist Daniel Jackson, speak modern English without any explanation (such as the universal translator in *Star Trek*). The extraterrestrial words are often just to add an otherworldly flavour.

But Goa'uld has a much richer linguistic background than the occasional words in the TV series would suggest. The TV series is a spin-off of the 1994 movie *Stargate* in which a young Egyptologist, Dr Daniel Jackson, manages to interpret the inscription on a large gate found on the Giza Plateau in Egypt, discovered in 1928 by archaeologist Paul Langford.

The gate turns out to be a 'Stargate'. Stargates open wormholes to different parts of the galaxy, transporting you to another planet in a single step. The gate that Dr Jackson manages to activate leads to a desert planet millions of light years away called Abydos.

The planet Abydos looks like Ancient Egypt during the time of the pharaohs and, after a while, Jackson also comes to understand the inhabitants' language, which turns out to be a so-called hieroglyphic dialect. Jackson can read hieroglyphs but has never heard the language spoken. It turns out that the inhabitants are indeed from Egypt, on Earth. The situation becomes serious when a creature pretending to be the Egyptian sun god Ra, who initially brought people to the planet from Ancient Egypt, arrives again in his pyramid-shaped spaceship.

To add credibility to the film's Egyptian environments, the film hired a genuine Egyptologist, Dr Stuart Tyson Smith, as a consultant and to produce an Ancient Egyptian dialect for the film. Although it has been possible to read hieroglyphs since 1822, when Jean-François Champollion published his study of the three parallel texts on the Rosetta Stone, Ancient Egyptian has not been spoken for many hundreds of years. The hieroglyphs are phonograms – written characters that convey sounds, but represent only consonants, so the vowel sounds of Ancient Egyptian are not known.

Stuart Tyson Smith used several sources to reconstruct Ancient Egyptian, including, among other things, a diplomatic correspondence written in cuneiform script in the ancient East Semitic language Akkadian. This text mentions some Egyptian names, vowels and all, and provides a small base of words of which the correct pronunciation is known.

With this knowledge of how the words are pronounced in Coptic Egyptian, Smith could then establish rules for how other vowels should be pronounced in Ancient Egyptian. This is because Coptic Egyptian, used as a liturgical language in the Coptic Church today, is an Afro-Asiatic language with Ancient Egyptian as its closest 'living' relative. So, Stuart Tyson Smith extrapolated Coptic rules back in time as a basis for the phonology of Ancient Egyptian. He also looked at other Afro-Asian languages such as Chadian, Ethiopian, Aramaic, Arabic and Hebrew for tips on pronunciation and grammar.

Based on this, Smith came up with a variant of Ancient Egyptian which he thought was a reasonable reconstruction of the language as it may have sounded in 1200 BCE. But the language spoken in the film would be an Egyptian dialect that had existed on the planet Abydos with no Egyptian contact for millennia, so Smith designed the language with an evolution all of its own, featuring more Coptic traits. It resulted in a dialect that anyone familiar with Ancient Egyptian could just about understand. So, with a little imagination, the spoken and written language in the movie *Stargate* should be fully understandable to Egyptologists, like Dr Jackson, in the film.

After *Stargate* became a success, a television series followed, with no fewer than 214 episodes between 1997 and 2007. It is revealed that Ra, the godly creature who enslaved the humans of Ancient Egypt and moved them to the planet Abydos, is from an extraterrestrial race called the Goa'uld. They are symbiotes and parasites and need other creatures such as humans to use as host bodies. The Goa'uld are actually a kind of super-eel that takes over the body and mind of its host – their favourite hosts being human. For thousands of years, the Goa'uld rule Earth, masquerading as or being mistaken for gods in the mythology of different cultures. Eventually, the earthlings manage to rebel and bury the Stargate in Giza.

The Stargates are a widespread transport network across the galaxy, through which the protagonists in the series can travel to a new planet in every episode, discovering and rescuing various alien cultures enslaved by the Goa'uld. In the TV series, we also know that the language we call Ancient Egyptian is actually Goa'uld, implying that proto-Ancient Egyptian came from another planet when the Goa'uld began using people as hosts.

The TV series didn't use Stuart Tyson Smith or his reconstructed Ancient Egyptian. Most of what is spoken in the TV series is gibberish invented by various screenwriters. But since certain words and phrases in the TV series have a translation, they are understandable and become a part of the language anyway. In the series, the language also appears in written form as decoration, using both hieroglyphs and Meroitic script, an Egyptian alphabet with its origin in hieroglyphs.

Stargate has also birthed a couple of spin-off series over the years, where other extraterrestrial beings have appeared. Loosely modelled on gods from other mythologies, these beings occasionally utter a word or two loosely based on, for example, Old Norse or Latin. But the languages these creatures use were certainly not developed in the same way as *Stargate*'s Ancient Egyptian was.

In 2018, a prequel was made to *Stargate* called *Stargate Origins*, which takes place in 1938. It revolves around Professor

Langford, who discovered the Stargate in 1928, and his daughter Catherine Langford. Originally a web series of ten episodes, each ten minutes long, it was later edited into a feature film. Interestingly, the production team re-hired Stuart Tyson Smith to get the Goa'uld dialogue right. So, now that the focus was once again on archaeologists and Egyptologists, the language returned to its Ancient Egyptian roots, after over twenty years of more or less ignoring them. At least one word from the vocabulary of the TV series has been loaned to Smith's Ancient Egyptian – **Goa'uld**.

A credible Ancient Egyptian language is a good start, but the language was made a little more alien with random words invented by various scriptwriters of the TV show. Any fans keen on learning the extraterrestrial Ancient Egyptian language have plenty to sink their teeth into. And as the dialect is based on legitimate scientific hypotheses about Ancient Egyptian and decorated with a few hundred extraterrestrial words from the TV series, a committed Goa'uld enthusiast could compile an interesting grammar and dictionary:

From the film:

> '**yimyu ma-yay naturru tee!**' – 'Look at your gods!'
> '**rrridiaouw woo oo rrri-ou!**' – 'There can only be one Ra!'
> '**di'bro, das weiafei, doo'wa.**' – 'People, welcome them, the gods have come.'
> '**na'noweia si'taia.**' – 'You are here to destroy me.'

From the TV series:

> '**a woo na nakhe.**' – 'The day of our victory.'
> '**yoi te sai moi.**' – 'I didn't tell them.'
> '**ne way na ga we.**' – 'We will not live as slaves.'
> '**Sha'uri, yi shi qi boy?**' – 'Sha'uri, what happened here?'

Fremen and Chakobsa

Deep in the wilderness of the desert planet Arrakis lives the secretive desert tribe the Fremen. They speak Fremen, a Semitic language related to Arabic. Frank Herbert, author of the classic *Dune* series, used Arabic terms and Bedouin people (as well as Native Americans) as a basis for the desert people and their languages. Arabic, as you might imagine, has a rich vocabulary to describe the desert and various types of sand formations. But the name **Fremen** itself is probably derived from English – in a first draft of *Dune*, Herbert called the Fremen 'Free Men'. In addition, the Tuareg people, one of the nomadic desert peoples that Herbert used as inspiration, do indeed call themselves 'free men'. The Fremen also speak Chakobsa, a second language used primarily for ritualistic and military purposes.

The Fremen are descendants of a persecuted group known as the Zensunni wanderers, a religious sect of Sunni Muslims strongly inspired by Zen Buddhism, as the name implies. The Zensunnis' religious ideas have evolved over time to the point where little of Islam or Buddhism remains in the religion and mythology of the Fremen.

The books also reveal the mystic intergalactic conspiracy and breeding sect of the Bene Gesserit. As part of their **Missionaria Protectiva**, the Bene Gesserit deliberately plant mythological elements in the Fremen religion to provide stranded Bene Gesserit sisters (like the protagonist's mother, Lady Jessica) with myths and titles they can apply to protect themselves in an emergency. As a result of this, Lady Jessica is able to quickly adopt the role of **sayyadina** ('priestess'), utilising the mythology to benefit herself and her son, Paul Atreides.

The Fremen language evolves throughout the course of their travels, spanning a millennium. Although rooted in Arabic, it becomes influenced by local languages on various planets inhabited by the Zensunni wanderers. When the Zensunni lived on the planet Rossak, a Fremen spiritual leader named Yarbuz managed to connect with the memories of their ancestors and realised how much their language had changed. Thus, a language reform process was initiated to revert it to its original form (probably quite close to Arabic). This meant rolling back 16,000 years(!) of language development.

When the Fremen finally settle on the planet Arrakis, the language has changed and developed again, and at this point Fremen seems closer to Arabic than one might imagine after 16,000 years of development. Here is an example of the same phrase translated into Arabic and Fremen:

English: 'A bird in the hand is worth two in the bush.'
Arabic: '*Kuntu sa'idan fi shabÂbi.*'
Fremen: '**Kuntu saghidan fi shababi.**'

Many Fremen words come from Arabic but are used differently. Khalid M. Baheyeldin, an Egyptian living in Canada, presents a thorough analysis of the similarities between Fremen and Arabic on his website and gives examples of words that have an Arabic root. The Fremen women's garment **aba**, for example, probably derived from *abaya* – a traditional Muslim women's garment. The Fremen communities live in well-hidden, well-guarded caves called **sietch**, which is similar to *seeq*, the Arabic name for the hidden city of Petra, carved into cliffs in the Jordanian desert.

Herbert took the priestess title **sayyadina** from *sayyed*, which means 'master' in Arabic, while other Fremen words are derived from Persian and Turkish. **Padishah** ('emperor') is a direct loan from Persian, and the cries of the Fremen water vendors, '**Soo-soo sook!**', is similar to the traditional cry heard from Turkish water vendors: '*Su, soğuk su!*' ('Water, cold water!')

Fremen also has borrowed words from languages spoken on other planets in the *Dune* universe, and those languages are in turn related to other terrestrial languages. The lingua franca is an Anglo-Slavic hybrid called Galach. This gave Fremen words such as **kanly** (a kind of formal vendetta), **chaumus** ('poisoned food') and **chaumurky** ('poisoned drink'), in which the Slavic origins of Galach are clear.

In *The Dune Encyclopedia*, compiled by Dr Willis McNelly in 1984, there is a piece written by student John Quijada that goes into some detail about Fremen which Frank Herbert supposedly approved. Quijada describes how the Fremen language has changed over time and, among other things, how many characteristic Arabic sounds disappeared. The pronunciation of Fremen became more Western, so to speak.

The Fremen script is based on written Arabic, but some characters have changed, most noticeably in that Fremen contains symbols for the vowels 'a', 'e', 'i', 'o' and 'u'. This makes the Fremen writing system an alphabet, as opposed to the Arabic writing system, which is an *abjad*, meaning it consists mainly of consonants, marking vowels with special diacritical marks. (These are like accents, apostrophes and dots that change the sound of a letter – like how the accent on the 'e' in café tells you how to pronounce it.)

The Dune Encyclopedia also gives a few longer sentences as examples of Fremen from a speech by Paul Muad'Dib (apparently rather lightly modified Egyptian Arabic). Intriguingly, there are two slightly different translations of this sentence:

Innama nishuf al-asir mayyit. u hiy ayish.	Though we deem the captive dead, yet does she live.
liana zaratha zarati. u gawlha gawli.	For her seed is my seed and her voice is my voice.
U tishuf hatt al-hudud alman albaid.	And she sees unto the farthest reaches of possibility.
aywa libarr adam al-malum tishuf liani.	Yea, unto the vale of the unknowable does she see because of me.

In the 2003 TV series *Children of Dune*, there was a song in Fremen that got linguists excited, **Inama Nushif** – 'She is Eternal'. However, upon closer inspection, it appeared that the Fremen text did not match the translation provided in the television series because the scriptwriter simply took random Fremen phrases from Paul Muad'Dib's aforementioned speech:

Fremen	*Children of Dune*	*Dune Encyclopedia*
Inama nushif	She is eternal	Even if we think
Al-asir hiy ayish	No malice can touch	The prisoner is dead, she lives on
Lia-anni	Singular and ageless	Because
Zaratha zarati	Perpetually bound	Her seed is my seed
hatt al-hudad	Through the tempest	… to the furthest parts
Al-maahn al-baiid	be it deluge or sand	Of what is possible
Ay-yah idare	A singlular voice	Yes, to the valley
Adamm malum	speaks through the torrent	For the unknown

Here we can see important differences in attitudes to languages in literature and film: it can either be a flourish, to add flavour and authenticity, or it can be linguistically genuine. As a way to create atmosphere and give an idea of how Fremen people sound, the song is fine, but if you consider Fremen to be a genuine language, you might feel a little cheated.

The second Fremen language, Chakobsa, known as the magnetic language, is derived from Bhotani Jib, a secret language used by the Bhotani assassins of ancient times. **Jib** seems to refer to a work-specific language or kind of slang, which Chakobsa also appears to be. The term is also used by non-Fremen groups, such as House Atreides, which names Chakobsa as its internal language. The Chakobsa of the Fremen is also described as a hunting language.

While the Arabic roots of Fremen are evident, it is harder to pinpoint a single earthly language that inspired Frank Herbert to create Chakobsa, although the name itself comes from a secret medieval Chechen language of the same name, meaning 'language of the hunters'. We have seen before that Frank Herbert has taken inspiration from Islamic cultures so it is no surprise that he would borrow the name of the Chakobsa hunting language from Chechnya.

As the language is used primarily in ritual contexts, there are some examples of ritualistic phrases, such as the Fremen funeral ceremony when the water of a deceased tribe member returns to the tribe:

> 'ima trava okolo!' – 'Here are the ashes!'
> 'i korenja okolo!' – 'and here are the roots!'
> 'ekkeri-akairi, fillissin-follas. Kivi a-kavi, nakalas!
> Nakalas! Ukair-an … jan, jan, jan.' – 'This is the water
> [of the new owner]. Never again will it be measured and
> counted by the heartbeat [of the water's previous owner]
> … go, go, go.'

For the first two sentences, Herbert was inspired by Serbian/Bosnian/Croatian, while the final chant was taken from Romani. The Serbian/Bosnian/Croatian phrases, in particular, have caused many a head to be scratched, and mean 'There is grass all around! There are roots around here!' Of course, this is *not* Serbo-Croat, rather it is a language spoken many thousands of years in the future. But isn't it curious that Herbert chose this particular phrase and translated it incorrectly?

The chant is even more baffling, and understandably so, given that it is from a magical nonsense rhyme that Herbert found in the book *Gypsy Sorcery and Fortune Telling* from the late 1800s.

In the book, the author Charles Godfrey Leland remembers a common nursery rhyme from his childhood:

ekkeri [or ickery], akkery, u-kéry an,
fillisi', follasy, Nicholas John,
queebee – quabee – Irishman [or, Irish Mary],
stingle 'em – stangle 'em – buck!

There are several slightly different versions, but according to Godfrey it is derived from a Romani nursery rhyme which, translated into English, becomes something like this:

First – here – you begin!
castle, gloves. You don't play!
go on!
a kettle. How are you?
stáni, buck.

It's still not particularly clear, but apparently Herbert thought it fit for ritual use by the Fremen, so he borrowed nonsense Romani and turned it into Chakobsa.

This old book also lets us solve the mystery of the strange, seemingly Serbo-Croat phrases. Either Frank Herbert made mistakes, or he simplified the phrase to make it sound better for his purposes. The two lines are from a song about unrequited love and how to make a love potion.

ima trava u okolo Savea,	There are herbs along Sava,
i korenja okolo jasenja	and roots around the ash trees.

According to Godfrey, the song originates from Slavonia in Croatia, where the River Sava flows, and it means 'ash' as in the tree, not as in 'ashes'. Herbert has removed the last words of each line – the River Save(a) and *jasenja*, which means 'ash' –

probably to make it sound more like chanting when he turned it into Chakobsa. Or, are these changes simply down to the language's evolution over the millennia?

At the time of writing, Denis Villeneuve has filmed a new version of *Dune*, for release in late 2021, which is awaited with much anticipation by anyone interested in the languages of Frank Herbert's universe. The production team hired David J. Peterson, who has been designing languages for film and television since 2009 when he created Dothraki for *Game of Thrones*. This guarantees that there will be a considered, faithful and interesting expansion of Fremen and Chakobsa, and possibly also a little Galach. Unlike most other languages created by David J. Peterson, there is already a lot of background and examples of Frank Herbert's language in books and surrounding material such as *The Dune Encyclopedia*.

Sullustan

In *Return of the Jedi* (1983), Lando Calrissian's co-pilot on the *Millennium Falcon* is called Nien Nunb and comes from the planet Sullust. As is to be expected when it comes to extra-terrestrial tongues of *Star Wars*, sound designer Ben Burtt was involved in the creation of his alien language. For Sullustan, Burtt simply had Kenyan exchange student Kipsang Rotich speak a few phrases in Kikuyu, Haya and Kalenjin. They didn't bother with a whole invented language for Nien Nunb's few lines. Burtt didn't expect anyone who saw the film to understand these languages, which are spoken primarily in Kenya and Tanzania.

Burtt used his usual technique for designing languages, recording Kipsang Rotich speaking about everyday things and planning to fiddle around with it in his studio later to eventually end up with alienese. However, when he asked Kipsang Rotich to read Nien Nunb's lines from the script he liked his reading so much he decided to use it just as it was.

Thus, Kipsang Rotich became the voice of Nien Nunb, while the body was a puppet played by Mike Quinn and a couple of other puppeteers. The puppet was silent during the filming of the scenes and Lando (Billy Dee Williams) had to speak his lines to no response. The name Nien Nunb is not quite as extra-terrestrial as it sounds; it was a spin on 'number nine' – the puppet's order in the packing list.

Burtt claims that the lines in Haya and Kikuyu, which were unchanged in the film, are straight out of the script and fully understandable to anyone who speaks the languages, but a stubborn rumour claims that the phrase, 'A thousand herds of elephants are standing on my foot' can be heard in Haya. I can't say whether or not this is true, but the first phrase that Nien Nunb utters is:

'atiriri, inyué haría murí haria muke haha ...'

This is clearly in Kikuyu but doesn't fit the context and probably didn't arise from the original script, which reads, 'All of you over there, come here.' To which Lando Calrissian replies, 'Don't worry, my friend's down there.'

'ong'ete akwek pichunguni?'

The line above is in Kipsang Rotich's native language, Kalenjin, but it doesn't make sense in the scene where the following line is spoken: 'Are you awake now, you there?' This scene with Nien Nunb always arouses great amusement in Kenya and Tanzania, where Kipsang Rotich has become something of a celebrity. However, he received no formal recognition and his name didn't appear in the film's credits.

The Force Awakens, Episode VII of the Star Wars saga, came out in 2015 and saw the return of many characters from Episode VI, released thirty years earlier. Director J.J. Abrams wanted Nien

Nunb to make a comeback and was adamant that Mike Quinn and Kipsang Rotich reprise the role. Quinn was easy to find, but Rotich, who had been an exchange student in 1983, had left the United States shortly after delivering Nien Nunb's lines.

They tried to track him down through his old university, the Kenyan Embassy and Ben Burtt's old archive, but got nothing but an automated reply that bounced back from an old email address. In the end, they tried to put out a very discreet request in a Facebook group for Kenyan actors without mentioning *Star Wars*. People put two and two together and soon bloggers and news sites picked up the story that 'American producer is looking for *Star Wars* voice actors'.

Eventually, they managed to find Kipsang Rotich and get him to a studio in Kenya to record dozens of new lines. The film team needed a few sentences to choose from so they could edit in two lines that matched the puppet's mouth movements, which had already been filmed. The next day, a new trailer for *The Force Awakens* was released, including Nien Nunb's newly recorded performance. After thrity-two years, Kipsang Rotich finally ended up in a *Star Wars* movie's credits!

The two lines in the film are in Kikuyu:

'**nĩmakũmũhũra**.' – 'It is to defeat you.'
'**acio mokĩte mũno**.' – 'They are coming soon.'

So, Kikuyu and Kalenjin form the basis for Sullustan, but it wouldn't be true *Star Wars* alienese unless Ben Burtt got involved with the final product. There is a short chapter on Sullustan hair-dressing terms, bizarrely enough, in Burtt's *Star Wars: Galactic Phrase Book & Travel Guide*. Apparently, the inhabitants of the planet Sullust – although they lack hair themselves – are famous throughout the galaxy for their hairdressing talents. So, besides the lines in the movies, the only known Sullustan is twenty-one phrases about hair removal!

'**a'foos mak bubon h'iok**.' – 'I'd like to get my head shaved.'
'**k'ying goh k'wang see**.' – 'Don't cut it too short.'
'**jima ja mooska wa Wookiee moo**.' – 'Give me a regular Wookiee haircut.'
'**m'ho towhunee moonee end zigwa**.' – 'I'd like to have my body shaved and polished.'

Basic Dialects

The language most commonly used in *Star Wars* is, of course, Galactic Basic – the language represented in the films by English. Such a galactic lingua franca would undoubtedly be coloured by different dialects, variants and pidgins from different corners of the galaxy. However, the filmmakers came under criticism for using non-Western dialects and accents to express otherworldliness, such as with Jar Jar Binks and his Gunganese creole. George Lucas apparently took inspiration from his 6-year-old son for Binks' way of speaking, but there are obvious similarities to Caribbean Creole languages, such as Jamaican Patois. Some believe that Gunganese, and the Gungans themselves, are a prejudiced caricature of Afro-Caribbean people. The characters and language are a little childlike and give the impression of a naive and somewhat gormless race.

The Neimoidian aliens and character Nute Gunray have received similar criticism. When finding an extraterrestrial dialect for Viceroy Gunray, actors from several different countries read the lines before they settled on a Thai actor who read the lines with a Thai accent. The actor then had to mimic this accent for Nute's dialogue. The Neimoidians have been criticised for 'Hollywood Orientalism' and presenting a stereotypical image of Asians.

Another well-known example is when the quick-witted blue-winged merchant Watto isn't speaking in Huttese, he pronounces Galactic Basic in a way that, in combination with his large nose, has been criticised for playing into anti-Semitic and anti-Arab stereotypes.

Still, the most interesting basic dialect is that of Jedi Master Yoda, which has no obvious model. He tends to speak with an unusual word order – object-subject-verb – which is rare in earthly languages. It gives Yoda's English a mystical, other-worldly shimmer and emphasises his habit of speaking in rid-dles. It has never been revealed what alien race Yoda belongs to, what planet he comes from, or what his home language is, but as professor of linguistics at Queen Mary University of London David Adger observes, it is obvious that Galactic Basic/English is not his native language.

David Adger thinks that we can say something about the lan-guage that Yoda grew up with, which he calls 'Yodic', by studying his unique way of speaking. Linguists call it 'linguistic inter-ference', referring to the different ways we transfer linguistic rules from the language we speak to new languages we learn. Hence Germans, Swedes and French people make characteristic German, Swedish and French errors when speaking English, because it is easy to fall into the grammatical rules from our respective languages.

After analysing Yoda's speech, David Adger concluded that his home language could be Hawaiian! Or an alien language reminiscent of Hawaiian in any case. There's a hot tip for the filmmakers anyway, in case they decide to visit Yoda's home planet in some future film …

Dog Latin and Other Macaronic Languages

Several languages are mentioned in this book, such as Quenya, High Valyrian and Hen Linge, which play the role of Latin in their fictional worlds, representing an older cultural language used for science, poetry, literature and, not least, magic.

In our own world, Latin is sometimes used as a linguistic prop, or rather a simplified or distorted variant of Latin – dog Latin. The classic magic chant 'hocus pocus' is a well-known example of dog Latin. This is probably something that church-goers thought they heard in mass, condensing *hoc est enim corpus meum* into 'hocus pocus', which came to signify something incomprehensible, exalted and magical. Obviously Latin – the language of priests – would be perceived as extraordinary and charged with power.

Latin still feels appropriate for magical incantations – it is strange and exotic, yet vaguely familiar and understandable for many readers. The most famous dog Latin spells today are from Hogwarts School of Witchcraft and Wizardry. '**Expelliarmus!**', '**Lumos!**' and '**Expecto Patronum!**' are well-known magic spells even beyond Harry Potter's universe. Most of the magical formulae that J.K. Rowling invented for her wizarding world were cobbled together in dog Latin. **Expelliarmus**, for example, consists of the Latin words *expello* ('banish') and *arma* ('weapon'). Therefore, it is a magic spell to banish weapons, i.e. to disarm. **Lumos**, from the Latin *lumen* ('light'), is a spell to make a magic wand emit light. Extinguishing the light from the wand again requires the word **Nox**, from the Latin for 'night'. **Expecto Patronum**, from *expecto* ('I wait') and *patronus* ('protector'), is an effective magic spell for invoking protector spirits to defend oneself from the soul-sucking dementors. **Dementor**, incidentally, is also a term derived from Latin: *demens* – 'insane'.

Many of Rowling's spells are close to Latin, while other phrases clearly show that magic has a language unto itself. In **Wingardium Leviosa**, the spell to make objects levitate, we can see the word 'wing' from English joined with the Latin *arduus* ('steep', 'high') and a Latin-esque ending *-ium*. **Leviosa** comes from the Latin *levi* ('light', as in weight). In a protective spell against enchantment, **Salvio hexia**, we can see *salvus* from Latin, which means 'healthy' or 'safe', and also forms the greeting *salve*, but the second word seems to derive from the German *hexe* with a Latin ending *–ia*. In the spell **Riddikulus**, the spelling seems to be significant as it differs from both the Latin *ridiculus* and the English 'ridiculous'.

The magic language used by wizards and witches is not classical Latin. Could magical Latin perhaps be even older than Muggle Latin? Or is it a variant of Latin that continued to evolve as Latin solidified into its traditional form in the Muggle world? There seems to be classic Latin in the *Harry Potter* world as well, such as Hogwarts' school motto: *Draco dormiens nunquam titillandus* – 'Never tickle a sleeping dragon'.

Maybe magic spells have to follow their own grammatical rules to work?

Other spells do not originate from Latin. **Anapneo**, which removes something stuck in the throat, seems to stem from the Greek for 'I breathe'. The dancing spell **Tarantallegra** appears to be derived from the Italian dance *tarantella* and another Italian word *allegro* – a musical tempo designation meaning 'cheerfully, with speed'. The most terrible of all curses, **Avada Kedavra**, seems to be related to another more common, and far less horrible, incantation: *abracadabra*. This probably comes from *avra kehdabra* from the Aramaic, meaning something like 'I create as I speak'. One last strange magic spell, which indicates that the magical language of witches and wizards is more interesting than it first appears, is **Alohomora**. This magical word that opens locks and doors seems to originate from Madagascar, oddly enough. In Madagascar, they practise a divination method known as *Sikidy*, in which they create patterns with seeds and grains to predict the future based on sixteen possible figures. One of these figures is called *alohomora* and its appearance in a reading can be interpreted as 'favourable to thieves'. And what could be more favourable to thieves than a lock-opening spell?

Latatian

On the slightly convex Discworld, which rests on the backs of four giant elephants, who in turn stand on the back of the huge turtle Great A'Tuin, there is a language called Latatian. Latatian is the Latin of Discworld, or the dog Latin, to be precise. Discworld creator Terry Pratchett even called the language 'very bad doggy Latin'.

In Discworld they mainly speak Morporkian, which corresponds to English, but also a number of other languages that have counterparts in our spherical world: Quirmian (French), Überwaldian (German), Ephebian (Greek) and Klatchian (Arabic). There are also examples of a language for trolls and the Dwarf language Kad'k (which is somewhat reminiscent of Tolkien's Khuzdûl).

Latatian is a dead language mainly used in mottos, and many are the organisations, guilds and families that have mottos in Discworld:

Quanti Canicula Ille In Fenestra – 'How Much is that Doggy in the Window' (the city of Ankh-Morpork)
Id Murmuratis, Id Ludamus – 'You Hum It, We'll Play It' (the Musicians' Guild)
Moneta Supervacanea, Magister? – 'Spare Change, Guv'nor?' (the Beggars' Guild)
Nunc Id Vides, Nunc Ne Vides – 'Now You See It, Now You Don't' (the Unseen University)
Fabricati Diem, Pvnc – 'To Protect and Serve' (Ankh-Morpork City Watch)

The Watch claim that their motto means 'yo protect and serve', but if you translate the Latatian with a rudimentary knowledge of Latin it might be interpreted as 'make my day, punk' – although really the motto is an abbreviation of **Fabricati Diem, Pvncti Agvnt Celeriter** – 'Make the Day, the Moments Pass

Quickly'! There are also a few Latatian phrases here and there in Pratchett's extensive Discworld treasury, such as the character Rincewind's exclamation, '**Stercus, Stercus, Morituri Sum**!' – 'Oh shit, oh shit, I'm going to die!'

As you can see, Terry Pratchett inserts Latin as witty titbits for those in the know, and it is fair to say that humour is probably the main use of dog Latin. The term 'dog Latin' can be used for bad Latin, such as in homemade mottos intended to be proper Latin wherein the comedy is unintentional, but it is mainly used intentionally for comic effect in fiction and journalism.

The tradition of using Latin for humorous purposes goes back a long way. English poet and actor George Alexander Stevens' *Lecture on Heads* (1765) parodies legal Latin in the description of a kitchen:

Camera necessaria pro usus cookare, cum saucepannis, stewpannis, scullero, dressero, coalholo,	A necessary room for the purpose of cooking, with saucepans, stewpans, scullery, dresser, coalhole, stoves,
stovis, smoak-jacko; pro roastandum, boilandum, fryandum, et plumpudding mixandum, pro turtle	smoke-jack; for roasting, boiling, frying, and mixing plum pudding, for turtle
soupos, calves-head-hashibus, cum calipee et calepashibus.	soups, calves-head hashes, with calipee and calipashes.

Dog Latin can also be called Macaronic Latin, which ties it into the Macaronic language family. This is a term coined in the sixteenth century by the monk Teofilo Folengo as a reference to his description of macaroni as 'a thick, artificial and rustic stew made from a mixture of flour, cheese and butter'. In other words, Macaronics are a sort of language stew.

In the Middle Ages, Macaronic verse was usually a combination of Latin and the vernacular, sometimes mixing individual words and sentences, or using Latin forms of inflection with modern words. The traditional hymn '*In Dulci Jubilo*' is a good example of such a language hodgepodge. It is a choral Christmas carol written in a Macaronic mix of German and Latin in 1328. It first appeared fully translated into English – therefore omitting the Macaronic element – in the sixteenth century. The first verse of the English/Latin Macaronic version from 1827 is:

In dulci jubilo
Let us our homage show
Our heart's joy reclineth
In praesepio
And like a bright star shineth
Matris in gremio!
Alpha es et O!

This Macaronic language was also a favourite of bored school children and students scribbling quick, witty verse when lessons began to drag. Indeed, this is most likely to be the origin of dog Latin's use within a certain kind of academic humour. It requires a level of education to keep up with both the Latin humour and the Macaronic mixed-language jokes.

Of course, not all Latin jokes have to be academic. In the comic book series *Asterix*, the pirates laconically cite correct Latin sentences, like *errare humanum est*, when their ships are repeatedly sunk by the Gauls. There are also some simpler linguistic jokes in the characters' names, like the Romans, Gluteus Maximus, Giveusabonus, Crismus Bonus and Magnumopus. This is not too dissimilar from the rudimentary Latin jokes in Monty Python's *Life of Brian*, in which they build a whole scene around the names Biggus Dickus and Incontinentia Buttocks.

There are a whole host of other, rather simple, jokes that rely on the audience interpreting Latin from another language:

E pluribus unum – Plumbers united (Out of many, one)
Cave canem – Cave of the dog (Beware of the dog)
Cogito ergo sum – I think I've added that up correctly (I think, therefore I am)

Caesar adsum jam forte	*Caesar 'ad some jam for tea*	I, Caesar, am already here by chance
Brutus aderat	*Brutus 'ad a rat*	Brutus was present
Caesar sic in omnibus	*Caesar sick in omnibus*	Caesar thus in all things
Brutus sic in at	*Brutus sick in 'at*	Brutus thus in but

But for longer sentences in Latin, or dog Latin, some knowledge of Latin or modern Romance languages such as French or Spanish is soon required to keep up with the jokes.

For example, British satirical magazine *Private Eye* has a recurring column, 'That honorary degree citation in full', which prints slightly longer playful texts in made-up Latin that require a little more knowledge on the part of the reader. The standing joke alludes to academic titles and honorary doctorates where Latin is still used in academic ceremonies and on documents and diplomas.

When Bob Dylan was awarded an honorary doctorate in music at St Andrew's University (which he came to receive in person!), naturally some parts of the ceremony were performed in Latin. In response to this, *Private Eye* published the tongue-in-cheek, 'That Bob Dylan honorary degree citation in full':

Robertus Dylanum (natum Zimmermanicum) cantorum americanus folkerensis et harmonica virtuosum. Celebratissimus anno sexuagensis cum hitto maximo 'ave homo tamburinus', 'tempores mutando' et naturaliter 'responsus est, amicus meus, pufferandum in vento'.

We salute Robert Dylan (born Zimmerman) American folk singer and harmonica virtuoso. A most celebrated man of sixty years with big hit 'Hey Mr Tambourine Man', 'The Times They Are A-Changing' and naturally 'The Answer, My Friend, is Blowing in the Wind'.

Perhaps Terry Pratchett was doffing his cap to this regular column with his made-up Latin in an honorary doctorate in one of his books, **Doctorum Adamus cum Flabello Dulci** – 'Doctor of Sweet Fanny Adams'; that is to say, of absolutely nothing.

Eine Language Europese

Europanto, like other Macaronic languages, is based on humour – only it didn't originate from a satirical magazine or humorous author, but rather from another winsome assembly: the Council of the European Union. It was invented by author Diego Marani when he worked as a translator for the EU Council in 1996. Like other Macaronic languages, it is based on the arbitrary use of a variety of European languages and leaves it up to the speaker to make themselves understood by using words that are recognisable to the listener or reader.

As an example, here are a couple of questions from an EU quiz put together by Diego Marani:

Welches esse der objective des Europese Unione?
• Finde eine alternative aan Jeux sans frontiers

- **Integrate Europese countries**
- **Make dinero mit autostradale tolls**

Wat esse Euro?
- **Eine stop des Frankfurt metro**
- **Eine brand lessive detergente**
- **Der common Europese money**

The presentation is tongue-in-cheek, but Marani is highlighting the need for an international language other than English. This is the same need that Esperanto, Interlingua and others have tried to address, using a common international (Western) vocabulary. Europanto does so without any grammatical rules, leaving it up to the communicators themselves to make themselves comprehensible. In a multilingual workplace such as the Council of the European Union, there is likely to be a de facto sort of Europanto in use, with people switching between languages for clarification. A sentence in French, a word in German, and then English.

Apart from a few articles and the novel *Las Adventures des Inspector Cabillot* (1998), Europanto hasn't been of any concrete use – yet.

Minionese

Minions – the little yellow creatures from the *Despicable Me* franchise – got their own prequel, *Minions*, in 2015, so naturally they got their own language too. The Minions are a rather unintelligent species who have made it their lives' mission to serve various evil geniuses or supervillains.

In the film, we learn about the Minions' origin and back story, following them through history, from the time they first crawled out of the sea, to serving one villain after another. The Minions continually mess things up so that the villain fails, fires the Minions, or simply dies. After being employed by a dinosaur, a caveman, an Egyptian pharaoh, Genghis Khan and Napoleon, the Minions exile themselves to Antarctica. It is not until 1968 that they venture out again to look for a new supervillain employer. Finally, they find the world's first female supervillain, Scarlet Overkill, at a supervillain fair in Orlando.

Director and voice actor Pierre Coffin is the person behind Minionese, or Banana Language, as it is also known. According to Coffin, the Minions' language can be explained by their nomadic history, snapping up words from different languages and cultures over the centuries, which is why Minionese contains certain words and phrases that are very similar to other languages. Really, the language is a kind of grammelot that Coffin made up retroactively as he recorded the voices, but he had the idea of inserting real words and phrases from a variety of languages for the sake of recognition and a sense of real language, as opposed to gibberish.

Pierre Coffin has joked that he used Indian and Chinese restaurant menus for ideas, and several dishes are indeed distinguishable in Minionese if you listen carefully, like **poulet tiki masala**. But Coffin has clearly taken inspiration from more than just takeaway menus:

terima kasih – 'thank you' (from Indonesian)
kampai – 'cheers' (from Japanese)
pwede na? – 'can we begin?' (from Tagalog)
naje – 'take it' (from Chinese)
tulaliloo ti amo! – 'We love you!' (from Italian: *ti amo* – 'I love you')
gelato – ice cream (from Italian)
para tu – 'for you' (from Spanish: *para ti*)
la boda – wedding (from Spanish)
hana – one (Korean)
dul – two (Korean)
sae – three (Korean)

There are many other phrases inspired by different languages, but they don't always make sense within the context. Coffin chose them because they sounded good and fitted in with the melody of Minionese. The Minion language has a distinct child-like flavour, and it sounds as cute as the adorable yellow characters look. Some words are childishly onomatopoeic, or just a child's variant of a word:

'**bee do bee do bee do**!' – 'Fire!'
'**poopaye**.' – 'Goodbye.'
'**bello**.' – 'Hello.'
baboi – toy
babble – apple
'**under wear**' – 'I swear'

The Minionese word for 'I' is **me**, which fits in with the baby-ish style, given how commonly children mix up these words in English. 'I'm hungry' in Minionese becomes '**Me want banana**'!

In another scene, some Minions try to lift something and one of them says, '**me le due, spetta**' – 'wait, I'll do it' – which sounds Italian-inspired: *Io lo faccio, aspetta*. By adding **me** and **due**, Coffin makes the phrase sound like something an English toddler might say – 'Me do it!'

We probably haven't seen the last of the Minions on either the silver screen or television, so we probably haven't heard the last of Minionese either.

Cityspeak

The neo-noir classic *Blade Runner* (1982), directed by Ridley Scott, depicts a dark, rainy Los Angeles in the year 2019. It is a gigantic city with breathtaking architecture towering over a toxic, dystopian landscape existing in perpetual twilight with a retro-futuristic aesthetic. There, old technology exists alongside flying cars, spaceships and, most importantly, replicants.

Replicants are artificial copies of human beings that are used as slaves – if such a term can be applied to manufactured objects – when humans colonise other planets. Replicants lack emotions but have the ability to develop human emotions over time. Their lifespan is therefore limited to four years. A special police force called Blade Runners are assigned to identify and 'retire' (read: 'kill') all replicants who are on Earth illegally.

The existential question of what makes a human being and where to draw the line between biological and artificial intelligence was rather new in 1982. In recent years, it has been explored further in science fiction, such as the TV series *Humans* (2015) and *Westworld* (2016). So, it was perhaps not surprising that director Denis Villeneuve returned to the Los Angeles of thirty years later in *Blade Runner 2049* (2017).

In 2049, the climate hasn't improved, the ecosystem has collapsed, and those who can afford to have settled on one of the space colonies. The manufacture of replicants has taken great strides and become even more sophisticated so that they are now hardly distinguishable from people. Are the replicants human? Do replicants deserve human rights?

The society depicted in both 2019 and 2049 is truly multicultural and a real melting pot of cultures and languages. Advertising signs that dominate the public space are in Japanese, Hebrew, Chinese, Russian, Hindi, Korean, etc. As is to be expected in such an environment, a street slang, dialect, or perhaps a new language altogether, has emerged. They call it Cityspeak. We mainly hear the character Gaff, a Blade Runner, speak the language to the film's protagonist Deckard, who does not answer but lets us know in a voiceover, 'That gibberish he talked was Cityspeak, gutter talk, a mish-mash of Japanese, Spanish, German, what have you. I didn't really need a translator. I knew the lingo; every good cop did.'

In the *Blade Runner* world, people generally seem to be multilingual. Gaff's Cityspeak dialogue is translated into English by a Japanese-speaking sushi chef who, just seconds before, was speaking Japanese to Deckard, who answered only in English. We see similar examples of multilingualism in the follow-up film where Finnish actress Krista Kosonen makes herself understood in Finnish. In 2049, the protagonist K (a nod to K in Kafka's *Metamorphosis*, perhaps?) also has no problems understanding the character Badger, who speaks Somali. It is reminiscent of *Star Wars*, where Han Solo easily understands Chewbacca's growls in Shyriiwook, but responds in English.

Cityspeak was designed by Edward James Olmos, who plays Gaff, and because Olmos is of Hungarian origin a lot of the Cityspeak we hear in the film is based on Hungarian. The only real lines we hear of this language are Korean-Hungarian-Japanese-French-German:

'**Hey, idi-wa.**' – 'Hey, come here.' (Korean)
'**Monsieur, azonnal kövessen engem bitte.**' – 'Sir, please come with me at once.' (Hungarian, with a little French and German)
'**Lófaszt, nehogy már. Te vagy a blade … blade runner.**' – 'Horsedick, no chance. You are a blade … blade runner.' (Hungarian)
'**Captain Bryant toka. Me ni omae yo.**' – 'Captain Bryant wants to meet you.' (Japanese)

In the scene after Gaff drives Deckard to the police station, behind Vangelis' music you can hear air-traffic information mainly in German, but mixed with sentences in Chinese, Russian and even two sentences in Swedish.

Cityspeak is not a developed language but rather is supposed to give the impression of a hybrid language that originated in a truly multicultural metropolis. The Philip K. Dick book on which the film is based contains no mention of Cityspeak, but we can assume that the filmmakers use the many languages as a sound effect to lay an exotic language tapestry over the film. In 1982, it would surely have been a frightening picture: a vision of the United States where English was in decline.

Syldavian, Bordurian, Arumbaya

'Blue blistering barnacles!', 'Cachinnating cockatoo!', 'Doddering donkeys!' – there is no doubt that Captain Haddock's salty expressions are unique contributions to our modern swearing culture, and one of the two major contributions that the stories of young journalist Tintin have made to language history. The other is a Germanic/Slavic language with branches in South America and the Middle East.

Tintin creator Georges Remi, better known as Hergé, was an avid armchair traveller. While *Tintin* travelled the world in strikingly realistic and detailed environments, the young Hergé remained at home. Hergé researched these far-flung locations for Tintin in newspapers and books, and much of his research is preserved in his archives, which Michael Farr has made available in his book, *Tintin: The Complete Guide*. There, you can see the templates for a variety of items and phenomena that appear in *The Adventures of Tintin: The Broken Ear*, such as South American temples, boats and aircraft.

One of Hergé's masterpieces is the fictional monarchy of Syldavia (Зылдавыа or Zyldavia), which features in five volumes. The readers are given a thorough introduction to the country and its history when Tintin embarks on a flight to Syldavia and picks up a tourist brochure from the seat pocket. The following pages give the reader the same information that Tintin gets in the brochure.

We are told that from the sixth century, Syldavia became populated by nomads of unknown origin. In the ninth century, they were driven up into the mountains by Turks who then settled there, in the fertile valleys. In 1127, Chief Hveghi led the nomads back down from the mountains and defeated the Turks in a battle outside the capital Zilehorum. Hveghi became King Muskar, meaning 'the brave', and Zilehorum was renamed Klow. Today's Klow, which is located where the rivers Moltus and Wladir converge, is home to 122,000 of the country's 642,000 inhabitants. And so it goes on. The tourist brochure is much like the typical Wikipedia entry for any real country, richly illustrated with pictures of the country, historical paintings with motifs from the Battle of Zilehorum, and enticing tourist images.

The geography of Syldavia brings to mind the Balkans but also contains aspects of more Central European landscapes. Its history is reminiscent of Poland's. It has place names that point to Poland and perhaps Croatia, and countryside mosques that suggest Hergé modelled it on Albania or the country formerly known as Yugoslavia. Syldavia's yellow flag featuring a black pelican is of course inspired by Albania's red flag with a black double-headed eagle. It is also worth noting that the castle in Syldavia's Kropow is modelled on the fifteenth-century Olofsborg Castle in Savonlinna in Finland. The Royal Castle in Klow is strongly inspired by the Royal Castle in Brussels.

Thus, in a volume of only sixty-four pages, we are introduced to an extremely well-constructed fictional country that feels authentic in every detail. The images that Hergé uses to showcase Syldavia – often newspaper clippings – hint at the fact that he took inspiration from many countries. For example, the Royal Guards' uniforms are inspired by, although far from identical to, Beefeaters at the Tower of London. The royal carriage is almost identical to a newspaper clipping from Hergé's archive showing the carriage of King George V, but for the pelican details, which give more of a Polish flavour, and so on.

Then, its crowning glory – a unique Germanic–Slavic language: Syldavian. Nowadays, Syldavian is often written with the Cyrillic alphabet, but an old document from the time of Ottokar IV (the 1300s), represented in the tourist brochure, teaches us that it was previously written in Latin script – a custom that has been upheld in the courts of Syldavia:

Pir Ottokar, dûs pollsz ez könikstz, dan tronn eszt pho mâ. Czeillâ czäídâ ön eltcâr alpû, »Kzommetz pakkeho lapzâda.« Könikstz itd o alpû klöppz: Staszr vitchz erom szûbel ö. Dâzsbíck fällta öpp o cârrö.

This is how the Old Syldavian text reads in the manuscript. Hergé does not offer any translation, but leading Syldavian linguist Mark Rosenfelder has translated it into French and English:

'Father Ottokar, thou falsely art king; the throne is for me.' This one said thus to the other, 'Come seize the sceptre'. The king thus hit him, Staszrvitch, on his head. The villain fell onto the floor.

This scene from Syldavian history has become part of the national mythology and is also related to the official motto: **Eih bennek, eih blavek**, which means, 'Here I am, here I stay'.

When Syldavian is written in Cyrillic letters it gives a clearly Slavic impression, but this is also apparent when the language is written in Latin letters. The suffixes 'sz', 'cz', 'itchz', and 'ow' are intended to give an Eastern European feeling. The place names do the same thing: **Klow (Клов)**, **Tesznik (Тесзнік)**, **Sbrodj**, **Istow**, **Dbrnouk** and **Zlip (Злiп)**, to name a few major Syldavian locations. Is **Klow** inspired by the Polish cities of Kraków/Lwów, and **Dbrnouk** and **Zlip** by the Croatian cities of Dubrovnik and Split? Could the Syldavian River **Moltus** be modelled on the Moldau, which flows through Prague?

Once you begin studying Syldavian, its Germanic roots soon become apparent, as in the following sentence:

'**Kzommet micz omhz, noh dascz gendarmaskaïa.**' – 'Come with us to the police station.'

It sounds strikingly German, but we also see a French influence in **gendarmaskaïa** (or **гендармаскаиа**, as it is written in Cyrillic) from the French word for 'police' – *gendarme*. However, Syldavian also uses the word **politzs** for a single police officer and the abbreviation for the Syldavian secret service is ZEPO (**Zekrett Politzs**).

Hergé was Belgian, so would obviously have been familiar with Flemish and Dutch, and his grandmother spoke Marollian, the Flemish dialect of Brussels. For this reason, some people rather lazily assume that Syldavian is just Marollian with funny letters. Although Marollian is clearly an influence, if you look more closely you can see that Syldavian is a language in its own right and that Hergé has drawn inspiration from several directions.

'**Czesztot on klebcz.**' – 'It's a dog.'

Here, Hergé has taken inspiration from Walloon-French slang *c'esteût on clebs*. There might also be a connection to the Arabic word for 'dog' – *kalb*, which may be due to an Islamic influence during the period when Syldavia belonged to the Turks. More French-related words in Syldavian include:

pir – father (*père*)
zsálu – hello (*salut*)
karrö – floor (*carreau*)

The linguistically intriguing word **zrälùkzen** ('to see') is a combination of the French *regarder* and a Dutch word *locken*, both of which mean 'to see'.

Certain grammatical features of Syldavian have greater similarities with German than with Flemish, such as the rich bouquet of its definite articles: **dascz, dze, dzem, dza, dzoe**. Certain names are closer to German.

Polish influence can be seen in the suffix -**ow**, meaning 'city', and the meat dish **szlaszeck** looks very similar to *szaszłyk*, the Polish word for 'shish kebab', which in turn comes from Turkish. Then there is **szprädj** ('red wine'), which is etymologically trickier but may come from the Marollian *sproeit*, which means 'dash' or 'squirt'. Hergé probably also came up with some words himself, like the gloriously onomatopoeic: '**szcht**!' – 'silence!'

The kingdom of Syldavia shares a border with the military dictatorship of Borduria. The neighbouring countries have long been in conflict, with the Bordurians occupying Syldavia between 1195 and 1275. Hergé has given this country its own character too, although it is not described in as much detail as Syldavia. Of course, Borduria has its own language. The neighbouring languages are closely related, but while Syldavian has some Slavic spelling traits, Bordurian appears closer to German and is not written in Cyrillic. Only a handful of Bordurian words are known, for example:

> **hôitgang** – exit (Dutch: *uitgang*)
> **platz** – town square (German: *platz*)
> **tzhôl** – toll (German: *zoll*)

From the little that is known about Bordurian, it seems that the language lies somewhere between the Germanic–Slavic Syldavian and a German dialect.

So Hergé has given us two languages that are largely based on the Flemish dialect of Marollian. But, as if that wasn't enough, Marollian also appears several times within representations of Arabic and the indigenous South American languages, Arumbaya and Bibaros.

The capital of Khemed is Wadesdah, and it doesn't take a huge leap of the imagination to see Hergé's Marollian or German vocabulary: 'Wat is das?' (*Was ist das?* – 'What is that?'). The wordplay in Khemed is harder to see, but it's likely to be the Marollian '*Ik heb het* or *K hem het*' – 'I have it'. The country's second city is called Khemk-hah, surely a take on the Marollian '*Ik heb het koud*' – 'I'm cold'.

The characters also have witty names. Emir Mohammed Ben Kalish Ezab sounds like *kalische zap*, a drink made from liquorice root. Emir's sworn enemy, Sheikh Bab El Ehr, calls to mind *babbeleer* – 'babbler', 'chatterbox'. Hergé also throws in two Belgian name puns with French origin:

Bir El Ambik – *bière lambic* (a Belgian beer)
Youssof Ben Moulfrid – *moules-frites* (Belgium's national dish of mussels and French fries)

So, we can't really say that Hergé designed a Marollian–Arabic language, but in the adventures that take place in Khemed (*Land of Black Gold* and *The Red Sea Sharks*) he uses Marollian wordplay as an in-joke between himself and a small circle of readers from Brussels.

When it comes to the language of the Arumbaya people in the South American country of San Theodoros, it is a completely different matter. The Arumbaya language has two unique and fascinating dialects, as we might call them: a Marollian–Spanish variant, and an English cockney one.

Let's start from the beginning and take a trip to South America, to San Theodoros, a fascinating little military dictatorship with operetta uniforms and 3,487 colonels but only forty-nine corporals. San Theodoros is one of Hergé's most masterfully crafted countries, perfectly capturing the atmosphere of many Latin American nations, or more accurately, playing on our Western image of 'banana republics'.

General Tapioca ruled in the 1930s, which we can read about in *The Broken Ear* (1937), but was overthrown by General Alcazar, who was at some point overthrown by Tapioca again before *The Seven Crystal Balls*, released in 1948. Then, Alcazar comes back into power at the end of the *The Red Sea Sharks* (1958). It is impossible to say just how many coups take place during the forty years it takes for Tintin to return to San Theodoros, but in 1976, in *Tintin and the Picaros*, General Tapioca reigns once again in San Theodoros.

The South American republic comes to resemble a typical Latin American country in the shadow of the Cold War: a military dictatorship, influenced by military advisers from the USSR – sorry, Borduria – who, judging by the presence of their moustache emblem on the San Theodorean uniforms, have spread Plexicism (named after Bordurian dictator Plekszy-Gladz) to San Theodoros. Furthermore, General Alcazar's revolutionaries in his jungle camp are more than a little reminiscent of Fidel Castro, Che Guevara and other Latin American guerrilla leaders.

There is also a hint of pre-Colombian history. Before the Spanish came to San Theodoros, the country was inhabited by the Pazteca Empire (French: *pastèque* – 'watermelon'), an ancient high culture that built astonishing pyramids such as Trenxcoatl (English: 'trenchcoat') which Tintin, Captain Haddock and Professor Calculus visit.

For the Paztecas, Hergé took inspiration from the Aztec and Mayan cultures. The name of the pyramid also points to the fact that the Pazteca language is related to Nahuatl, which belongs to the Uto-Aztec language family.

The Arumbaya people living in the San Theodoros rainforest along the Badurayal River may be descendants of the Paztecas, although Hergé also drew inspiration from other Native American people. Arumbaya's arch-enemies are the Bibaros people, and the word **Bibaros** (Latin: *bibere* – 'to drink') is very similar to *Jívaro*, a term that denotes several indigenous peoples of the Amazon.

While the main language of San Theodoros is Spanish, the Arumbaya people speak an indigenous South American language, which is fundamentally Marollian–Spanish with several different 'branches', depending on which translation of *Tintin* you read. The most famous language branch is cockney–Spanish.

The Broken Ear was the first time Hergé used the Brussels dialect Marollian in his construction of a foreign language. He tried to make Marollian read like a native South American language and thus added what he perceived to be a few indigenous touches with some Spanish suffixes. Hergé continued to develop the Arumbaya language just over forty years later, in *Tintin and the Picaros*.

'Nokho. Ara no pikuri klana opoh? Tintin zouka da pikuri. Wetche douvanêt?'

Most people probably only think of Hergé's use of Marollian in the context of Syldavian. However, the Arumbaya language lacks the Slavic features of Syldavian, and as a layman myself I personally perceive it as a credible indigenous language. The Syldavians and Arumbayans could probably communicate with each other with little trouble.

Swedes were left guessing about what the sentence above meant until 2004, when Björn Wahlberg's new *Tintin* translation came out:

'Tell me. This is about the fetish from our tribe. Tintin is looking for the fetish. What do you know about it?'

In the old Swedish edition, the Arumbaya language had to speak for itself, but with a translation to hand and a little understanding of how Hergé built fictional languages with the Flemish/ Dutch dialect, it is possible to identify a few words:

ara – are
klana – clan, tribe
zouka – search (Dutch: *zoeke*)
'**wetche?**' – 'do you know?' (Dutch: *weet je?*)
douvanêt – by, about it (Dutch: *daarvan*)

The relationship between the Arumbaya language and Syldavian (or rather, Hergé's variation on Marollian) is even clearer if we look at Chief Avakuki's lines from *Tintin and the Picaros*:

'**Nagoum wazehn! Yommo! Nagoum ennegang!**'

In the new Swedish edition, which bases its interpretation of Arumbaya on Frédéric Soumoi's analysis in his book *Dossier Tintin*, this translates as:

'Drink then! Condemned! You just have to drink!'

This is a perfectly reasonable interpretation in the context, but if we take a closer look at the sentence, we might translate it more like this:

'Now we shall see! Oh yes! Now we move on.'

This is specifically when comparing it with the Marollian:

'*Naa goeme wa seen! Jo mo! Naa good ne gang.*'

Considering the main language in San Theodoros is Spanish, it is no wonder that the Arumbaya language borrowed a few Hispanic words, such as the phrase '**Stoum érikos!**', which was translated to 'Idiots!' in *The Broken Ear*. Christophe Helmke, an associate professor of indigenous languages and cultures at the University of Copenhagen, interpreted this as a curse that came out of a derogatory term for people from Nuevo-Rico, i.e. 'new money'. It is not impossible that Hergé had that idea in the back of his mind, but the word is also found in Flemish/Dutch: *stommerick* – 'idiot'.

As previously mentioned, there are two quite distinct branches of Arumbaya. If we take the first sentence we looked at and compare the two linguistic variants, we can see that these are two completely different languages:

> **'Nokho. Ara no pikuri klana opoh? Tintin zouka da pikuri. Wetche douvanêt?'**
> **'Naluk. Djarem membah dabrah nai dul? Tintin zluk infu rit'h. Kanyah elpim?'**

To most, both sentences are completely incomprehensible unless we have the keys to decipher them. The second sentence does not come directly from Hergé's pen, but from Michael Turner and Leslie Lonsdale-Cooper's 1975 English translation. And it is absolutely brilliant! If you read the sentences aloud, you realise that they are a kind of phonetic variant of the London cockney dialect.

> **'Naluk. Djarem membah dabrah nai dul? Tintin zluk infu rit'h. Kanyah elpim?'**
> 'Now look. Do you remember the brown idol? Tintin's looking for it. Can you help him?'

It was a brilliant translation solution that let more people in on the linguistic jokes than just Hergé and an inner circle of Brussels residents, allowing this variant of the Arumbaya language to look as foreign as the Franco-Marollian version. Word for word, the language is incomprehensible – it is only when you read the words out loud and try to emulate the cockney rhythm that it becomes understandable.

From the outset, Michael Turner and Leslie Lonsdale-Cooper decided not to attempt a word-for-word translation of Hergé's work, instead putting their efforts into an anglicised version. The characters' names were translated into more native versions than in many other translations: the Castle Moulinsart became Marlinspike Hall, Milou became Snowy, and Dupont and Dupond became Thomson and Thompson.

Hergé redrew parts of *The Black Island* at Turner and Lonsdale-Cooper's request to get the English and Scottish details right. They also added Gaelic words that were missing from the original. Hergé, a great anglophile, was amused by the English translation and worked closely with Turner and Lonsdale-Cooper.

It is therefore likely that this alternative branch of the Arumbaya language had Hergé's blessing and approval. Here are a few more examples of the cockney-influenced Arumbaya language:

'**Owzah g'rubai?**' – 'How's the grub?'
'**Oozfa sek' unds?**' – 'Who's for seconds?'
'**Ava 'n ip?**' – 'Have a nip?'

The Broken Ear also features a sentence in the language of the Bibaro people:

'**Toth koropos ropotopo barak'h!**' – 'Soon your heads will be shrunk! What a joy!'

It is probably related to the Arumbaya language, and we can at least see that both languages use the word **toth**. In the English version, the relationship with cockney is clear:

'**Ahw, wada lu'vali bahn chaco conats!**'
'Oh, what a lovely bunch of coconuts!'

The Adventures of Tintin have been translated into over 100 languages and three volumes have actually been translated into Marollian, but these don't feature Hergé's constructed languages. It is a pity – it would have been interesting to see how the Marollian translator dealt with the Syldavian, Arumbaya and Marollian wordplay.

Wakandan

Director Ryan Coogler's older cousin introduced him to comic books when he was a kid in the 1990s living in Oakland, California, and it was *X-Men* and *Spider-Man* that first got him hooked. It wasn't long until the young Coogler went to his local comic-book store and asked if they had any featuring African American superheroes. That was when he discovered *Black Panther*. Coogler's interest in comics, and particularly *Black Panther*, followed him through college to his burgeoning film career. From the very beginning, he always had the idea at the back of his mind that, one day, he might be able to direct a superhero movie.

And so it was – Coogler became the first African American to direct a superhero movie. He made it about his childhood hero: the first-ever black superhero, Black Panther.

In East Africa lies the small fictional kingdom of Wakanda. It borders Kenya, Uganda, South Sudan and Ethiopia, but few know of its existence because its residents have chosen to isolate themselves. To the outside world, Wakanda appears only as a stereotypical image of a developing country, but hidden behind its high mountains and deep forests (and forcefields) is an extremely prosperous country. As one of the few countries in Africa not affected by colonialism, Wakanda has developed its own super-high-tech society.

In Wakanda, the king is known as the Black Panther. Along with this title, the monarch gets a ceremonial panther-like costume, reinforced with the rare metal vibranium, a natural resource found only in Wakanda. The monarch also has the right to drink a concoction made from a very rare heart-shaped herb that grows only in Wakanda and bestows superpowers on anyone who drinks it. The herb is said to be a gift from the panther god Bast, but is actually a mutation caused by a vibranium meteor that struck near where the herb grows.

So, the African Marvel character Black Panther, who made his debut in a *Fantastic Four* comic book in 1966, is not only a superhero – he is also the head of state. This means he has to commute between his two jobs – from the Avengers superhero group in the USA to his official duties in Wakanda.

When the series about the first African superhero was created by Stan Lee and Jack Kirby in the 1960s, Africa and Africans were portrayed with exoticised, stereotypical images. The series has had several writers over the years and has had its highs and lows. In 2016, it was successfully relaunched by bringing in award-winning journalist and author Ta-Nehisi Coates. He has since passed the baton of head writer to female Nigerian-American sci-fi writer Nnedi Okorafor.

Once Ryan Coogler got to sink his teeth into directing *Black Panther* (2018), the film became a huge global success. It is one of the fastest money-making Hollywood films in history. As a result, Black Panther, or 'T'Challa', as the incumbent is called, became well known beyond comic-book circles.

Seeing as T'Challa's homeland Wakanda has developed a highly advanced civilisation without Western influence, the film offers a fascinating Afro-futuristic depiction of the country. Ryan Coogler combines African history with science fiction to build a world where tribal communities exist side by side with super-high-tech infrastructure.

In this fictional world, Wakanda is an unprecedented African success story, but even in our world, the film production is a success story for African culture, African actors (especially women) and the African Americans who make up a large part of the film crew. Ryan Coogler is now the most successful African American director of all time – monetarily speaking, at least. The National Museum of African American History and Culture, which is part of the world's largest museum and research complex, the Smithsonian, has even procured props from the film to exhibit precisely because of the film's great importance to African American culture.

One of the few members of the film team without African origins was Swedish composer Ludwig Göransson, who wrote the film score. He had worked with Ryan Coogler on previous films, so it made sense that Coogler wanted Ludwig Göransson to write the music for *Black Panther* as well. Since he had no previous knowledge of African music, Göransson spent months travelling around the continent, learning about and recording instruments and vocals. He even accompanied Senegalese star Baaba Maal on a tour of Mauritania. In South Africa, Göransson visited the International Library of African Music, which has a collection of 500 African musical instruments that are no longer in use and have largely disappeared. This was an opportunity for Ludwig Göransson to record sounds rarely heard today. As a result, the music in the film came to be inspired by a huge range of African music styles, and therefore can be described as uniquely Wakandan. So, Ludwig Göransson's Oscar for Best Original Score in 2019 doesn't seem like as much of an honour for Sweden or the municipal music school as it does for the people and unique musical tradition of Wakanda itself.

Naturally, Wakanda also has its own language. Before 2018, however, little was known about Wakandan and few had heard it spoken; the comic books only featured occasional words in the language, or languages, spoken in the country. But in a film that takes place in Wakanda, there was no getting around the fact that Wakandan must be heard spoken in the background.

Besides Wakandan, there are also reports that some tribes in the country speak the West African languages Yoruba and Hausa. In addition, the film's title track is performed in artist Baaba Maal's mother tongue, Pulaar, so presumably this language is also spoken in Wakanda.

In fact, the language that came to be heard in Wakanda on the silver screen already appeared in the movie *Captain America: Civil War* (2016). In this film, Black Panther plays a supporting role but, more importantly, his father, T'Chaka, makes an appearance. It was South African actor John Kani who pointed out that it seemed silly for T'Chaka and T'Challa to speak to each other in English in an intimate father-and-son scene. The filmmakers agreed and had John Kani perform the lines in his native tongue, Xhosa. As a result, when it was time to film *Black Panther*, it was already established that the inhabitants of Wakanda spoke Xhosa, one of the eleven official languages of South Africa. Appropriately enough, John Kani and his son were also hired as language consultants, and to teach the other actors to speak their lines in Xhosa.

While Xhosa is the language heard in the film, it is unclear if this is exactly the same as Wakandan. If we look at local names, like the capital Birnin Zana, there seem to be elements of Hausa – *birnin* means 'city' in Hausa and *zana* means 'drawing'. Could this be a hidden joke from the comic-book writer: **Birnin Zana** – 'cartoon city'? In Wakanda, at least, they call the capital 'the Golden City', so **zana** likely means 'golden' in Wakandan.

There are other words from the comic series that do not seem to be related to Xhosa and appear to have originated from other African languages such as Swahili and Rwandan. Additionally, the late actor Chadwick Boseman, who played T'Challa, tried to give the Xhosa an East African rather than a South African pronunciation, taking into account where Wakanda is located on maps in the comic books.

Some Wakandan words not derived from Xhosa include:

Dora Milaje – The Loved Ones (the king's female guards, from whom the king historically chose his wife)
hatut zeraze – dogs of war
n'cos – thank you
mena ngai – the big hill (which contains vibranium. *Ngai* is the mountain-dwelling supreme god of the Maasai faith)
Birnin – city (in Hausa)
Damisa-Sarki – The Black Panther (means 'Panther King' in Hausa)
rutuku – derogatory word for white people (Rwandan)
jambazi – bandit (Swahili)
majambazi – bandits (Swahili)
kimoyo – of the spirit (compare with Zulu: *womoya*)
taifa nagao – shield of the nation (Swahili)
nyanza – lake (in many countries in the region, Victoria Lake is called '*Victoria Nyanza*')

Of Wakanda's five tribes, four of them appear to speak Wakandan (Xhosa in the film), while the fifth tribe – the Jabari people, who live in isolation in the mountains – speak Igbo, a West African language. The Jabari, who belong to the cult of the white gorilla, differ greatly from the other tribes in Wakanda. For one, they don't worship the panther god Bast, but the gorilla god Ghekre, called Hanuman in the film – a clear reference to Indian mythology. Perhaps they worship both a gorilla and a monkey god. To mark this difference, Ryan Coogler wanted the white gorilla people to speak another language in the film. He looked for a West African language and landed on Igbo.

Interestingly, the written Wakandan seen in the film also originates from West Africa and perhaps suggests that the white gorilla tribe had a greater influence historically, at least in the written language. The old Wakandan script has its roots in the ideographic scriptural language Nsibidi used in south-east

Nigeria and south-west Cameroon. Today, Igbo is written in the Roman alphabet.

Nsibidi also spread across the Atlantic carried by slaves, inspiring Cuban Anaforuana writing and Haitian veve symbols. It then spread further to Wakanda, whose linguistic roots otherwise originate from southern Africa. In the royal palace in Birnin Zana, for example, we see Nsibidi signs as decoration on the pillars of the throne room.

The modern alphabet seen everywhere in the film on billboards, shops or buttons in the laboratory, etc., was developed by Hannah Beachler, the film's production designer, and her colleagues. Beachler took 400-year-old symbols from Nigeria and supplemented them with symbols of the Dogon and Mursi people; symbols from Tifinagh, an alphabetic script used by the Berber Tuaregs in North Africa; and symbols from an Old South Arabian script containing twenty-nine characters for consonants.

Finally, another script was used, from the ancient kingdom of Bamun in Cameroon. The sixteenth king of Bamun, Ibrahim Njoya, designed his own written language based on older characters in the early 1900s. The script was used to write down the people's history and knowledge of local herbal medicine. Bamun characters are also used in the film as embellishments on the blue clothing of the border tribe.

Hannah Beachler passed on this research into written language to her colleagues, who then sketched out the unique Wakandan alphabet we see in the film. It's accompanied by another completely different set of Wakandan characters – numerals – which are one of the only things shared between the older and more modern written languages.

Hannah Beachler is also the person behind many of the props. She came up with what she calls a bible for the movie – a visual history and sourcebook so that every designer in the team got a feeling for Wakanda. For this, Beachler drew inspiration from various parts of Africa for her Afro-futuristic designs.

It's notable in the design of Ruth E. Carter's Oscar-winning costumes, which are unique for each of Wakanda's various tribes.

As a result, the African futurism in the film is based on researching and drawing inspiration from a blend of different cultures. Admittedly, it has all been put through a Hollywood filter, but nevertheless gives rise to a rather distinctive Wakandan culture that can be found in everything, from its music and architecture to its clothing and language. Considering the huge success of the film, we are more than likely to see a sequel or two, where perhaps we may hear a little more of the Wakandan language. The filmmakers might also put a little more effort into making the spoken language as unique as the rest of Wakandan culture.

If so, I would imagine Wakandan will turn out to be a unique form of Bantu language (like Xhosa) with elements of other languages of West Africa, such as Hausa and Igbo. The Igbo speakers in Wakanda, the Jabari tribe, seem to be the originators of the country's older writing system. This historical background suggests Wakandan is a language in its own right, made of a unique blend of eastern, western and southern Africa. The modern written form of Wakandan, which is inspired by scripts from around the African continent, appears both beautiful and distinctive, and is synced to the English alphabet. So for anyone who considers Wakanda their spiritual home, the language is there to be used and extrapolated upon. Wakanda forever!

Hen Linge – Elder Speech

Geralt of Rivia is a witcher in the medieval Poland of a parallel universe, who makes his living by bewitching people and killing all kinds of monsters. In the successful Netflix series, he is played by Henry Cavill. Prior to that, Geralt was seen in the well-known computer game *The Witcher*, which is in turn a sort of continuation of the short stories and books by Polish author

Andrzej Sapkowski. Netflix has high hopes for the fantasy series and has said from the outset that it has plans for seven seasons.

Like a Polish Tolkien, Sapkowski takes his inspiration from Polish and Baltic folklore. It's a world that's not only populated by elves and dwarves, but also by monsters like strigas, sylvans, vodniks, vampires, dopplers, werewolves, leshys, djinns, bloedzuigers, foglers and dragons – green, black and red dragons. But witchers don't hunt dragons. Not if they can avoid it …

It's a concept that fits short stories and television series well. Geralt of Rivia comes to a village plagued by a monster, fights it, defeats it and then moves on to the next episode. Owing to the fact that *The Witcher* has remained on screens since the 1990s and has been the main character in three video games, there is a well-constructed mythology on which a TV series can be built. And perhaps most importantly – a language.

Most in *The Witcher*'s world speak the common language, the lingua franca, represented as English in the TV series, but there is an even older language, the world's equivalent of 'Latin'. Elder speech, or **Hen Llinge**, is spoken by **aen seidhe**, 'the hill folk' or 'Elves', and the **aen woedbeanna**, 'the nymphs of the woods' or 'the Dryads'. The Elves populated the world at the beginning of time, but now they are few in number and live exiled in the time of men. Elder Speech is also used, as it should be, by mages and scholars.

For his version of Elvish, Andrzej Sapkowski took elements mainly from Celtic languages – Welsh, Irish and Gaelic. That is not unusual for Elvish languages, as it's associated with Tolkien, who took inspiration for Sindarin from Welsh. Tolkien has set the standard for how elves are represented in literature after him; his Elvish language continues to influence how other authors create languages for their elves.

As well as Latin, Elder Speech takes inspiration from German, French and English. For example, Sapkowski took two important verbs, 'to be' and 'to have', from the Latin *esse* and *habet*. In the original books, it's Polish that represents the common language and, to give readers a completely different feel for Elder Speech, Sapkowski simply took inspiration from non-Slavic languages. At least one word comes from Tolkien's Sindarin – **pherian** (Hobbit). From Swedish, Sapkowski has taken the word for spy, *angivare* ('informer') – **an'givare**! (Perhaps not so flattering for Swedes like me, who are more accustomed to loans from our extensive legalese, i.e. 'ombudsman'.)

Some phrases in Elder Speech:

> **'mir' me vara.'** – 'Show me your goods.'
> **'que suecc's?'** – 'What's going on?'
> **'a d'yaebl aép arse!'** – 'A devil up your arse!'
> **'ire lokke, ire tedd.'** – 'Another place, another time.'
> **'ymladda dh'oine. Ess'tedd, esse creasa.'** – 'Fight the humans. It is time, it will be the place.'

Even though there's a lot of use of the language in the books, Sapkowski has not so much developed a complete, 'real' language, but rather a well-thought-out constructed language. Sapkowski was inspired by Tolkien to write fantasy, but he had no ambitions to create a similarly elaborate language. However, he also didn't want to create a nonsense language which would later have to be cleared up in a footnote. Instead, he took from many languages when he constructed phrases in his Elvish, in the hope that an educated reader could understand the content. His thinking was that using real languages in a unique mix should then make his constructed language feel real and be at least partly intelligible.

TV producers realised that there was quite simply not enough Elder Speech in the books to serve the dialogue in the TV series, so they employed none other than David J. Peterson to give the Elves a genuine language. To build Hen Llinge, or Hen Linge, after Peterson changed the spelling for clarity of pronunciation, into a fully functional and detailed language, he went through and analysed everything Andrzej Sapkowski wrote about the language in the books and built on that. He gathered all the words in a list, where he carefully inserted new words, which were often derived from Sapkowski's own. He also invented a detailed grammar so that all the words are conjugated correctly.

Sapkowski's spelling was not completely consistent and, more importantly, he used apostrophes a lot, which has the potential to confuse actors. David J. Peterson streamlined this using his standardised way of Latinising unfamiliar languages.

Peterson also created a rune-like written language for Hen Linge which is used in the TV series. The written language uses Sapkowski's spelling from the books. So, if we take, for example, '**Thaess aep!**' ('Shut up!') from the books, we find that it is spelled like that with the runic alphabet, but with Latin letters in the script it is '**Theis eip!**', which makes it easier for actors to pronounce correctly.

> '**Aven it vete.**' – 'We heard it.'
> '**Het es luned.**' – 'She's a girl.'
> '**Keim irig, wed.**' – 'Come back, child.'
> '**Blödei dung!**' – 'Damn it!'
> '**Avreid me, aheil me.**' – 'Feed me, heal me.'

In the same way that Latin has given rise to languages like Italian, French and Spanish, Elder Speech has also given rise to the languages/dialects they speak in Nilfgaard, Zerrikania and the Skellige Isles.

Elder Speech is equivalent to Valyrian in *Game of Thrones*, which David J. Peterson is also behind. For the TV series, Peterson developed multiple dialects: one part was the classic Valyrian and then other derivatives like Astapori Valyrian, Meereenese Valyrian and the other dialects spoken in the city states in Essos. So, the hope is that we will see a similar development of Elder Speech in *The Witcher*; that is, that Peterson gets an opportunity to develop the Dryad and Zerrikanian dialects, for example. In the books there are words that are specific to different dialects but it's not particularly developed. In this case, Peterson's handiwork would be worth its weight in gold for all who are interested in the language of this world. Development of the language will take time, so we cross our fingers that there really will be seven seasons as the producers have so confidently suggested.

Incidentally, it's not the first time David J. Peterson has developed an Elvish language. At least three of them have already been heard on the silver screen:

Shiväisith – the language of the Dark Elves in *Thor: The Dark World*
Övüsi Kieru – the Elvish language from *Bright*
Yulish – the language of Santa's elves in *The Christmas Chronicles.*

4

A Priori

LANGUAGES THAT ARE A LITTLE MORE OUT OF THIS WORLD

Shyriiwook, Geonosian, Mando'a, Tamarian, Rihan and Romulan, Na'vi, Poleepkwa, Mangani, Barsoom, Heptapod

---

Many of the languages mentioned in this book are a priori languages. It is the nature of science fiction and fantasy to want to depict alien worlds and exemplify this otherness through alien languages, so these genres are teeming with examples of languages that are truly out of this world. A priori language is one in which the constructed vocabulary is not based on any previously existing language. In these cases, the creator has invented every word from scratch. Perhaps this gives them a more extraterrestrial flavour as compared to a posteriori languages.

However, it is rarely black and white. Many conlangs borrow their grammar or other linguistic features from existing languages. Tolkien, for example, was inspired by real languages and legends when he created his universe. Much of Quenya's vocabulary is not entirely 'original'; Tolkien gladly acknowledged that the lexicon of his Elvish languages was 'inevitably full of … memories' of older languages – Indo-European, Semitic and Welsh words and roots can be clearly distinguished in Tolkien's linguistic world. In the Elvish language Sindarin, there are many words with a direct correlation to Welsh.

Sometimes, there is a direct nod to existing myths and languages – for example in Tolkien's own Atlantic legend about the island of Númenor, also called **Atalantë** – 'the fallen'. The Dwarves' names in *The Hobbit* are taken from ancient Norse myths. Orcs were named after the Roman god of death, Orcus, and *orc* in Old English means 'evil spirit'. But despite these various influences, Tolkien's languages are usually considered a priori. There is a chapter in this book dedicated to the languages of Tolkien because, arguably, the most fascinating thing about these tongues is their linguistic evolution – both in Tolkien's fictional world and our own.

The otherworldliness of Klingon as an a priori language is more obvious, but it is also well known that its creator, Marc Okrand, snuck a number of jokes into it, implying that Klingon is indeed related to terrestrial language, or at least influenced by it.

There are direct similarities, such as **qavIn** ('coffee') and **qettlhup** (a type of sauce (from 'ketchup')), but most are more obscure references: for example the word for 'fish' – **ghotI**. This alludes to a classic English joke, often attributed to George Bernard Shaw, about the illogic of English spelling. The joke goes that **ghotI** could be an alternative spelling of 'fish' if you pronounce the 'gh' as in 'enough', 'o' as in 'women', and 'ti' as in 'nation'. The word for 'pair' in Klingon is **chang'eng**, after Chang and Eng Bunker, a famous pair of Siamese twins. Other jokes are more personal and difficult to detect, such as **jIl** – 'neighbour', because Marc Okrand had a neighbour named Jill. There are also onomatopoeic jokes like:

'ugh – heavy
'oy' – pain
'uH – hungover

As soon as the Klingonists get a new word from Marc Okrand, the hunt is on to find the joke behind it, sometimes resulting in people perceiving pretty far-fetched, contrived jokes.

Truly extraterrestrial languages, which is to say those with no basis on Earth, will first appear when we look at some of the languages of *Star Wars*. These languages took a different approach from those of, say, *Star Trek*, *Game of Thrones* or Tolkien's world, all of which gave rise to real working languages. In *Star Wars*, the languages are just adornments or sound effects. In most cases, they are only meant to *sound* like real languages. Sound designer Ben Burtt created the extraterrestrial speech in *Star Wars* just as he created the famous sounds of light sabres, starships and blasters.

Some of the languages, such as Huttese, are grammelot – intended to be heard and perceived as believable languages even though they are not. Other languages are simply sound effects. For example, in the first film, Burtt created the extraterrestrial hubbub at the Mos Eisley cantina by mixing a range of animal sounds and manipulated human voices. A hippopotamus grunt was used for a laughing alien, a tree frog croak was the voice of another space creature, and a spliced recording of a man reading a Latin text was just one of the components of the bar's background hum. Burtt also got a group of colleagues to breathe in helium and have an everyday conversation in high-pitched voices. Male and female participants were recorded separately so that Burtt could slow down the recording speed to lower the pitch for the women and speed it up to raise the pitch for the men. These sounds all worked together to become the bar's background chatter, which Burtt calls the 'cantina walla'.

Although the languages in *Star Wars* were not systematically developed from a linguistic point of view, a lot of work went into making them sound like real extraterrestrial languages. And as if that wasn't enough of a challenge, all the languages had to be different enough for the cinema audience not to confuse them.

Shyriiwook

Han Solo's large hairy companion, Chewbacca, is a Wookiee who communicates in what sounds to human ears like gargling, whining, snorting and roaring. This is actually Shyriiwook, the language of the Wookiees as spoken on the planet Kashyyyk. Seeing as Han Solo understands what Chewie says, and even utters the odd phrase, it should be possible for us to learn the language too.

When Ben Burtt set out to design the Wookiees' language in the first *Star Wars* movie, he wanted it to be completely different from human language. His first thought was that of animal sounds, but he was also keen for the language to be perceived as more than just noises, rather as a language with grammar and vocabulary. George Lucas suggested that Burtt use bear sounds to give Chewbacca a voice.

After attempting to record several bears, Burtt eventually found Pooh, a bear used in Hollywood films. By recording Pooh when he was hungry and being tempted with food, he got a variety of sounds. Burtt then brought these into his home studio to cut and edit. He divided the sounds into short snippets according to what he felt they expressed. Some sounded happy, angry or discontented.

In this way, Burtt built up a 'glossary' of various Wookiee sounds. He then adjusted the pitch in his studio and manipulated the sounds in the various ways made possible by the analogue technology of the 1970s. Then, by combining these words or snippets of sound, he was able to construct short sentences that seemed to convey a message and feeling. But this audio material alone was not enough to give the Wookiees a complete language. Burtt had to go out with his tape recorder again to collect additional bear and animal noises. Walrus sounds made a good addition, which Burtt managed to record on a day when a zoo was moving the animals out of their enclosure for pool cleaning. By the end, his considerable 'glossary' of Wookiee words/sounds included bears, walruses, dogs, lions and seals.

The choice of usable sounds was limited by the mask worn by actor Peter Mayhew, who played Chewbacca in the 1970s. Pretty much all Mayhew could do was open and close his mouth, so any sounds that required more complex lip movements were out. This is why the bear noises came in handy – because they come from further back in the throat.

The language of the Wookiees was further developed in the legendary 1978 TV production, *Star Wars Holiday Special*, in which the audience got to meet Chewbacca's family: his wife Malla, son Lumpy and grandfather Itchy. The grumpy grandfather's vocabulary included a good dose of grizzly bear noises. Black bears provided the sounds for Malla, and Ben Burtt found a cub to voice little Lumpy.

In the movie *Solo: A Star Wars Story* (2018), in which Han Solo and Chewbacca meet for the first time, new actors took on these iconic roles. Chewbacca is played by Finnish basketball player and actor Joonas Suotamo and Han Solo by Alden Ehrenreich.

For Chewbacca's speech, the same method was used as in the early films: Suotamo delivered his lines in English, swearing like a sailor, and they were dubbed in post-production into Shyriiwook, consisting of a newly recorded mix of bear, seal and lion sounds. This is also the first time we get confirmation that not only can Han Solo understand Shyriiwook, he can also make himself understood in the language. Ehrenreich delivers a couple of lines in Shyriiwook, mainly improvising Wookiee noises and a fixed line that he had to repeat for several different takes.

Shyriiwook is mainly a sound effect, but we can gain a little insight into its vocabulary with the help of Burtt's *Star Wars: Galactic Phrase Book & Travel Guide*, including how to transcribe the words into Roman letters. In 2011, an introduction to the language was published for children, *How to Speak Wookiee: A Manual for Intergalactic Communication*, which is richly illustrated and comes complete with a sound module to demonstrate the pronunciation of the ten basic phrases in the book. For example, you can learn to distinguish between the two rather slippery phrases, '**Aarrr wwgggh waahh**' and '**Aaaarrr wgh ggwaaah**', meaning 'jump into hyperspace' and 'I'm feeling travel-sick', respectively. Here's what counting to ten sounds like for Wookiees:

1 – **ah**
2 – **ah-ah**
3 – **a-oo-ah**
4 – **wyoorg**
5 – **ah wyoorg**
6 – **hu wyoorg**
7 – **muwaa yourg**
8 – **ah muwaa yourg**
9 – **a-oo-mu**
10 – **a-oo-mu wyaarg**

Geonosian

The digital revolution had a huge impact on the *Star Wars* films of the 2000s. Complex aliens could be computer animated instead of only using puppets, and sounds could be altered to a much greater degree than playing with tape recorders previously allowed. One result of these advances was the insectoid race of the planet Geonosis. These creatures are giant sapient insects that live in a hive-like society. The drones lack wings, while the warrior caste is winged. They also have exoskeletons and mandibles.

They have been given the most exotic language in the *Star Wars* universe – a true extraterrestrial language that would probably be very difficult for people to pronounce. Admittedly, the animal sounds of Shyriiwook and the language of the Sand People are also pretty hard for humans to imitate, but with Geonosian, Burtt went one step further. In addition to words,

Geonosian also consists of honking, clucking and clicking sounds. The honks and clucks can probably be attributed to Burtt's digital sound creation, while the clicks are reminiscent of the click sounds that can be found in languages of southern Africa, such as the Khoisan languages, Xhosa and Zulu. Geonosians produce these unusual sounds with their two sets of mandibles, one moving vertically and the other horizontally.

All Geonosian dialogue is subtitled, so while some parts can be understood and a few individual words identified, very little is otherwise known about the language. Burtt hasn't revealed much and doesn't feature it in his phrasebook (which came out before the Geonosians appeared on screen). Burtt's colleague, Matthew Wood (who also voiced General Grievous), was also involved in the creation of the language and said that the sounds recorded for it were among the strangest he had ever heard, which he revealed included the mating calls of penguins and a swarm of fruit bats fighting over a banana.

Mando'a

Boba Fett's native language, Mando'a, or Mandalorian, is very different from the other languages in *Star Wars*, first and foremost because it is a real language with grammar and a deliberate vocabulary. Ben Burtt was not involved in its creation, so the language is neither a sound effect nor grammelot.

Boba Fett is a minor character in the first three films and not particularly interesting. Mainly, he just stands in the corner looking tough, until he is eaten by a desert monster known as the Sarlacc. However, thanks to his cool helmet and the mysterious air he has about him, he became something of a fan favourite. The films from the early 2000s took the opportunity to develop young Boba Fett's role, and in particular, his father Jango Fett got more screen time – wearing the same helmet as his son, just to be on the safe side.

In the supplementary literature created around *Star Wars* – the books, comics and games usually referred to as 'the expanded universe' – the character of Boba Fett had already been developed further than in the early films. We learned that he belonged to the Mandalorians – a tough, warriorlike people.

Unusually, the Mandalorian language Mando'a came into existence in written form first and spoken form second. The written language originated in the film world when Philip Metschan developed a Mandalorian alphabet for use in *Episode II: Attack of the Clones*, with the appearance of Jango Fett and his spaceship. There might also be a single sentence of spoken Mando'a in the movie when Jango tells little Boba to close a door. But this could also be a secret code language between father and son.

After this, we move away from the film world to the expanded universe and the video game *Republic Commando* for which Jesse Harlin wrote the music. The game's introductory music was a Mandalorian song called **Vode An** – 'Brothers All'. Here is the first verse:

Kote!	Glory!
Kandosii sa ka'rta, Vode an.	One indomitable heart, Brothers all.
Coruscanta a'den mhi, Vode an.	We, the wrath of Coruscant, Brothers all.
Bal kote, darasuum kote,	And glory, eternal glory,
Jorso'ran kando a tome.	We shall bear its weight together.
Sa kyr'am nau tracyn kad, Vode an.	Forged like the sabre in the fires of death, Brothers all.

Based on these lyrics, English author Karen Traviss was given the task of developing Mando'a into a working language. The alien language came to be used in a number of novels as well as the animated series, *Knights of the Old Republic* by John Jackson Miller, author of three *Star Wars* novels between 2005 and 2014 and several comic books.

Finally, the *Star Wars* universe had a real language that didn't start life as a sound effect. The vocabulary of Mando'a grew and some fans began to study and use it.

Then the language development came to a halt. Karen Traviss stopped working for Lucasfilm because of 'creative differences' and stepped away from developing the language. On her website, she has posted all existing information on Mando'a: a glossary of over 1,000 words and a set of grammatical rules. She points out that she is no longer involved in the language, and that it doesn't even belong to her, as Lucasfilm owns the copyright. Traviss also states, somewhat wearily, that there is no point in emailing her questions, new words or anything else do with Mando'a.

The fansite *Mando'a Dictionary* is an attempt to bring fans together and share resources. There, they debate how to expand the vocabulary, and most seem to agree that it is acceptable to do so as long as the new terms are composed of existing Mando'a words. But many fans are also in favour of carefully adding to the glossary when they come across words with no other possibility for translation. The site has received a sort of blessing from Lucasfilm – or at the very least, they have not been ordered to shut down. In this way, the language can live on and develop among the fans, and maybe even hibernate until it can re-emerge within its natural habitat: movies.

In 2014 it finally happened, if not yet on the silver screen. Two sentences of Mando'a were spoken in the animated television series *Star Wars Rebels*, by the Mandalorian character Sabine Wren.

'Su'cuy aliit Wren. Ibic Sabine Wren. Ara'novor gedet'ye. Me'vaar ti gar?'
'Hailing Clan Wren. This is Sabine Wren, to approach. Status please.'

'Elek, Sabine Wren. Ke parer.'
'Copy Sabine Wren. Standby.'

This is actually quite good and understandable Mando'a.

In *The Mandalorian* (2019) – the first live-action television series in the *Star Wars* franchise and a space western – we follow the Mandalorian bounty hunter Din Djarin. He is the silent-hero type, but when he does speak it's in English and not Mando'a – at least not yet. The only phrase that might be in Mando'a is **Dank Farrik**, which means something like 'Goddammit'. If we get some spoken Mando'a in coming seasons, the language would get a boost, and the vocabulary and grammar could be developed further.

One interesting feature of Mando'a is its gender neutrality. **Buir** can mean 'mother' or 'father' – so, 'parent', basically. Similarly, they don't speak about 'sons' and 'daughters' but just **ad** ('children'). If, for some reason, you need to specify gender, you add **jagyc** or **dalyc** – 'masculine' or 'feminine'. Naturally, **ba'buir** signifies either 'grandmother' or 'grandfather'. **Buirkan** means 'responsible', which seems related to being a good parent for the Mandalorians.

Mandalorians do not use 'f', 'x', or 'z', even though these letters do appear in the alphabet. The explanation for this is that these letters were incorporated into the alphabet to facilitate the transcription of foreign languages. It is fair to assume that there was some kind of gap in communication between Metschan, who created the written language, and Traviss, who created the spoken language.

It is well known that both Jango and Boba Fett are tough guys without equal. The Mandalorians are a warrior people and that is clear in their language. There is no word in Mando'a for 'hero', because everyone is assumed to be heroes. If not, they are **hut 'uun** – 'a coward'.

We won't go into grammatical detail, but the following phrases give an idea of how Mando'a works.

ni – I
juri – to carry
kad – sword
'**ni juri kad**.' – 'I carry a sword.'
'**nu'ni juri kad**.' – 'I do not carry a sword.'
'**ni ven juri kad**.' – 'I will carry a sword.'
'**ni ru juri kad**.' – 'I did not carry a sword.'
'**ke jurir kad**!' – 'Carry the sword!'
'**ke'nu jurir kad**!' – 'Put down the sword!' (Literally: 'Don't carry the sword!')

Tamarian

In *The Hitchhiker's Guide to the Galaxy* there exists a very handy little yellow creature, the Babel fish, which once inserted into your ear will translate all kinds of extraterrestrial languages via its brainwaves. The TARDIS time machine does much the same thing in *Doctor Who*.

Star Trek came up with a similarly practical invention which, incidentally, is convenient for the TV producers, called the universal translator. This is a small device that is carried at all times by most beings of the future and translates, in real time, virtually all languages into its owner's mother tongue – think Google Translate, but perfect and always available. Oddly enough, this miracle machine does not always work and allows space creatures of various kinds to throw in the occasional untranslated word to garnish their outer-space identity with a touch of exoticism.

In the 1960s, we heard a few words of Mr Spock's native Vulcan, mostly in reference to Vulcan rituals and concepts. Then, when first contact is made with the Tamarians on the planet El-Adrel, the universal translation technology faces a peculiar problem. The software has no trouble with the vocabulary and grammar of the Tamarian language, but because they speak entirely in metaphors, and given that humanity (or rather, the Federation) has no prior knowledge of Tamarian culture and history, misunderstandings naturally ensue.

In the Darmok episode of *Star Trek: The Next Generation*, the *Enterprise* encounters the Tamarians and cannot communicate with them. Frustrated, Tamarian Captain Dathon teleports himself and Captain Picard to a planet and isolates them together within a forcefield so that they can only be teleported back when they have learned to understand each other. Dathon has two daggers, one of which he throws to Picard, uttering the phrase, '**Darmok and Jalad at Tanagra**'. Picard interprets this as challenge to a duel, which he refuses.

However, this phrase is a Tamarian expression for joining forces against a common enemy, as the mythological characters Darmok and Jalad did on the island of Tanagra. The Tamarian captain wants to signal co-operation, but Picard sees it as a challenge to a fight.

The ice begins to break when Picard fails to make a fire and Dathon invites him to join his campfire with the phrase **Temba his arms wide**. The two captains realise that a predatory animal is stalking them from the bushes, and they must work together to defeat it. Dathon is seriously injured and while Picard tends to his wounds, he recites the *Epic of Gilgamesh* (the whole episode is a nod to this ancient Mesopotamian classic) and begins to understand how the Tamarian language works. Dathon dies from his injuries, but Picard returns to the *Enterprise* in time to stave off a war with the Tamarians by speaking to them in their own language. The Tamarians are impressed and create a new phrase, '**Picard and Dathon at El-Adrel**', meaning successful communication through co-operation.

Fans have found the Tamarian language fascinating, and the unusual concept of an entire language based solely on allegory has boggled many a mind. It gives a real insight into a totally alien culture. But questions soon arise. How would such a language work in practice? How could Tamarian children learn to speak it, knowing the historical references on which the allegories are based? Can such a language be precise enough to achieve a culture that builds spaceships?

Of course, we know very little about the Tamarian language, so it's difficult to say. Could it be that this episode is really about technological shortcomings and the difficulties of effective machine translation? Anyone who has used Google Translate or similar services knows how comical it can be. Machine translation sometimes translates word for word, entirely missing the context, with culture-specific metaphors in particular being impossible to convey. Is this what happened between Dathon and Picard?

Then again, well-established allegories tend to gain a literal meaning over time. Take the example of 'toilet', which comes from the French word for a 'cloth or bag', *toile*, and its diminutive form, *toilette*, which was used to mean a small bag to store clothes or hygiene products. This came to signify grooming and personal hygiene in general, *faire la toilette*, 'to make one's toilet', which could mean washing, combing your hair, waxing your moustache, getting dressed and so on. Subsequently, it came to mean 'fine clothing' – 'she appeared at the ball in a fantastic toilet' – as well as a 'separate room (toilet room), in which you can arrange your clothes, etc', as described in the *Nordic Family Book* from 1892. So, the idea of a 'toilet room' was used as a euphemism, much like 'powder room' still is. So now this allegory has acquired a very specific meaning. It no longer has anything to do with outfits, bags or cloths.

So for a Tamarian child, one assumes the phrase '**The River Temarc, in winter!**' would simply mean 'be quiet!'. But if the metaphors have acquired precise meanings, this begs the question, can it really be classed as a language based on metaphor and allegory?

Therefore, with an upgrade, the universal translator probably could translate Tamarian metaphors into their more literal equivalent:

Darmok on the ocean – solitude, privacy
Darmok and Jalad at Tanagra – collaboration
the beast at Tanagra – a problem to solve
Temba, his arms open – to offer a gift
Temba, at rest – when an offered gift is rejected
Shaka, when the walls fell – failure
Rai and Jiri at Lungha (Rai of Lowani. Lowani under two moons. Jiri of Ubaya. Ubaya of crossroads, at Lungha. Lungha, her sky grey) – a greeting between two different cultures.

Two Romulan Dialects

The Romulans – the Vulcans' evil twins – first appeared in *Star Trek* in the 1960s, but they weren't given the space to seriously develop their culture and language until 2020. The Romulans are genetically related to the Vulcans, but the family lines split apart when the majority of the Vulcans started engaging in strict logic and suppressing their emotions. A minority who refused to submit to Surak's teachings left the planet Vulcan and settled on diverse planets before they colonised the planets Romulus and Remus and settled there.

In the TV series from the 1960s, Romulan society and culture were loosely modelled on ancient Rome, which can be heard in the name of the species and those of their home worlds. There is a Romulan senate, the highest leader's title is Praetor, and centurion is the name of a military rank. The Romulans are otherwise portrayed as empire builders – militarised, suspicious and isolationist.

In the 1980s and 1990s, the most striking thing about the Romulans was their checked uniform with enormous shoulder pads. But there were also scattered words and phrases in Romulan. For example, the greeting '**jolan tru**' has become widespread. In an episode of *The Next Generation*, a countdown to the self-destruct mechanism can be heard on a Romulan Warbird:

'**Setha-tri par trukatha.**'
'**Setha-ki par trukatha.**'
'**Setha-mille par trukatha.**'

A Romulan alphabet, **kzhad**, also appears, most likely as decoration. The occasional words and phrases from the TV series *The Next Generation* and *Enterprise* are not systematic and there is no thought to the linguistic structure behind them. They are probably the invention of various scriptwriters who simply made up Romulan words as and when needed by the script.

d'deridex – Warbird, a Romulan starship
veruul – an insult
vorta vor – source of all creation
tal shiar – Romulan secret police

In 2009, it looked like the Romulans would get a little bit more structure to their language. For the reboot of *Star Trek*, Marc Okrand was asked to create some Romulan dialogue, although it never made the movie's final cut. Okrand, who had previously created some phrases in Vulcan for different films, tried to design Romulan so that it would be interpreted as related to the Vulcan language.

Vulcan isn't a fully developed language in the TV series – the big Vulcan language development has taken place among the fans (see the section on Vulcan, p. 247). In a similar way, the first Romulan language revolution took place outside the TV shows – namely in a series of novels that are part of the *Star Trek* universe but not strictly canon. (Only what takes place on TV or the silver screen is considered official.)

In the *Rihannsu* novels, the Irish author Diane Duane developed a language for the Romulans which would later be used in other *Star Trek* books. In Duane's books, the Romulans call themselves **Rihannsu** and they call their language **Rihan**. Interestingly, even in Duane's world, Rihan is a constructed language. When the Romulans broke away from Vulcan they didn't want to speak the same language, and so they developed Rihan, based on Old High Vulcan. This then evolved differently to Modern Vulcan. Duane's language uses phrases from the TV series, for example, the greeting '**jolan tru**' and the name for the secret police, **Tal Shiar**. Naturally, due to its lineage, there are also features which are similar to Vulcan.

> Vulcan: '**Dif-tor heh smusma**.'
> Rihan: '**Thiichu tohr u'tehsmaeru**.'
> English: 'Live Long and Prosper.'

The fans started to add to Rihan, which was already a relatively well-developed language, and even inserted other Romulan words that were heard in later TV series and films. Some useful phrases:

> '**Veisa notht**?' – 'How are you?'
> '**Veisa vihroi**?' – 'What's your name?'

'**Vikra nnea au**?' – 'Where are you from?'
'**Mnekha havrae**.' – 'Bon voyage.'
'**Rhanne na docgae**.' – 'I don't understand.'
kheh'irho – Romulan ale

With the release of *Star Trek: Picard* in 2020, there was a quantum leap for both Romulan culture and the Romulan language. Gone were the 1980s shoulder pads. Instead, we were given countless representations of Romulan culture, and they were not just portrayed as militarised enemies to the Federation.

We get to know **Qowat Milat**, an order of female warrior nuns who fight the **Zhat Vash**, which most modern Romulans believe are a myth used to scare children. However, the **Zhat Vash** are an ancient and covert part of the powerful secret police, **Tal Shiar**. We also get a glimpse of the Romulan meditation ceremony, **Zhal Makh**, where a part of the labyrinthine ritual is called **lu shiar** – 'lifting the eyes' (cf. **Tal Shiar**).

And above all, of course, the Romulans got their own full language. At present, we only know that the language is fully developed and has a fascinating writing system. Fans sit and analyse it diligently, looking for snippets of Romulan in the background in *Picard*, trying to decipher writing on signs and in the set design. So far, it's not safe to say whether fans have found their Rosetta Stone (or perhaps their 'Romulett' Stone).

Some examples of deciphered Romulan:

shaipouin – false door
qalankhkai – Freeblade, a Qowat Milat warrior
tan qalanq – a sword the Qowat Milat use
tan zhekran – a Romulan Rubik's cube
qezh – a curse
qezhtihn – an insult
'**zha'rau hrrao luzh vos**!' – 'Bite me!'
'**tivTolRet veh pos**.' – 'May it happen soon.'

hazhMas menFar – Romulan Star Empire
der-iDekh – Warbird, the more correct spelling of **d'deridex**
melShat – Romulan whisky, a spirit distilled from a Romulan grain known as **GenMat**

It was conlanger and linguist Trent Pehrson who constructed Romulan for *Picard*, and it's hard to think of anyone more suitable for the task. For example, in the 1990s, Trent created a written language (Eiha) that's believed to be a fusion of the Vulcan and Romulan languages you see in the TV series. He was also involved in the Vulcan language that fans, led by Mark Gardner, systematised from the phrases of Vulcan heard on TV and in film throughout the years.

Trent Pehrson is best known for the conlang Idrani, which he has worked with for decades and for which he has created about fifty(!) different writing systems. Trent is a highly skilled calligrapher and has designed the most amazing and unique written languages imaginable.

Pehrson is bound by some sort of NDA in his contract with the producers of *Picard*. Apparently, they don't want him to talk about Romulan yet. Some fans hope this indicates that CBS could be publishing something about the Romulan language. What we know so far is that Pehrson, in addition to the snippets of Romulan heard in *Star Trek* throughout the years, has taken inspiration from the Vulcan heard in *Star Trek* to develop the Romulan language. Michael Chabon, author and showrunner for *Picard*, has disclosed that he and Pehrson considered using Diane Duane's Rihan language, but they thought that Romulan needed a more explicit connection to the Vulcan that was heard in earlier *Star Trek* adaptations.

So, based on what is known of the Vulcan fragments, created by Marc Okrand, and the fan-developed Vulcan language, it would be safe to assume that Pehrson first created an Old

High Vulcan from which he then developed modern Romulan. The fact that Trent Pehrson is involved gives great hope that we eventually will have an official Vulcan language in the coming seasons of *Picard*.

The most ambitious fan study so far, by Lyretha ir-Korthre t'Aieme, looks closer at the language. With her knowledge of Vulcan and Rihan, Lyretha has listened to the snippets of pronunciation on the TV series and tried to transcribe them with appropriate spelling. This study concludes that Pehrson's Romulan, as expected, is strongly related to Vulcan, but also to Diane Duane's Rihan. Romulan, as heard in *Picard*, clearly lies somewhere between Diane Duane's Rihan and Okrand/ Gardner's Vulcan, which is in keeping with Michael Chabon's statement that they didn't use Rihan straight away because they wanted to have a more explicit connection to Vulcan.

This short example gives a clear demonstration:

Rihan: '**Sa ma! Sa ma**!' – 'He comes! He comes!'
(**Sa** – 'he', **Ma** – 'comes')

You see a clear connection to the Vulcan, **sa-veh** – 'he', **mayri** – 'comes'. And here's another example of what Lyretha heard compared to the Rihan equivalent:

'**Hwidus vah dorfete vas kai Ganmadan**?'
'**Hwio fvah aledek dochaite khei Ganmadan**?'

'What can you tell us about Ganmadan?' (Ganmadan is a Romulan Ragnarok mythos.)

Lyretha ir-Korthre t'Aieme systematically examines all examples of Romulan and finds many similar points of contact between Romulan, Vulcan and Rihan. The three languages are clearly related to one another.

Of course, the Romulans have also been given their own intricate written language. The Romulans already had a written system, **kzhad**, which was seen in the TV series and the films and was later found to be connected to the English alphabet. As mentioned earlier, Trent experimented in the 1990s with different Vulcan writing systems in an attempt to fuse the Vulcan and Romulan written languages. Two of the systems Trent created for his own language Idrani – Eiha and Suweiha – are very similar to the Romulan system seen in *Picard*. It seems the symbols were taken from, or inspired by, **kzhad**, and they may act as consonants, complete with symbols for vowels.

Studies of Romulan are still in their infancy. Up to now, Romulan linguists have not come to a consensus on spelling or grammar. Hopefully, we will hear more of both Romulan and Vulcan in the upcoming series of *Picard*, and in all likelihood, CBS will loosen the muzzle on Trent Pehrson so he can explain everything about Romulan and how it was developed.

As we can see, it's a fantastic accomplishment that Trent Pehrson has not only made the fan-developed Vulcan canon 'through the backdoor', but he's also built the old, simple writing system into a new and creative one. And not only that – he has also invented a way to make Romulan related to Rihan! That means fans now have two Romulan languages to examine.

Of course, that much we knew already, as it's well established that the Starship *Enterprise*'s xenolinguist Nyota Uhura has mastered all three of the Romulan dialects.

Na'vi

There are several notable similarities between the Smurfs and their larger cousins, the Na'vi on the moon Pandora – they both have blue skin, reside in mushrooms/trees, live in harmony with nature and have their own language. However, while the language of the Smurfs is a kind of strange pidgin based on local human idiom with a smattering of Smurfisms, Na'vi is a far more advanced and exotic alien language. And it is growing every day, in both the scope of its vocabulary, and the number of speakers.

With several new *Avatar* films in the pipeline, the Na'vi language and culture is likely to develop in leaps and bounds to become a well-established language. Could Na'vi even challenge Klingon to become the world's most widely spoken extraterrestrial language?

This is language creator Paul Frommer's ultimate dream, at least – that Na'vi will become a 'new Klingon' and 'a living language in itself'. Frommer was obviously aware of Klingon and its history, being a fan of Klingon creator Marc Okrand long before he was commissioned to develop Na'vi for the movie *Avatar*, directed by James Cameron. Frommer even had a Klingon translation of *Hamlet* on his bookshelf. So, unlike Marc Okrand, who was surprised to see his constructed language come to life, Paul Frommer was aware of the fact that Na'vi could reach beyond the silver screen – and was determined that it should.

Director James Cameron might even be considered the founder of the language, as it was he who created the first thirty words, as well as the name 'Na'vi'. It was only when production on the film began that he sought out a linguist to develop it properly and found Paul Frommer, professor at the USC Marshall School of Business in California, and doctor of linguistics (Persian grammar).

Frommer thought Cameron's original vocabulary had a Polynesian flavour to it, and Cameron has confirmed that he did indeed have Maori, the language of the indigenous people of New Zealand, in mind when he created the first words of Na'vi. Frommer initially presented Cameron with three options, using example sentences made of nonsense words. One was a sort of tone language like Mandarin, while another was inspired by Mayan language and used different vowel lengths, and the third used what is known as ejective consonants (where the speaker catches air in the larynx and releases it immediately after the pronunciation of a consonant), which is common in some Native American languages like Lakota and Quechua. This third variant appealed to Cameron, and Frommer developed a first draft of the language based on Cameron's original glossary in 2005. The director was also adamant that the language sounded friendly, perhaps as a reaction to the somewhat rough-around-the-edges sound of Klingon.

In the film, the Na'vi people are as friendly as the Klingons are gruff, and represent a kind of nostalgic, idealised vision of humanity living in harmony with nature – polar opposites to the greedy, exploitative humans. The Na'vi can, perhaps, best be described with their own word, **fpom** – a sense of wellbeing and harmony with nature.

So, how did the Na'vi language come about? The thirty basic words initially produced by James Cameron drew inspiration from Maori, and Frommer has since said that the language has Afro-Polynesian-Native American influences. Just as in the case of Klingon, the idea is that Na'vi should be perceived as otherworldly mainly from a North American and Western European perspective. To achieve this, Frommer rejected the usual sounds and features of English. For example, Na'vi doesn't use 'b', 'd', 'j', 'ch', 'sh', or hard 'g' sounds. Instead, Na'vi uses the more unusual ejective consonants, which Frommer transcribes with the addition of an 'x', as in 'kx', 'px' and 'tx'. Sometimes ejectives are mixed with click sounds, as used in languages such as Xhosa in South Africa, but there are no click sounds in Na'vi. The popping sound is the ejectives.

Since some sounds used in English are missing in Na'vi, they had to be approximated in the pronunciation of English loan-words: 'doctor' becomes **toktor**, 'gunship' becomes **kunsip**, 'book' becomes **puk** (incidentally, **paq** in Klingon!) and the name 'Jake' is pronounced **Tseyk**. It is these sorts of little details that lend credibility to the film and to the Na'vi as an alien race. They need no loanword for 'human', however, and use the descriptive **tawtute** – 'person from the sky'.

Rather unusually, Na'vi also uses infixes. These are similar to a prefix or suffix (an addition at the beginning or end of a word to change the meaning), except they are inserted into the middle of the root word. The Na'vi word for 'hunting', for example, is **taron**, while 'hunted' is **tolaron**. The infix '-ol' (which marks a completed action) is inserted directly after the 't'.

The syntax doesn't depend on word order like it does in English or many European languages, but on cases, as in Russian or Latin, allowing for great flexibility in Na'vi word order. This means you can basically put the same words in any order in a sentence and get the same meaning! For example, the typical greeting phrase, 'I see you', can be expressed correctly in three ways:

'**Oel ngati kameie**.'
'**Ngati oel kameie**.'
'**Oel kameie ngati**.'
(**Oel** – 'I', **ngati** – 'you', **kameie** – 'see')

One truly extraterrestrial feature of the language is that Na'vi counting is not base-10, but base-8, because they have only four fingers on each hand. This is comparable to Huttese, which is also base-8 on account of its four-fingered speakers. Hence, counting in Na'vi is rather an alien skill for most earthlings:

0 – **kew**
1 – **'aw**
2 – **mune**
3 – **pxey**
4 – **tsìng**
5 – **mrr**

6 – **pukap**
7 – **kinä**
8 – **vol**

So far so good. 8 + 1 = 9, i.e. **vol** + **'aw** , so 9 is **volaw** and 12 is **volsing** (**vol** + **tsìng**, 8 + 4). Continue up to 15, until 16, which is is 2 × 8 – **mevol**. An example of a higher number would be **mrr volmrr** (5 × 8 + 5 = 45).

In an octal system, the counting base is different from a decimal system; for example: 64 is **zam**, 512 is **vozam** and 4,096 is **zazam**. So if we can get our tongues around the sounds, we can have a go at some larger numbers, such as: **vozamtsìzamvolaw**, or 777 as we would say (512 + 4 × 64 + 8 + 1 = 1 **vozam** + 4 **zam** + 1 **vol** + 1).

Of course, it is not clear just how high the Na'vi can actually count, seeing as they deal exclusively with mental calculations, and given that Na'vi is a completely unwritten language, they have no symbols for numbers or mathematical operations. (To be more precise, the fictitious language Na'vi on the moon Pandora [**Eywa'eveng**] is unwritten while the constructed language Na'vi on Earth is written in Latin letters.)

Ironically, this unwritten language is mainly disseminated through writing on internet forums and is rarely spoken. Just as in the case of Klingon, most people learn to read and write a language before learning to speak and understand it, which gives the spoken language a very formal, 'written' style.

As might be expected from a blockbuster like *Avatar*, interest in the Na'vi language and culture has spread like wildfire. Internet forums were already popping up just a couple of weeks after the film premiered, where Na'vi was hotly discussed and its fans joined forces to learn and explore the language. It wasn't long before language courses and dictionaries became available online.

How many Na'vi speakers there are is impossible to say, but the largest forum has over 5,000 members, and in addition to all the English-language forums, there are sub-forums in seventeen different languages, including Swedish, Chinese and Klingon. But many of the threads focus on discussions about the film *Avatar* more than the language itself.

Paul Frommer was more or less prepared for the language's success, but instead of publishing a grammar guide or dictionary – as was the starting point for Klingon – he embraced the enthusiastic gaggle of online fans and writes a blog with regular, extensive updates on new grammar and vocabulary. An initial expansion of Na'vi came shortly after the film's 2009 premiere with the new words required for the *Avatar* computer game, but the language continues to expand on the blog month by month.

At a Na'vi conference in autumn 2010, Paul Frommer suggested that fans form the Na'vi Vocabulary Committee to propose words to expand the lexicon. They aim to produce twenty to twenty-five new words a month and send them to Frommer for approval. In this way, the committee creates its own Na'vi words and proposes them to Frommer for him to adopt, reject or modify. There is also a Lexical Expansion Project, where fans list words that are noticeably missing from the language in various categories, which Frommer looks at regularly. Ten years after the film's initial release, the vocabulary is approaching 3,000 words.

The follow-up films have been delayed and postponed by James Cameron on several occasions, including as a result of the COVID-19 pandemic. However, Disney has made a Pandora-themed area in one of its amusement parks where visitors can walk around and take a boat ride through a constructed alien landscape. This has led to the creation of some new Na'vi for use in brochures and songs. For example, the safety regulations are bilingual.

'rä'ä yomtivìng ayioangur.' – Don't feed the animals.
'ke tung Na'vil futa tswìk kxenerit Mo'araka nìwotx.' – The Na'vi have banned smoking in Mo'ara.

A touring show set on Pandora also came about in collaboration with Cirque du Soleil and is called *Toruk – The First Flight*. This also required supplementary vocabulary.

In 2015, when it was thought that a new movie would be coming out soon, the film company launched an official SoundCloud stream and corresponding Instagram account where Frommer posted hundreds of clips on how to pronounce different words and sentences in Na'vi. So, despite the sequel's delay, the language has thrived and developed beyond its medium over the past decade. This means that much of the development necessary for the new films is already done. Unless, of course, the next film is about an entirely different language, because Cameron has revealed that it will partly follow another clan, the Metkayina, who apparently live on the reefs and ride large marine animals. Will Frommer be commissioned to develop one or more alternative Na'vi dialects?

As with other extraterrestrial languages spoken on Earth, Na'vi has acquired some earthly features because its speakers/ fans want to be able to talk about things of their own world. Or is it merely a coincidence that the Na'vi have a seven-day week beginning on a Sunday, just like in the USA?

Trr'awve – Sunday
Trrmuve – Monday
Trrpxeyve – Tuesday
Trrtsive – Wednesday
Trrmrrve – Thursday
Trrpuve – Friday
Trrkive – Saturday

Over the years, Frommer has been asked various questions, and dutifully translated words and phrases, in interviews. In one interview, he was asked if he could translate this well-known Klingon sentence from *Star Trek*:

'veQDuj 'oH DujIIj'e'.' – 'Your ship is a garbage scow.'

So now we know how to say this in Na'vi too:

'tawsìp ngeyä lu sngeltseng.'

Some Na'vi words have come about because the actors made mistakes or were unable to pronounce the words that Frommer intended. During shooting, director James Cameron also influenced the language's development with his own opinions on what the Na'vi would say, even though it wasn't always *technically* grammatically correct.

It is especially tickling and meta that actress Zoë Saldaña, who plays Neytiri, invented the verb **páte** – 'to arrive', through a slip of the tongue. In 2009, when *Avatar* was filmed, she was also playing the role Lieutenant Uhura in the remake of sci-fi classic *Star Trek*, herself a specialist in xenolinguistics – extra-terrestrial languages.

Poleepkwa – 'Prawn'

In the film *District 9* (2009), aliens come to South Africa in 1982, when a giant spaceship appears hovering above Johannesburg. While not a particularly unusual portrayal of first contact with space creatures, in *District 9*, this is all that happens. The spaceship simply parks above the city and nothing more. After three months without communication, the South African authorities decide to make contact and drill a hole in the hull of the spaceship. On entering the vessel, they are met by a multitude of dehydrated, emaciated space creatures living in misery on their ship. The aliens are evacuated and transported to a fenced-off area on the outskirts of Johannesburg, which over the years turns into a slum – a traditional South African township. The area is named District 9.

Thirty years pass from the appearance of the spaceship but still no one discovers what happened to it or why the space creatures appeared on Earth. It seems that an infectious disease broke out on their craft, taking the lives of the chief officers and the more educated crewmembers. The majority of survivors seem to be drones: a class of workers with limited intellectual abilities. It appears that the society of these insect-like space creatures is organised in a strictly hierarchical caste system, with few of the higher castes surviving. In the film, we follow an alien named Christopher Johnson who, unlike the other aliens in the film, is familiar with the spaceship's technology and knows how to operate the craft.

The creatures' appearance gives rise to a nickname: 'prawns'. This doesn't refer to the aquatic prawns you might be more familiar with, but rather a special kind of cricket: the Parktown Prawn (*Libanasidus vittatus*), found in southern Africa. The nickname is on account of the space creatures' likeness to said cricket, as well as the fact that they are regarded as unclean. The aliens' name for themselves could be **Poleepkwa**; at least, this is the accepted name among the fans. *District 9* is based on a short film on the same theme called *Alive in Joburg* (2006), made by director Neill Blomkamp three years earlier. In that film, the prawns are once referred to as Poleepkwa.

The prawns are taller than humans and resemble insects with their exoskeleton, antennae and three claws on each hand. But they also have a bunch of little tentacles around the mouth that are not at all insect-like, and eyes which appear very mammalian. The prawns seem to be hermaphrodites and lay a large number of eggs that are then nourished by suspended animal carcasses. They are mostly carnivorous but also have a penchant for car tyres, and are completely obsessed with cat food, which they find utterly irresistible. They become distracted by the mere sight of it and are willing to sell their high-tech weapons cheap in exchange for a few cans.

In the film, tensions exist between the prawns and human inhabitants of Johannesburg. The prawns are at the bottom of the social ladder, along with Nigerian criminals, and live in poverty in the slums. The authorities decide to evict the residents of District 9 and move them to a new place of residence, District 10, far out in the wilderness.

Setting the film in South Africa is, of course, a reference to apartheid and its aftermath. The film title is a direct allusion to District 6, a residential area of Cape Town. It was a rather mixed and cosmopolitan area by South African standards, inhabited mainly by coloured people, but also home to diverse cultures including Xhosa, Indian and white Afrikaans. In 1966, the district was declared 'white' by the apartheid regime and 60,000 residents were forced to move to a newly constructed area. Almost all the buildings were demolished. Many of the town scenes in the film were shot in a town that really had been evacuated, but in this case, it was because the inhabitants were offered a better standard of housing elsewhere.

Naturally, the prawns have a language that can also be understood by humans, while some prawns seem to understand English as well. The film doesn't make it clear whether or not they speak English, but if they can, they seldom do.

It was New Zealand sound designer Dave Whitehead, who went on to create the extraterrestrial language in *Arrival*, who was behind the prawn language. The first version he produced was based on the sounds of marine mammals, such as echolocation clicks and other characteristic dolphin sounds. This language seemed to work even with the insect-like appearance of the space creatures. However, it turned out that people couldn't accept these sounds as a language – it was simply too different from human communication.

So, Dave Whitehead got to work and created a language, or at least enough for the few lines required by the script. Whitehead produced 'hundreds' of words and was eventually able to communicate with his colleague in his new language. Next, he recorded all the lines in his own voice and altered the recordings. He built a small insect studio where he recorded the sounds of bees and other insects he happened upon. He left a dead chicken in his backyard and recorded the buzz of the swarm of flies around its rotting body. The various consonant sounds in the recorded lines were then replaced with a suitable insect noise or clicking sound from whales and dolphins. Whitehead then added in the sounds made by rubbing or crushing different types of vegetables. The vowels were recorded separately, but most of the original recording can still be heard, although obviously distorted by various filters and reduced in volume. Dave Whitehead has estimated that about 10 per cent of the prawns' languages is derived from human speech.

The end result is that the lines that formed the basis of the prawns' language don't feel quite as exotic and alien. It seems that Whitehead wanted a conlang as a foundation on which to create his tapestry of sounds. Some sentences are somewhat playful and based on English, and sometimes Poleepkwa directly borrows English words, such as '**Yuku satchu si chu kazi kami**' – 'You said it was a suicide mission'. **Yuku satchu** is suspiciously similar to 'you said' and **kazi kami** seems to be the prawn version of *kamikaze* (Japanese suicide attacks during the Second World War). In any case, the written sentences available in Poleepkwa probably shouldn't be seen as a genuine extraterrestrial language, rather a precursor to one. Some examples:

'**Wegotz Kasibooyas tika?**' – 'We're going home now?'
'**Zami zagool gala laksika yuul?**' – 'How many moons does our planet have?'
'**Siya gala xibitu ooda.**' – 'This planet has only one.'
savhee – yes
kau – no
jek – quiet

ki'sa – there
prrru – friend
kasibooyas – him
zeepol – seven
gala – planet

The prawns also have a writing system and several extraterrestrial written characters appear in the film, which fans have analysed to compare with the English alphabet – naturally …

Mangani

Mangani is the name of the species of great apes that adopt little Lord Greystoke, better known as Tarzan, after his parents die in the African jungle, and can also be used to refer to their language. **Man** means 'big' and **gani** means 'apes/people', and it is the name they have given themselves. They name little Lord Greystoke 'Whiteskin': **tar** – 'white', **zan** – 'skin'.

It is clear that the Mangani view humans as relatives to them, much like any other great ape, because their name for humans is also **mangani**, but with the prefix **tar**- to denote 'light-skinned' or **go**- for 'dark-skinned': **tarmangani** and **gomangani** – 'white big people' and 'black big people'.

It is generally thought that this division of people according to skin colour and the fact that Tarzan is called 'Whiteskin' was a sign of the racism of the times (*Tarzan of the Apes* came out in 1912), but it is also conceivable that author Edgar Rice Burroughs reasoned that the great apes would find Lord Greystoke's white skin unusual and therefore think it was the little tot's most remarkable feature. By the age of 10, Tarzan is worried about not being as hairy as his ape friends. He tries to fit in by rubbing himself with clay, but it doesn't work very well.

Either way, the Mangani consider humans to be people or apes just like them. They make no distinction except in terms of colour. Gorillas, on the other hand, are not perceived as 'big people' of the same kind and are called **bolgani** – 'ground people'. This is presumably because gorillas don't climb trees.

The origin of the great apes is interesting in itself and has been the subject of much speculation. Burroughs describes them as human-apes who are related to the gorilla, giving rise to the idea that the Mangani might be a cross between gorillas and chimpanzees. I wonder if Edgar Rice Burroughs knew about the Bili apes that were 'discovered' in the Bili district of the Democratic Republic of Congo in the 1990s. These apes are larger than chimpanzees and build their homes on the ground, like gorillas, causing scientists to debate over whether they were a previously unknown primate or some sort of chimpanzee–gorilla cross. However, DNA analysis has shown that the Bili apes are a type of unusually large chimpanzee that exhibits habits more reminiscent of gorillas. Could this solve the mystery of Tarzan's adoptive parents? Could the Mangani, in fact, be Bili apes?

As Tarzan grows up, he realises that he is different from his Mangani family, especially regarding his capacity for logic and thought. He finds his biological parents' house in the jungle and eventually learns to read the books in their house. He realises that the great apes' language and capacity for thought is not enough, 'So limited was their vocabulary that Tarzan could not even talk with them of the many new truths, and the great fields of thought that his reading had opened up before his longing eyes.' The hairless ape is superior to the great apes and he assumes the role of king of the tribe.

Burroughs describes the Mangani language as very basic and mostly consisting of grunts, growls, body language and gestures. The grammar is simple, with individual words mainly just appearing one after the other. There are no numbers, but the great apes use **tand-ho** ('few') and **ho** ('many'). And to emphasise 'very many', they simply repeat the word for 'many': **ho-ho**.

But the simplicity of the language is somewhat contradicted by the relatively large glossary presented by Burroughs, indicating that the language may be more advanced than it seems. In any case, Tarzan manages to express relatively complex sentences. When Tarzan defeats his rival, Tubal, he gives a victory speech to the others in the tribe. The speech appears in English in the book, but Mangani linguist Peter Coogan attempted a translation:

Tarzan [pointing to himself]: '**Tarzan ko-korak. Yato-nala Tarzan-ul-Mangani. Yato-nala Kala, kalu-ul-Tarzan. Tand** [pointing to the audience] **ko-Tarzan** [pointing to himself]. **Tand-yo kreeg-ah**.'

Literal back-translation: 'Whiteskin. Whiteskin mighty killer. Watch out for Whiteskin of the great apes. Watch out for Kala, mother of Whiteskin. Not mighty white skin. No-friend warning.'

'I am Tarzan … I am a great killer. Let all respect Tarzan of the Apes and Kala, his mother. There be none among you as mighty as Tarzan· Let his enemies beware.'

Coogan, like several other Manganists, has cobbled together fragments of Mangani from the books and comics to develop as complete a vocabulary as possible, although not everyone recognises the same sources, and some argue over which words should be included. Burroughs describes several languages in his Tarzan books and mentions that they are related to Mangani, which has led to some people including words adapted from the language Pal-ul-don, for example, in their Mangani glossary.

This is a typical phenomenon when fans start using a conlang. Differing versions can lead to confusion, but fan versions are often built in collaboration with each other; as some lexicons and interpretations gain legitimacy over others, they go on to become the basis for further development.

Here are a few examples of the language of the great apes:

'**kreeg-ah bundolo**!' – 'Warning! (I) kill!'
bund – dead
kreeg-ah – warning
kreeg-gor – scream
'**ka-goda**?' – 'Do you give up?' or 'I give up!'
dum-dum – drum
gogo – speak
eta-gogo – whisper
eta – small
nala – up
tand-nala – down
tand – not

Barsoom

In 1912, the same year that the language of the great apes spoken by Tarzan first appeared, Edgar Rice Burroughs also began work on an extraterrestrial language. Barsoom is spoken by a variety of creatures of varying colours on the planet Barsoom (Mars) and Burroughs' earthling hero, John Carter, soon learns the language and puts it to good use in the eleven-book series set on the red planet.

Carter's Martian adventures, complete with alien princesses and strange new cultures, gained huge success and have fascinated readers for over a century. Burroughs used his constructed language mainly to add a bit of flavour and otherness to his books. As a result, there isn't that much Barsoom in the books, other than the characters and place names on Mars. There are also some plants, numerals and units of measurement. The only word spoken, other than names and places, is '**sak**!' – 'jump!'.

Around 420 Barsoom words have been identified in the books. This meant that in the early 1900s, there wasn't much of a language to speak of yet. However, almost 100 years later, great strides were made in Barsoom's development when the film *John Carter* was released, and the Martian vocabulary was expanded into a language. The filmmakers used Paul Frommer, the man behind Na'vi in the movie *Avatar*, to make Barsoom workable for the silver screen.

Frommer started by reviewing what the fans had already done. Of course, over the years, fans had analysed Barsoom and used what little there was as creatively as they could. Frommer's greatest source was John Flint Roy's *A Guide to Barsoom*, which was a compilation of the entire Barsoom vocabulary. Based on Burroughs' 420 words, Frommer got a good idea of the phonetics and phonology; in other words, the sound of the language.

But Burroughs wasn't always consistent in his spelling, so it required some guesswork on Frommer's part. For example, Burroughs used 'ph' in some places and 'f' in others, and it was unclear if there was any difference in pronunciation. How, for example, would 'ch', 'tj' and 'gh' be pronounced? Frommer decided that 'ch' is pronounced as in 'Bach', 'tj' as in 'church' and 'gh' as a guttural French 'r' (like in Klingon). These decisions on the pronunciation were based on educated guesses about what Burroughs would have had in mind a century previous, concluding that he probably had a working good knowledge of Latin and probably took inspiration from there.

In the first two books about John Carter on Mars, the language is described as partially telepathic. Frommer tried to make the language simple because, not only is it described that way in the books, but John Carter learns to speak it more or less in a week, implying that the grammar can't be all that complicated. So it was never his intention to make the language too otherworldly.

The Barsoom word order, verb-subject-object, is quite common in terrestrial languages like Hebrew, Arabic and Welsh, but is different enough from the English subject-verb-object for the language not to be perceived as a simple code language (by English-speaking cinema-goers, of course). This didn't appear in Burroughs' books, given it was simply a choice made by Frommer. The simplicity of the language was probably Frommer's way of staying as faithful as possible to the original Barsoom while being respectful to Burroughs' creation. He strove to extrapolate Burroughs' Barsoom instead of inventing his own version from scratch.

This is probably why Barsoom is not as elaborate as other languages in Frommer's repertoire. He chose to produce only as much of the language as was needed for the script, so the lines spoken in the film are the only new Barsoom that was added to the 420 original words from the books. Frommer also provided explanations for some of the more interesting grammatical features of Barsoom. 'I' in Barsoom is **tu**, and to say 'me' you simply repeat the beginning letter at the end: **tut**; thus, 'he' – **ki**, 'him' – **kik**. For plurals, 't' and 'k' change into their voiced counterparts, 'd' and hard 'g': 'we' – **du**; 'us' – **dud**.

Titles in Barsoom give a good idea of the kind of adventures John Carter has in store on Mars:

than – soldier
panthan – mercenary
gorthan – assassin
kadar – guard
padwar – lieutenant
dwar – captain
odwar – general
jedwar – commander-in-chief
jed – king
jeddak – emperor
jeddara – empress

John Carter didn't turn out to be a blockbuster and no sequels are planned, so what might become of Barsoom and whether it will get a second wind remains a mystery. Seeing as the language has already survived for over 100 years, it's likely to stick around for a while yet ...

Heptapod

The hit film *Arrival* (2016) is unusual among the ranks of sci-fi movies because it puts language at its centre and is one of the few films in which a linguist plays the starring role – and a credible linguist, at that! By putting language at its centre, I do not mean a well-designed, fully developed extraterrestrial language such as Klingon or Na'vi. Rather, this film focuses on the very concept of communication with aliens, and if it might be possible at all – whether we could find a common language or learn each other's.

Throughout history, people have had extensive experience of encountering unknown languages – both extinct and living – but their speakers have always been human, with recognisable human behaviour. The same applies even to languages no longer spoken. Human thoughts and brains have been shaped by our encounters with the world, and are adapted to the environmental conditions of Earth. Similarly, aliens would be the product of their own evolutionary and cultural history and be shaped by their planet, which may have a different atmosphere, different gravity, or different light conditions.

Although we humans share a planet and evolutionary history with dolphins, monkeys, dogs, and intelligent birds such as rooks, we haven't learned much of their languages, despite being able to communicate with them on a very basic level. What's more, there are creatures on Earth that can communicate through fragrances, electrical impulses, changes in colour, heat signals and vibrations, with whom we are nowhere near being able to hold an interesting conversation. The intelligence and language of aliens would likely be even more difficult to understand.

This is easily solved in science fiction, thanks to handy devices such as the Babel fish of *A Hitchhiker's Guide to the Galaxy*, which translates in real time once stuck in your ear, or the universal translator in *Star Trek*, where the Starfleet crew each have the device attached to their uniform – easy-peasy.

But there is also a lot of science fiction that deals directly with the problem of communicating with aliens. One such example is Suzette Haden Elgin's *Native Tongue*, which gives linguists the starring role precisely because it is so difficult to communicate with aliens. In her book, linguists have become a kind of upper class, since they are the only ones capable of learning alien languages, and only then because they are exposed to aliens for most of their waking hours from an early age (read more about this in the chapter on dystopian languages).

A popular solution to the problem of how best to communicate with aliens is to use mathematics or physics. This is based on the idea that the laws of mathematics and physics would be universal and assumes all spacefaring civilisations would have a grasp of Pythagorean theories and prime numbers. By establishing a common ground through mathematics, it should be possible to establish contact and build communication. It stands to reason that intelligent spacefaring civilisations should be able to solve for X.

Humanity's most famous attempt to send a message to extraterrestrial civilisations was the Golden Record (like an LP record), which was attached to Voyager of 1977, the first Earth vessel to leave our solar system, which has been travelling deeper and deeper into space ever since. The Golden Record contains over 100 images, ninety minutes of all kinds of music, from whale song to Mozart, and greetings in fifty-five languages. It also contains the recorded brainwaves of author Ann Druyan. The cover has engraved schematic instructions for how the content should be interpreted, how to see the pictures and play the sounds. There is also a pulsar map showing the position of our solar system and a symbol for a hydrogen atom. For aliens to be able to determine how long the vessel has been travelling through space, there is also radioactive uranium-238 on the front of the case, the idea being that its discoverers can calculate the half-life of the uranium.

But no one will know whether this attempt at communication will work, at least not in our lifetime, because of the immense distances involved. And even though we would probably share a similar level of knowledge about the workings of the universe with any creature that might happen to encounter Voyager, there is nothing to say that we would describe physical laws in the same way – nor that this particular alien civilisation would happen to have a record player …

One member of the committee who selected the messages on the Golden Record for NASA was astrophysicist Carl Sagan (1934–96). He later developed the theme of mathematics as a universal language in his novel *Contact* (1985), which was then made into a film ten years later. A young radio astronomer picks up mysterious signals from a star cluster. The message initially consists of the first 261 prime numbers. When the message is deciphered it turns out to be old TV broadcasts that reached the aliens twenty-six light years away, which they then sent back to Earth together with the blueprints of a vessel. Once made, this machine allows the heroine to travel through time and space to a place in the Vega constellation.

Like mathematics, music is also said to be a universal language, and it is certainly no coincidence that so much music was sent with Voyager. In Steven Spielberg's film *Close Encounters of the Third Kind* (1977), which came out the same year as Voyager was released into space, music proves to be the way to make contact with aliens. To establish contact with a spaceship that appears on Earth, communication is initiated with five musical notes and flashing lights. Once contact is made with the alien mothership, this simple message quickly turns into a veritable concert of sound and light. It is hard to say how much of this is really about concrete communication and how much is just playing around.

In the film, researcher Claude Lacombe is the man who first figures out how to communicate with the aliens, and he uses hand signals to represent the five musical notes. This has led to speculation that his method is based on Solresol, Jean-François Sudre's musical constructed language, created in the 1830s with a view to becoming an international auxiliary language. As previously mentioned, Solresol can be played, written, sung and conveyed with colours or hand signals. It is possible the filmmakers were either directly inspired by Solresol, or simply had it in the back of their minds, but the five notes were developed by composer John Williams. Apparently, Williams and Spielberg chose this particular sequence of notes from over 300 combinations he composed. The hand symbols Claude Lacombe uses in the film, however, are the same as in Solresol. It is a musical pedagogical technique method called Tonic Sol-fa, developed by Englishman John Curwen in the nineteenth century.

Denis Villeneuve's film *Arrival* has a similar premise to several other films about first contact with an alien civilisation: large spaceships that suddenly appear around the globe. In *Arrival*, a dozen mysterious spacecraft appear at seemingly random points around the Earth. The US Army quickly contacts linguist Louise Banks to find out what the aliens want but, not trusting a linguist to establish contact on her own, they throw physicist Ian Donnelly into the mix too.

The film revolves around their efforts to learn how to communicate with the 'heptapods', which is what they call the space creatures. The gigantic seven-legged beings seem to have a spoken language that sounds like rippling water, static and something reminiscent of whale song. They also communicate visually by releasing smoke signals that form into a kind of misty ring, producing images similar to Rorschach ink blots.

Villeneuve has endeavoured to portray the first attempts at contact with an extraterrestrial civilisation as plausibly as possible. Linguist Louise Banks' work on cracking the alien code is compelling. However, it all happens a lot faster than it probably would in reality, and much of the real linguistic work is seen only in the background, in the glimpses of Banks' materials and analysis programs visible on computer screens.

Linguist Jessica Coon from McGill University in Canada was hired as a linguistic consultant to make the work look credible. Some books from her own bookshelf even featured in the movie. The filmmakers also used computer scientist and consultant Stephen Wolfram to add 'scientific texture' to the film. One thing he designed, together with his son Christopher, was a program to analyse the written language of the heptapods. We catch a glimpse of this code in the film, meaning that all of the code and analysis of the smoke plumes are, so to speak, authentic.

Louise Banks and Ian Donnelly work primarily on trying to analyse the aliens' written language, Heptapod B, and seem to completely ignore their spoken language, Heptapod A. We don't get to see any of the work done in the other countries where the large spaceships appeared, but they contribute with their own perspectives on how best to establish contact. South America tries to make contact through sign language, Japan by playing the cello, while the Chinese army teaches the heptapods to play the game Mahjong. Heptapod B seems to consist of logograms, similar to Chinese characters, which form segments of the smoke rings with different 'ink blots'.

The idea that the written language should be based on circles came from screenwriter Eric Heisserer, who tried in vain to describe his vision in text and sketched out different solutions himself without finding the right one. His idea was that the circle should link to another of the film's central themes: circular versus linear time. This task was entrusted to the film's art direc-tor, Patrice Vermette, who sketched out five different proposals for the aliens' written language. But he wasn't satisfied with any of them – they all felt either too human, too mathematical or too reminiscent of hieroglyphs. The designers then looked for inspiration in ancient Asian writing systems, Arabic script and the various writing systems of North Africa, but the smoke-ring language of the heptapods needed to be more extraterrestrial and mysterious.

Eric Heisserer found the solution one morning at his kitchen table. His wife, artist Martine Bertrand, had produced fifteen sketches during the night, and he showed one to director Denis Villeneuve. Everyone agreed – the heptapods' written language had been found. It wasn't just the shape of the ink blots that was significant, but their thickness and various small additions, such as a mark to denote a question. From there, they began developing the script, building up a lexicon of around 100 different logograms, each with a defined meaning. The film features seventy-one of these 100 characters. Patrice Vermette even learned how to write Heptapod B by hand.

So, Heptapod B can be clearly analysed and understood in the film, but the film's heroes barely even try to crack their spoken language, Heptapod A, and understandably so. It would be much more difficult for humans to decode.

Heptapod A was developed by two sound designers from New Zealand, couple Dave Whitehead and Michelle Child. Whitehead had previously produced a fascinating alien language for the film *District 9*. When they came to tackle the spoken language of the heptapods, they based it on their physical form. They are gigantic creatures with a large body mass (the seven legs visible in the film make up only a quarter of the aliens' bodies) and have no appar-ent mouth, so the sound of their spoken language would need to be generated another way. They thought of the body as a reso-nance chamber, with two internal bones producing the sounds.

Their starting point was that the aliens needed to come across as elegant, graceful and 'holy', rather than frightening. Whitehead and Child's thoughts were led in the direction of choirs, organs and meditative woodland walks with distant bird song. Indeed, they took a long forest hike to find a sound they wanted to use as the basis of the extraterrestrial language. After a three-day hike on New Zealand's North Island, they eventually found the rare North Island kōkako bird and were able to record its sound. Together with the song from another bird, the tui, this formed the foundation of Heptapod A. The frequency of the bird sounds was significantly reduced and mixed with other sounds, such as the snorts of a camel. They also used various instruments such as pūtōrino, a didgeridoo (played by Child), and experimented with a number of sounds from a disassembled bagpipe. A large 'lung' was also built out of rice paper, which they filled with water and used to produce the sound that became the heptapods' breathing.

The two heptapods we meet in the film are named Abbot and Costello. They are difficult to tell apart visibly and it is next to impossible to tell which is speaking. However, Whitehead and Child made every effort to give each of the extraterrestrial voices their own character. One has a slightly higher frequency than the other and a more fluttery sound, while the other has a deeper, more throbbing sound.

Dave Whitehead said that the biggest challenge was to not just make the sounds exotic, but also something that could pass for genuine communication between intelligent beings, even if it is not a language per se. The exact link between Heptapod A and B is still not entirely clear, as they appear to be quite distinct from each other. Director Denis Villeneuve has said of Heptapod A, 'In fact, it's not talking, it's expressing emotions through sound.'

Louise Banks and Ian Donnelly decode the heptapods' smoke rings one by one and gradually begin to make themselves understood with simple sentences, but the big breakthrough comes in a different, quite unexpected way. One day, Louise removes her protective suit inside the spaceship, approaches the large glass pane that separates the people from the aliens and presses her hand against it. One of the aliens moves its tentacle to touch her palm from the other side – and somehow conveys its language to Louise Banks. This is the moment that changes Louise, and Earth, forever. Once Louise understands the language of the heptapods, her image of reality changes radically. The film thus plays into the Sapir–Whorf hypothesis in its purest form, where a different language can reprogramme the brain to experience the world in a radically different way. Now Louise can see into the future, as the heptapods don't see time as linear. Heptapods have come to Earth specifically to teach people their language, giving them the gift of experiencing time as they do. This is apparently because humanity is going to save the heptapods in 3,000 years' time.

Suddenly, the viewers also understand that the scenes throughout the film that seemed at first to be flashbacks, in which Louise cares for her daughter Hannah who is dying of cancer, have not yet occurred. These are images that Louise, with her changed perception of time, can now see from her own future.

5

Dystopian Languages

FULL-SCALE LITERARY EXPERIMENTS

Newspeak, Láadan, Nadsat

Utopia is an ancient concept, as old as the notion of life after death or any number of heavenly realms. After the struggles of life we will eventually be rewarded with an idyllic, divine world, relieved of suffering of any kind, from starvation to everyday annoyances: a world where everyone is happy, the sun is shining and the birds are chirping – all the time.

The term 'utopia' comes from Thomas More's *Utopia*, but the dream of a paradisical society has gone by many names: Atlantis, Lemuria, Mu, Shangri-la, the Communist society and even the Nazi Thousand-Year Reich. Utopia is strongly associated with vision and desire, and throughout the ages people have felt its pull, dreaming up religious, ecological, economic and, not least, political utopias.

But, as we all know, one person's utopia is another person's prison.

Or, as John the Savage puts it when addressing the infallible World Controller, Mustapha Mond, in Aldous Huxley's *Brave New World*:

'I *want God, I want poetry*, I want real danger, I want freedom, I want goodness. I want sin.'

'In fact,' said Mustapha Mond, 'you're claiming the right
to be unhappy.'

A society where everyone is happy does not and cannot exist,
by definition. Appropriately enough, the word 'utopia' literally
means 'nowhere', and 'utopian' has come to denote an unrealis-
able dream. Utopian literature is sparse in modern times, rather
science fiction tends towards its opposite: dystopia. This is partially because utopia makes for a boring read. Perfection is not
exactly thrilling.

If utopia is a perfect world, then dystopia is its nightmar-
ish opposite. Significantly, utopia and dystopia often go hand in
hand. The visionary's concept of utopia often becomes dystopia
for its citizens. Dystopia is therefore particularly well suited to
critical sci-fi literature, where the author can take the trends that
they find disturbing in current society and extrapolate them into
full-scale trials in literary form.

Dystopian stories often reflect the time when they were written and the fears prevalent in that specific period. Technology
turning on humans is a recurring theme. During the nineteenth
century, when the world was marvelling at new technology and
all its possibilities, many dystopian stories were written about
machines eventually leading to the downfall of humanity. This
theme is still prevalent in more modern dystopian literature,
as well as environmental destruction, excessive consumption,
overpopulation and surveillance. With new advances in technology happening all the time, perhaps it is no wonder that we
fear science spinning out of our control.

Dystopian, and to some extent also utopian, societies need
to control and monitor their citizens to keep the peace. Any
discontents must be located and brainwashed or medicated into
accepting the system – or be got rid of so as not to ruin things for
citizens who are content and satisfied with the status quo, often
the elites. Propaganda and surveillance technology are common

tools used in dystopian society, and language can also play an important role in dystopian literature.

The Theory of Linguistic Relativity

In general, science-fiction literature is an ideal testing ground for the theory of linguistic relativity, the Sapir–Whorf hypothesis, which states that the grammar and vocabulary of each language contains within it an inherent world view that characterises the way its speakers think. Human culture determines language, and in turn, language determines how we categorise our experiences and thoughts. In Suzette Haden Elgin's *Native Tongue* and in the Cthulhu Mythos of H.P. Lovecraft's works, the difference between alien and human language/thought is so great that people risk losing their minds or even dying if exposed to extraterrestrial language or logic.

The Sapir–Whorf hypothesis can either be interpreted very literally or more loosely. The literal interpretation – that language controls our perception of the outside world completely and determines or limits how and what we can think – has no support in modern research. However, this is the most interesting interpretation to explore within science fiction. The looser interpretation, that language has a certain influence on our thoughts and perceptions of our surroundings, is less controversial, but this is difficult to prove outside of lab conditions.

For example, some credence is given to the theory of linguistic relativity in terms of how different cultures perceive colours. One study showed that English-speaking participants could easily define blue-green hues as either blue or green, whereas this was significantly more difficult for the Tarahumara indigenous people of Mexico whose language makes no distinction between the two colours.

Another example is the Berinmo language, spoken in Papua New Guinea, which has only five basic colours. Berinmo doesn't distinguish between green and blue, and in one study, research-ers found that Berinmo speakers had difficulty determining whether two shades in the blue-green spectrum were the same or different. English speakers showed faster response times at the border between green and blue, whereas Berinmo speakers were better at distinguishing nuances not expressed in their own language than the English speakers.

The distinction between blue and green is significant in many languages. The traditional Welsh definition of green and blue, for example, doesn't match English, as the word *glas* can mean green, blue or grey. In Russian, there are two words for blue: *goluboy* and *siniy* (light blue and dark blue). The Vikings made no distinction between blue and black, and Vikings who encountered Africans described them as 'blue men'. The Dani people of New Guinea only have two words for colours: light and dark.

According to a widely accepted theory, the distinction between light and dark, or black and white, is common to all languages. These are the two basic 'colours' in all languages. If the language expresses a third colour, it is red. The fourth is either yellow or green, and if there is a fifth there will be words for both yellow and green. The sixth colour, according to this theory, is blue and then brown. Purple, pink, orange and grey appear when a language has eight or more terms for colours.

This human way of describing colours is challenged in science fiction via extraterrestrial languages. For example, the Klingons only distinguish between four colours expressed as verbs:

Doq – orange/red
SuD – green/blue/yellow
chIS – white
qIj – black

The colour **SuD** is alien because there is no language or culture on our planet that classifies yellow as the same colour as blue or green. As the aforementioned theory shows, if a (human) language has four colours then the fourth is *either* yellow or green. This is one of several unearthly features of Klingon.

The idea behind the theory of linguistic relativity is that each of us experiences colours (and the world) in different ways depending on what, and how many, terms exist in our language. If my language has no word for 'pink', I am unlikely to register a pink toy like a 6-year-old in a colour-coded toy shop would.

There are, of course, more examples of linguistic differences than colours alone. Unlike English, French and German, Swedish distinguishes between two types of berry – *jordgubb* (the larger kind of strawberry usually found in shops) and *smultron* (smaller wild strawberries that grow in forests). The hypothesis would then be that speakers of English, German and French regard wild strawberries as just another type of strawberry, while Swedes would see them as two different types of fruit.

Chinese numerals are another example, although this might be more a case of culturally conditioned superstition. In China, some numbers are considered to be more auspicious than others because they are loaded with meaning. The especially good numbers are zero, six, eight and nine. The Mandarin word for 'eight' sounds like the word for 'wealth', and the number 518 is pronounced *wo yao fa*, which sounds like 'I want to become very rich'. The worst figure is four, which is pronounced in the same way as 'death' and therefore is an unlucky number. It is not uncommon for hotels to lack a fourth floor, just as some hotels in the Western world lack a thirteenth floor. Companies selling any product with a four in the name often change it specifically for the Chinese market.

This means that telephone numbers in China vary greatly in price according to how coveted the digit combinations are. A phone number including an eight can fetch a hefty sum, while one with multiple fours probably goes for a song. Who wants to say 'death-death-death' when giving out their number to someone they've just met in a bar?

In China, time is also viewed somewhat differently than in the West. The Chinese concept of time is vertical, unlike in the West where time goes from left to right, because that is the direction we write. Chinese people, who read and write vertically, tend to see the past as upwards. Similarly, those who write Hebrew and Arabic regard time as going from right to left. Psychologist Lera Boroditsky was able to demonstrate this with an experiment in which she gave subjects a series of photographs of her grandfather at different ages, from childhood to old age, and asked them to arrange them chronologically.

There are also languages that place the past as something that lies ahead of the individual, whereas we in the West tend to see the future as ahead of us and past as behind. In the language of the Aymara people in the Andes, the past is ahead because it is known and therefore something we can 'see'. The future, on the other hand, is unknown, so is located behind us where we cannot see it. Similar views of past and future are found among speakers of Malagasy in Madagascar. The linguist behind Valyrian in *Game of Thrones* took this into consideration and used a vertical cultural metaphor for time, as in Chinese, except the past is below and the future is above. This is a possible indication that Valyrian would be written from bottom to top, but its writing system is currently unknown.

So, it does seem that our concept of time depends on which language we speak. This is a prominent theme in the film *Arrival* – how language can affect our experience of time. But there are many ways for writers and filmmakers to explore the Sapir–Whorf hypothesis, not least by using language as a means of power.

Newspeak

In George Orwell's dystopia *1984*, the regime's leader has clearly adopted the Sapir–Whorf hypothesis and uses language as an instrument to secure power and suppress any form of dissent against the prevailing elite. By controlling the language, political party Ingsoc tries to control citizens' thoughts. Or, more precisely, to limit their capacity for incorrect thinking, which is to say, free thinking.

In the province of Airstrip One (Great Britain), in the totalitarian state of Oceania, citizens face comprehensive oppression under the great leader Big Brother. Torture, violence, indoctrination and relentless, round-the-clock surveillance via telescreens are commonplace in Oceania, so language is just one component of the oppression. But the idea is that by eliminating undesirable words from the language, and removing synonyms, opposites and nuances, the party hopes it will make it harder, and eventually impossible, to express or even think dissenting thoughts.

The party's Newspeak should make all thoughts that are not in line with the 'correct' ideology impossible: 'Orthodoxy means not thinking – not needing to think.' Newspeak is unique among languages in that its vocabulary decreases as it develops. In *1984*, they are working on the eleventh edition of the Newspeak dictionary where more words than ever have now been removed.

Let's take the word 'good' as an example. Any synonyms such as 'great', 'excellent', 'wonderful', etc., have been removed from Newspeak. According to the party, 'good' says it all. To show the opposite meaning of a word, 'un' is added in front of the adjective. Thus, **ungood** means 'bad'. To add emphasis, you put a 'plus' in front of the adjective to make **plusgood**. If you really want to go to town, you can add further emphasis with 'double' before the adjective. **Doubleplusgood**, wouldn't you say?

Similarly, **unlight** means 'dark' and **uncold** means 'hot'. A really sweltering summer's day could be described as **doubleplusuncold**.

It is an unusual construction in English, but this is precisely how real agglutinating languages work to form meaning.

There is also no word in Newspeak for just 'sex', because it has been replaced by two new words: **crimesex** and **goodsex**. Goodsex can only mean sex between a man and woman in order to produce a child. Everything else comes under **crimesex**. Young party members are expected to join the Junior Anti-Sex League to uphold morality.

Crimethink denotes a criminal thought. It doesn't even have to be something you think consciously – your children might turn you in for something you say unknowingly in your sleep. The children of the party members are part of the youth organisation The Spies, which trains children to report on their own parents. **Doublethink** means the ability to accept two contradictory statements as both true, without question.

Think is a Newspeak word that can mean both the noun 'thought' and verb 'to think'. Sometimes a Newspeak word comes from the verb and sometimes from the noun. For example, 'cut' is replaced with **knife**. Irregular inflections have been removed from Newspeak, so the past tense of 'give' and 'bring' are **gived** and **bringed**. Similarly, there are no irregular comparative forms: **good, gooder, goodest**. There is also only one plural ending: **man – mans, life – lifes**.

The word 'free' remains in Newspeak but may only be used in the sense of 'The dog is free from lice'. The second meaning of 'free' – as in political or intellectual freedom – can no longer be used, 'since *political and intellectual freedom no longer existed even* as *concepts*, and were *therefore* of necessity nameless'. The phrase 'all mans are equal' is also regarded as an incorrect phrase, but only because 'it expressed a palpable untruth – i.e. that all men are of equal size, weight, or strength'. The more general concept of equality no longer exists.

Even though it is grammatically possible to construct the unorthodox phrase 'Big Brother is ungood' in Newspeak, it would sound absurd and unthinkable to the ear of an adherent. Besides, it would be difficult, if not impossible, to really expand on or defend the sentence, since all such definitions (that is, all words to describe opinion that may oppose Big Brother) have been removed.

The vocabulary is divided into three categories: A for everyday speech, B for political terms and C for technical purposes. The latter is divided by subject so that each expert has a list of the words they need in their profession. There are no direct examples of words in the C categories, but they are said to resemble the expert terminology of Oldspeak (English).

The prescribed ideal way of speaking as a party member is to blurt Newspeak in rapid, staccato sentences without thinking, known as **duckspeak**. The specific purpose of Newspeak is to produce **duckspeakers** – citizens who produce ideologically correct phrases without any conscious thought.

Nobody in *1984* really speaks Newspeak fluently. They still use Oldspeak with a smattering of Newspeak words. The only thing that appears entirely in Newspeak is the leading article in the daily newspaper, *The Times*. The novel's protagonist Winston Smith works at the Ministry of Truth where he edits history. He is able to write in Newspeak, although he doesn't speak it fluently.

Winston Smith's job is to revise, or rather falsify, history. As soon as something happens that contradicts earlier newspaper articles, the archives must be changed and printed to replace the old ones. Thus, he is continually told that **unpersons** – people who disappear – never existed to begin with. Oceania has always been at war with one of the two other super states that take turns in being its enemy and ally.

In his work, Winston receives newspaper texts to correct, written in 'not actually Newspeak, but consisting largely of Newspeak words', for example:

> times 17.3.84 bb speech malreported africa rectify
> times 19.12.83 forecasts 3 yp 4th quarter 83 misprints
> verify current issue
> times 14.2.84 miniplenty malquoted chocolate rectify
> times 3.12.83 reporting bb dayorder doubleplusungood
> refs unpersons rewrite fullwise upsub antefiling

Party members expect Newspeak to have completely replaced Oldspeak by 2050. Presumably, this is because the first generation to have Newspeak as their mother tongue should have grown up by then. **Proles**, the Oceania masses, are not members of the Party and are not expected to learn Newspeak, at least not yet. Thus, the **proles** still converse in Oldpseak with no Newspeak words mixed in.

George Orwell was a dedicated socialist and became very concerned about how he saw communist states developing. It won't come as a surprise to anyone that the Soviet Union was the model for the oppressive state in *1984*. Newspeak was based on another artificial language: Basic English. This international auxiliary language, created by Charles Kay Ogden, is a simplified variant of English. It contains only the 850 words you need in everyday life, plus a few hundred words for more specialised areas such as education and scientific terms. Does that three-part division of vocabulary remind you of anything?

Basic English has only eighteen verbs and a greatly simplified, regular grammar. Ogden's idea was that Basic English would be easy to learn as a second language and could function as an international auxiliary language, as well as a warm-up before learning the full English language. Orwell was initially a keen proponent of Basic English but turned against it a few years before he wrote *1984*.

Newspeak words, and the word 'Newspeak' itself, have become loanwords in several modern languages. 'Newspeak' has become a catchword in political debate when events are renamed, often with euphemisms, for political reasons, or when words are created or replaced with other terms considered more 'politically correct'.

Other Orwellian words that have become part of our collective mind include Big Brother, unperson, thought police and doublethink. Interestingly, one Newspeak word has reached a wide sphere beyond the novel: doublespeak. A teachers' organisation in the USA gives out the ironic Doublespeak Award annually. Doublespeak means purposefully using euphemistic expressions to make bad things sound better – 'let go' instead of 'fire', 'collateral damage' instead of 'multiple fatalities', etc. I wonder whether the new generation of reality TV aficionados knows what the title of *Big Brother* actually refers to …

Láadan

It could be argued that the true protagonist of Suzette Haden Elgin's *Native Tongue* trilogy is the theory of linguistic relativity itself. This is partly because the main premise of the story is in itself the ultimate test of this theory – encounters with entirely alien languages – and partly because Elgin was performing a deliberate linguistic experiment with her women's language, Láadan. She wanted to see whether it would grow beyond the scope of her books.

The first book in the *Native Tongue* trilogy was published in 1984 (a suitable year for dystopia) and is set in a near, but very different, dystopian future. In the series, in 1991 women's rights and suffrage are abolished in the United States. Women are classed as minors and must have a male guardian: father, husband, brother or male relative. Women cannot have a passport, travel freely or be in possession of anything more than pocket money. In other words, a status somewhere between nineteenth-century Europe and modern-day Saudi Arabia.

Even though 1991 is far in the past now, and these sorts of changes in law may feel unbelievable and absurd, it is worth bearing in mind that women's rights, human rights in general, and universal suffrage are not a given, even today. From a historical perspective, these rights are not even particularly old or well established.

In Elgin's world, men are in charge and protect 'their' women from professional life and other exertions. Women are housewives or sometimes allowed to be nurses (and maybe a few other professions). Other than this old-fashioned attitude to women, their society is modern: humankind has gone into space, colonised other worlds and made contact with extraterrestrials of many different types.

This is where it gets really interesting. In the 1950s, the linguistic focus on the differences between languages diminished when American linguist Noam Chomsky launched a new theory. He strove to find a universal grammar that is innate and common to all languages. Chomsky believed that the differences between languages are mostly superficial – or earthly languages, anyway. Chomsky said, 'If a Martian scientist looked at us the way that we look at frogs he might well conclude that with marginal, minor modifications, there is only one language.'

The philosopher Ludwig Wittgenstein thought along the same lines and wrote, in *Philosophical Investigations*, 'If a lion could speak, we would not understand him'. Wittgenstein argues that language is first and foremost a social phenomenon that arises from interaction within a language community. A language developed among lions (or frogs or aliens) is thus only understandable to lions; when human language emerges through interpersonal interaction, it is only understandable to humans.

I couldn't say whether Suzette Haden Elgin was inspired by these quotes, but as a doctor of linguistics, she was undoubtedly familiar with the logic behind them. For this very reason, in the *Native Tongue* trilogy linguists have become a kind of upper class. After all, communication with aliens is incredibly difficult, even once contact has been made – they are just so different from humans.

In Elgin's dystopia, therefore, linguists have become an elite, and thirteen special families or 'lines' of linguists maintain all contact with aliens. The linguists' heavy workload means they must live separate from society, and their culture resembles a sort of sect. They almost exclusively marry other linguists. Since there is a shortage of linguists, the women (and children) are also allowed to work – anyone who is able to interpret is needed. This reinforces the linguists' isolation from the rest of society because the average citizen looks suspiciously at these strange linguists who let their women work!

Other than that, the lives of the female linguists don't differ greatly from those of the other women in the book. They are not allowed to keep the money they earn and are expected to produce at least six or seven children who can be raised to learn new alien languages. When the linguist women can no longer reproduce, they are moved to a special house for infertile women. There, they are allowed a certain freedom in an all-female environment and this is where Láadan, a language by and for women, develops in secret.

Back to Chomsky's and Wittgenstein's ideas about aliens, frogs and lions, and their application in science fiction. Aliens and people would be said to differ so greatly that it is near impossible to learn each other's languages beyond the most basic and super-ficial. And herein lies the great power of the linguists in Elgin's stories: they have developed a technology that they call 'the Interface'. From a technical point of view, the way the Interface works is not described in detail, but on one side of a glass wall the linguists create an environment and atmosphere suitable for the alien in question (AIRY – Alien-in-Residence), and on the other, they create an environment suitable for a human. Linguists' children (both boys and girls) are put in the Interface when they are just a few weeks old and continue to spend a large portion of their time in it, typically eight hours a day, until they are teenagers. They grow up with an alien as their main contact and therefore learn the alien language as their native tongue.

The idea is to take advantage of children's natural and inimitable ability to learn language. This is also in line with Chomsky's theories, which claim that humans have an intrinsic propensity for language – a kind of pre-programming to grammar. It is said that children are able to learn seven or eight languages fluently before the age of 10. This exceptional skill disappears as the child approaches puberty. It is debatable whether this ability can be described as innate, but children and adults certainly do learn languages in different ways. Strangely, a major factor in children's aptitude for language is the fact that they don't work hard at it – they learn unconsciously, more or less.

On the other hand, adults who learn languages struggle with this. We are very aware of the fact that we are learning Spanish so we can move to the Costa del Sol, or so we can converse with business contacts, or whatever our motives might be. This awareness doesn't favour language learning at all. On the contrary, it inhibits it.

Additionally, we may have too much respect for foreign languages, which manifests as a fear of making mistakes. Children aren't afraid of making mistakes; they will make any number of them – 'me want', 'I thinked', 'two sheeps'. In fact, it is their mistakes that allow them to learn so quickly.

Elgin drew on this idea in her trilogy – but there is more to it. Human and alien logic are so different that it is difficult for a human brain to comprehend how the aliens think at all. When a state agency tries to circumvent the thirteen lines of linguists and build their own Interface, the children they use either die or become vacant zombies when paired with an alien. Only the linguists have developed techniques and strategies to allow the children's brains to cope with the conceptual world of the aliens.

Within the linguist families, everything revolves around language and linguistics, so children are socialised into the world of linguistics and grammar from day one.

This means that by the age of 6, a child might be the only available interpreter for a certain extraterrestrial language. As the child gets older, they can teach another child to speak the language fluently, and other people to speak it to a reasonable level. In addition to their extraterrestrial language, all linguists speak half a dozen Earth languages fluently and have a working knowledge of a further dozen.

In Elgin's dystopia, there is virtually no public opposition to the social order. Individual women protest by doing 'unwomanly' things or running away from home, but they are considered insane and put in institutions. The real resistance is of a completely different, long-term nature. The women of the Chornyak linguist family secretly develop a language to better express women's thinking; a language that allows women to express themselves more accurately. Elgin wanted to test the Sapir–Whorf-inspired hypothesis that language generally has a male bias, making it more difficult for women to express themselves. This might be a backdrop to the stereotype that women talk too much – since language is not designed to meet women's needs, they need more words to express themselves.

Another source of inspiration for Elgin was *Gödel, Escher, Bach: An Eternal Golden Braid*, a book by Douglas Hofstadter published in 1979. Hofstadter is an American physicist and polymath who is interested in mind and spirit, consciousness, self-reference, translation and mathematical games, and his book inspired a generation of engineers to devote themselves to artificial intelligence. Elgin drew on one of Hofstadter's lines of argument when he rephrased a theorem named after mathematician Kurt Gödel: 'For any *record player*, there are records which it cannot play because they will cause its indirect self-destruction'. Elgin was intrigued by this idea and transferred it to language.

183

What if each language contained specific notions that cannot be expressed because they would indirectly lead to the language being erased? And what if each culture had languages that could not be used or they would destroy that culture?

The interesting thing about Suzette Haden Elgin's Láadan project is that it extends beyond the world of the trilogy. She wanted to test if the language could have a bearing outside fiction. *Native Tongue* came out in 1984, and although the book doesn't contain all that many concrete examples of the language, Elgin nevertheless constructed Láadan thoroughly. She planned to give the experiment ten years to see how it would be received by women, and whether it would prove successful. How might a language that is adapted for women change society? Would American culture self-destruct?

In the fictional world, the Chornyak women keep the language secret from everyone except the women of the other linguistic families. They also teach it to their daughters so that it might develop from an academic conlang into a native tongue, as the title suggests. The female linguists thus use their expertise in languages to effect long-term societal reform: changing ways of thinking through changing ways of speaking. It is about the power of language.

In the real world, the results were not quite so dramatic. A small group formed to study the language, write poetry, and suggest new words and grammatical rules. In the late 1980s, a science-fiction association released a Láadan dictionary, but the language never caught on, so in 1994 Elgin declared the experiment unsuccessful. There simply wasn't enough interest in a women's language. Meanwhile, she wryly pointed out that the 'hyper-masculine' warrior language of Klingon was growing and flourishing.

Láadan has continued to lead a life on the margins but new words have gradually been added. The glossary was updated in both 2003 and 2009, and attempts were made to develop a new grammar. Suzette Haden Elgin passed away in 2015, so the question becomes – how to manage a language now its creator is gone. The language has many words for nuanced emotions: for example, the different ways you can feel angry. It is a tonal language, so an accent over a vowel marks a higher tone.

bma – anger for a reason, but with no one to blame, but that is not pointless
bana – anger for a reason, but with no one to blame, but that is pointless
bara – anger for a reason, with someone to blame, but that is pointless

Love is also an area that Elgin believed needs more shades of meaning, so Láadan draws a distinction between seven types:

azh – love for one sexually desired at the time
áazh – love for one sexually desired at one time, but not now
ab – love for one liked but not respected
ad – love for one respected but not liked
am – love for one related by blood
ashon – love for someone you feel related to but are not related to by blood
aye – love that is an unwelcome burden

Clarity and avoidance of misunderstanding are the foundation of Láadan. The idea is that there should be no room for the sort of arguments in which a person would need to defend themselves (herself) with, 'Yes, I know I said that, but I didn't mean it like that!' This is why every sentence in Láadan begins with what Elgin called a speech-act particle:

'**bíi**' – 'I say this to you as a statement.'
'**báa**' – 'I ask you.'
bó – indicates a command, unusual except to children

bóo – indicates a request, imperative
bé – indicates a promise
bée – indicates a warning
'**bíid**' – 'I say this to you in anger.'
'**bíili**' – 'I say this to you with love.'
'**bíiya**' – 'I say this to you in fear.'

There are many more speech-act particles, specifically suffixes, that can add nuance to the feeling of the sentence.

'**bíi shóod le wa**.' – 'I'm busy.'
'**bíid shóod le wa**!' – 'I say this in anger: I'm busy!' (**-d** indicates anger)
'**bíida shóod le wa**!' – 'I say this as a joke: I'm busy!' (**-da** indicates playfulness)

You get the idea. It should be entirely impossible to misconstrue the intentions behind someone's words. This is the exact opposite approach of Orwell's Newspeak, which removes words and nuances in order to prevent 'misunderstandings'!

There is another compulsory feature of Láadan that adds further nuance to a sentence. To avoid possible misinterpretation, Láadan indicates evidentiality. This means that it requires the speaker to make clear how they have received the information they are imparting – whether it is something they have seen with their own eyes, heard through hearsay, and so on. These grammatical elements are inserted last in the sentence:

-wa – experienced by the speaker
-wi – known by the speaker because it is self-evident
-we – experienced by the speaker in a dream
-waa – the speaker thinks the statement is false because they mistrust the source

-wálh – the speaker thinks the statement is false because they mistrust the source and think the source has malicious intent

-wo – the speaker's hypothesis

Elgin clearly thought grammatical tricks to reduce the chances of misinterpretation are necessary in a women's language. I am unsure as to whether this is truly a gender-specific thing, or whether Elgin, as a linguist, simply found these linguistic building blocks fascinating and couldn't resist the chance to include them in her language. She also invented new words to better describe female experiences such as menstruation, menopause and pregnancy:

lawida – to be pregnant
lalewida – to be pregnant and joyful
lóda – to be pregnant and tired
lewidan – to be pregnant for the first time
widazhad – to be at the end of pregnancy and eager to give birth

And finally, two Láadan words that I think are more telling of the culture of the time, but which I think many can relate to regardless of gender:

radíidin – non-holiday; a time supposed to be a holiday that becomes a dreaded burden because of all the work and preparations. Especially when there are too many guests and none of them help.

rathoo – non-guest; someone who comes to visit even though they are well aware that they are barging in and being an inconvenience.

Nadsat

Our third dystopian language, Nadsat, differs greatly from Newspeak and Láadan, as most of Anthony Burgess' 1962 book *A Clockwork Orange* is actually written in the language. Anti-hero Alex, the protagonist and first-person narrator of the book, speaks in the teenage slang dialect Nadsat (which is the Russian equivalent of '-teen' in thirteen, fourteen, etc.), so the language is picked up by the reader as they go along – or the viewer, for that matter, because in many ways the film has become more famous and influential than the book. Burgess is quoted as saying that one of his intentions with the book and language was to brainwash readers into unconsciously learning a little Russian.

In the shadow of the Cold War, Anthony Burgess constructed a distinctive slang with significant Russian influence, thus his dystopian depiction of the future gives readers a strong impression of the direction he saw society heading, without so much as a mention of the Soviet Union.

Burgess' dystopia bears little resemblance to the Soviet Union, but via Nadsat we can see a significant element of Russian in its society. This is also implied via passing mentions of 'Gagarin Street' (after the Soviet cosmonaut) and chart-topper Johnny Zhivago, a **russki koschka** (Russian cat, read: 'cool cat'). Nadsat is a fusion of the two world languages of the Cold War.

A character in the book called Dr Branom describes Nadsat as follows, 'Odd bits of rhyming slang ... A bit of gipsy talk, too. Most of the roots are Slav. Propaganda. Subliminal penetration.' So, while the Communists/Russians don't seem to be in power in Britain, their propaganda is influential enough that **nadsats** – 'teenagers' – soak it up. Since the Russian element of Nadsat is so significant, it might also indicate the desires of defiant teens to distance themselves from the older generation by using words that their parents and the authorities wouldn't.

Burgess also had another, more authorial, reason for creating a fictional teenage slang. Youth jargon ages extremely quickly and becomes a very clear time marker. If Burgess had made Alex and his gang speak genuine 1960s slang, today we would probably have scoffed at their expressions.

In another dystopian work, the epic space poem *Aniara*, Swedish author Harry Martinsson created a highly effective terminology to describe futuristic technology, such as the supercomputer **Mima** and her attendant the **Mimarobe**. In Klass and Sjöberg's English translation, **Mima** uses 'screener-cells', 'electro-lenses', 'focus-works' and 'tacis of the third indifferent webe'. These words and concepts seem believable, but when Harry Martinsson gives examples of Dorisburg slang in verse, via Daisy Doody, it becomes clear how hard it would be to make it sound timeless:

> **You're gamming out and getting vile and snowzy.**
> **But do like me, I never sit and frowzy.**
> **I'm no sleeping chadwick, Daisy pouts,**
> **my pipes are working, I am flamm and gondel,**
> **my date's a gander and my fate's a rondel**
> **and wathed in taris, gland in delt and yondel.**

To my ears this sounds rather old-fashioned, both in original and translation.

Nadsat, on the other hand, has done a better job of creating a sense of timelessness, as when Alex describes the Korova Milkbar, a **mesto** with **milk-plus**, on the first page:

> They had no license for selling liquor, but there was no law yet against prodding some of the new **vesches** which they used to put into the old **moloko**, so you could **peet** it with **vellocet** or **synthemesc** or **drencrom** or one or two other **veshches** which would give you a nice quiet **horror-show** fifteen minutes admiring **Bog** …

Despite several foreign words, the meaning is understandable. We don't yet know that **moloko** is 'milk' in Russian or that **vesch** comes from Russian *veshch* ('thing'), but we start to pick up Nadsat from the very first page. **Horrorshow**, together with **ultra-violence**, are the two most well-known Nadsat words, and have been adopted by other languages. Burgess took the Russian word for 'good' (*khorosho*) and anglicised it to become **horrorshow**.

This was Burgess' technique for shaping the Russian loanwords, adapting them to roll off the English tongue. Sometimes the Russianness is barely perceptible, as in the examples of **gulliver** ('head' – from Russian *golovo*) or **gloss** ('voice' – from *golos*).

Many of Nadsat's 200 words describe the violent lifestyle of Alex and his gang:

krovis – blood
bitva – fight
britva – razor
tolshock – punch
nors – knife
krasta – rob

Glaringly absent from Nadsat's vocabulary are more abstract concepts that relate to knowledge, philosophy or love. As a result, when Alex needs to discuss something more intellectually demanding, he has to use English and noticeably struggles to find the right words, despite his clear intelligence. There is also a childlike element to Nadsat, which highlights the immaturity of Alex and his **droogs** ('friends', from Russian *droog*). Examples such as **eggy weggs** ('eggs'), **skolliwol** ('school') and **interestovated** ('interested') emphasise that Alex is very young. In many ways, he is immature, even for a 15-year-old. But this is contradictory, because Nadsat also includes some old-fashioned, almost Shakespearean language.

Alex is eventually jailed and sentenced to fourteen years in prison, but soon hears about the new Ludovico Technique and is selected after volunteering as a guinea pig. The technique is a kind of psychological conditioning experiment using drugs and sensory stimuli to alter a person's behaviour, transforming them from a psychotic, violent criminal to a harmless, non-violent vegetable. Alex is forced to watch films of violence and abuse while being injected with drugs that make him physically ill. After fourteen days of treatment, the conditional reflex is ingrained – Alex can't so much as think about violence without becoming severely nauseated. He has thus ceased to be a danger to society.

An unfortunate side effect for Alex is that the sound of his favourite composer, Ludwig van Beethoven, now makes him feel sick, as his music and that of other classical composers are used as the atmospheric score for the violent film scenes.

Beyond the Seven Kingdoms

HOW TV SPARKS LANGUAGE DEVELOPMENT

Lekh Dothraki, Valyrio Udrir, Mag Nuk, Gerna Moussha

Dothraki

George R.R. Martin, author of the popular fantasy series *A Song of Ice and Fire*, which was made into the hugely successful TV series *Game of Thrones*, has lamented that he doesn't share fellow fantasy author J.R.R. Tolkien's gift for language. This is understandable because, just like Tolkien, Martin has created a fantasy world that is believable down to the last detail, apart from one noticeably missing piece of the puzzle: language. Martin refers to the various tongues spoken in Westeros, Essos and the free cities of his fantasy world, circumventing the language barrier by writing, '… she said in Valyrian'. However, Martin did make some effort with the Dothraki language, inventing a handful of words in this harsh warrior tongue and even providing a few example sentences. But when HBO developed the books into a TV series, they compensated for George R.R. Martin's regretted lack of language talent and the subsequent rift in realism by deciding that Dothraki should be developed into a real language.

It would hardly have been possible to make a TV series like *Game of Thrones* without the Dothraki speaking their own language. Seeing as Martin's fantasy epic is reminiscent in many ways of Tolkien's genre-defining literature, and in the tradition of Elvish, Na'vi and Klingon, it is unavoidable that today's viewers expect to hear invented peoples speaking invented languages.

The Dothraki are modelled on the notion of an exotic 'warrior people' and somewhat resemble the original Klingons in the 1960s *Star Trek* when they had something of the Genghis Khan about them, as well as the more modern Klingons, who have long luscious hair like the Dothraki. When dreaming up the Dothraki and Klingons, both Martin and *Star Trek* creator Gene Roddenberry likely drew inspiration from Genghis Khan's famous mounted warriors. It is not inconceivable that Martin was also influenced by Klingons when he started writing about the Dothraki.

The Klingons have a legendary first emperor, whom they revere almost as a god, called Kahless, which is similar to the Dothraki word for 'queen' (**khaleesi**). The Dothraki word for king is **khal**, which is not a million miles away from *khan*, as in Genghis Khan …

When the production company decided that the Dothraki needed a developed language, naturally the question arose of the best way to go about inventing one. These days, it is very unlikely that major TV or film production companies would risk letting the scriptwriters just invent a few cool-sounding words. Today, authenticity standards are higher for fictional languages. So, HBO didn't just go out and contract any old linguist; they held an audition. Or rather, they contacted a bunch of enthusiastic conlangers through the Language Creation Society and asked if they could help. And, unsurprisingly, they could.

They announced a contest and received around thirty-five entries with draft versions of a Dothraki language. All contributions were anonymously assessed by a group of experts in engineered languages, and in the end, four finalists were invited to meet HBO representatives, who were deeply impressed by the love the linguists had put into their projects. The winner was David J. Peterson, chairman of the Language Creation Society, and one of its founders in 2007. Not only had he already created twelve artificial languages, but also held a Masters degree in linguistics. Some might suspect that Peterson 'happened to' win the contest because of his senior role in the Language Creation Society, but all the submissions were anonymous, and the producers chose his language from the four best finalists. With the languages of *Game of Thrones*, Peterson embarked on a decade-long journey and the beginning of a professional career as language engineer for television and film.

So now, George R.R. Martin was getting help with his language building. He had previously only come up with fifty-six words in Dothraki, twenty-four of which were proper nouns, plus a few short sentences. But these were enough to give Peterson a good idea of the language's sound, or phonology, and a glimpse of a few pieces in the grammatical puzzle. For example, Peterson could see that 'u' never appeared as a vowel but only as 'qu', and there were no examples of consonants 'p' and 'b', so he decided to omit them from the language altogether. He reasoned that the sounds 'p' and 'b' did once exist in Dothraki but were transformed into 'f' and 'v', respectively. But then when Peterson had finished the language, he discovered he had been wrong: the book features the names Pono and Bharbo! Peterson quickly decided that these were dialectical anomalies.

The longest sentence in the book is '**Khalakka dothrae mr'anha**!' – 'A prince rides within me!', which one of the book's protagonists Daenerys Targaryen says during a ceremony for the baby she is carrying. We can see in the sentence above that **dothrae** means 'ride', just as the mounted nomads' name for themselves is **Dothraki** – 'riders'. Another word mentioned in the book is **Vaes Dothrak** ('City of the Riders'), the only city of the Dothraki people. From these two pieces of information, Peterson assumed that -k, -i and -e were suffixes attached to the root **dothra**-. Some words were relatively simple for Peterson to create, such as the frequently used 'blood rider', a kind of close bodyguard – **dothrakhqoyi** – since both **Dothraki** ('riders') and **qoy** ('blood') were among the words Martin had invented himself.

In other cases, Peterson developed the grammar from seemingly small details. For example, the word **khalasar** from the book led Peterson to assume that -r was a plural suffix, which then inspired the creation of the **ath- -zar** circumfix that creates an abstract noun from a base verb or adjective: for example, **davra** – 'good'; **athdavrazar** – 'excellence'; and **jahak** – 'braid'; **athjahakar** – 'pride'.

In addition to analysing the Dothraki words contained in the books, Peterson also went through everything the Dothraki said in English, noting the way they spoke the 'Common Tongue'. For example, Khal Drogo says 'Iron Chair' instead of 'Iron Throne', leading Peterson to conclude that Dothraki has no word for 'throne'.

He then broadened his perspective to try to capture the Dothraki spirit, getting to grips with their culture as depicted by Martin while imagining how this would affect their language. At their core, the Dothraki are nomadic warriors like the Mongols and Native Americans of ancient times, sharing a symbiotic relationship with their horses. So it stands to reason that a lot of their terminology would have to do with horses and riding. That said, the horses are not just for riding – the Dothraki worship a horse god, ferment horse milk into alcohol (**lamekh ohazho**), eat horse meat, and measure a person's merit in horses. The word for 'powerful and important', **vezhzen**, derives from the word for 'stallion' (**vezh**), implying that to be powerful is to be stallion-like. It is also not surprising that a horse-centric culture would have a lot of specific terms for horses. One word isn't enough; they need a whole herd:

hrazef – horse
tehin – bay/reddish-brown horse
qahlan – palomino/dun-coloured horse
ocha – black horse
nozho – chestnut horse
messhih – perlino/cream-coloured horse
fansa – grey/roan horse
cheyao – dark brown horse

It's no wonder really – any avid equestrian could probably list more horse descriptions in English.

The Dothraki terms for distance are derived directly from their terms for horses' gaits. From **karlinat** ('gallop') comes the unit of measurement, **karlina**, meaning the distance a horse can gallop before they get tired, which takes around two minutes, or **leshitof**, as the Dothraki say. For simplicity's sake, David J. Peterson assumes that one **karlina** is about a mile or 1.6 kilometres:

karlinat – gallop
karlina – as far as a horse can gallop in about two minutes
chetirate – canter
chetira – half of the distance a horse can gallop in two minutes
ir vosat – trot
ir vosa – a quarter of the distance a horse can gallop in two minutes
onqothat – walk
onqotha – an eighth of the distance a horse can gallop in two minutes

These are not particularly practical or satisfying units of measurement for modern people but entirely logical for horse people in a steppe landscape.

Unlike constructed extraterrestrial languages, there has been no endeavour to make Dothraki sound like alienese nor have intrinsic grammatical oddities the likes of which have never been seen in human languages. In fact, in order to emphasise the human feeling of Dothraki, Peterson even designed a kind of proto-Dothraki, as they may have spoken 1,000 years previous, developing the modern language from there to give it a sense of organic growth. Peterson also had the objective of constructing a language to suit the Dothraki as they appear in the book, which would sound foreign enough without immediately bringing to mind associations with existing languages. Dothraki sounds a bit like a mixture of Arabic and Spanish.

But there are certain nuances to Dothraki grammar that are remarkable to an English speaker. For example, Dothraki lacks a type of verb central to many languages – copula verbs. Copula verbs are empty interconnecting verbs such as 'is', 'become', 'get'. Can you imagine English without them? However, the structure of Dothraki simply doesn't allow for them.

When David J. Peterson delivered Dothraki for the TV series in 2009, the language consisted of 1,700 words, but just before the third season of *Game of Thrones*, Dothraki had surpassed the 3,600-word mark and is now approaching 4,000. Peterson has said he is aiming to develop the vocabulary to 10,000 words, which is about as many words as someone who studies a foreign language in school might use. It is worth bearing in mind that Peterson is a conlanger and is passionate about developing languages. For the purposes of the books and TV series, the first 1,700 words were probably more than enough.

Peterson has also produced a language course for the horse-masters' tongue, *Living Language Dothraki* (2014), a book and CD that even has a complementary phone app for effective practice.

Valyrian

Before the third season of the *Game of Thrones* TV series, David J. Peterson was commissioned to create Valyrian, or rather, the Valyrian languages. High Valyrian occupies the same position in George R.R. Martin's world as Latin historically does in ours. It is no longer spoken in daily life but is still used in art, science and education. Once upon a time, High Valyrian was spoken throughout the Valyrian Freehold on the continent of Essos, which lasted for 5,000 years. The educated nobility of Westeros seems to possess knowledge of the ancient language and several of the characters such as Tyrion Lannister and Samwell Tarly read books in High Valyrian. Daenerys Targaryen speaks High Valyrian and several Low Valyrian dialects of the free cities.

Unlike the fall of the Roman Empire, which occurred gradually over a few hundred years, Valyria suffered a cataclysmic downfall when fourteen volcanoes erupted, covering the land in lava and ash. Earthquakes ravaged buildings and walls, and a great tsunami drenched the entire Valyrian peninsula like gravy on mashed potato. It was a collapse of a civilisation on an Atlantean scale.

Although classical High Valyrian is no longer spoken, Low Valyrian is spoken in the free cities and in most places where the former Valyrian Freehold extended. Low Valyrian is a collective name for a variety of dialects and languages that evolved from High Valyrian. This is much like, for example, how Spanish, French, Italian, Portuguese and Romanian stem from Latin. In the free cities of Volantis, Braavos, Myr, Pentos and Lys, they speak similar Valyrian dialects, while the Valyrian spoken in Astapor, Meereen, and other areas of Slaver's Bay has emerged as a sort of creole mixed with the language spoken in Old Ghis.

The city of Ghis, an even older power than Valyria, ruled over a vast empire and waged constant war with Valyria, until the Valyrians obliterated the city with their secret weapon: dragons. In the time the books are set, Ghiscari is more or less extinct, but

Ghiscari words remain in the creole-Valyrian spoken around Slaver's Bay. One word is known: **mysha** ('mother'), which the liberated slaves in the city of Yunkai call Daenerys in the 'pure tongue' of Ghis. In its Low Valyrian variant, the loanword is spelled as **mysa**, and in classic High Valryian 'mother' is **muña**. **Muñar**, by the way, means 'parents'.

By the time David J. Peterson was given the task of developing Valyrian dialogue, he had already made a small start on the language. He needed a word for 'bread' in Dothraki, but since the Dothraki are nomadic riders and very unlikely to engage in agriculture, he considered it unrealistic that it would have a native Dothraki word. Rather, the Dothraki would have borrowed a word from another language when they encountered bread for the first time, so Peterson decided that their loanword for 'bread' would come from Valyrian: **havon**. Later, the Dothraki took more loanwords from Valyrian, such as 'book' – **timvir**, from the High Valyrian **tembyr**. But **havon** was not the first Valyrian word ever made. George R.R. Martin provided a sprinkling in his books, but not nearly enough for Peterson to go on as was the case for Dothraki.

Most of the words that formed the basis for Peterson's development were the names of people and cities, but there were also a few well-known Valyrian expressions: **valar morghulis** – 'all men must die'; **valar dohaeris** – 'all men must serve'; and **dracarys** – 'dragon fire'. The first two terms gave Peterson something to work with. He concluded that the ending **-is** means 'must' and used this as a basis for the whole Valyrian inflection system.

Dracarys led him in another direction. George R.R. Martin has likened Valryian to Latin on several occasions, and Peterson thought it was unfortunate that **dracarys** was so similar to the Latin word for 'dragon' (*draco*). He decided this was a coincidence, however, and made **dracarys** mean 'the kind of fire a dragon breathes', and the Valyrian word for 'dragon' instead became **zaldrīzes**. Peterson also decided to spell the word with a 'k' – **drakarys**. In his blog, Peterson speculates that **drakarys** may have given rise to the word 'dragon' in the Common Tongue of Westeros after all. When the Targaryens (the only noble family and dragons to survive the collapse of Valyria) invaded Westeros with their dragons several centuries before the books are set, **drakarys** was used as a command for the dragons to attack. It stands to reason that this would soon become a word that people associated with the beasts and perhaps become their name. So linguistically speaking, High Valyrian has nothing to do with Latin, but Peterson strived to make High Valyrian sound like Latin anyway.

Let us return to the most famous High Valyrian phrase, '**valar morghulis**', a greeting to which the standard reply is '**valar dohaeris**'. We have already established that the suffix **-is** means 'must'. **Morghulis** comes from the verb **morghūljagon** ('to die'), and **dohaeris** from the verb **dohaeragon** ('to serve'). As **valar** is included in both phrases, we can understand it to mean 'all men'. If, on the other hand, you wanted to say, 'All women must die', you would use the plural form of **ābra** ('woman'), and it would become '**ābrar morghulis**', but this can also mean, 'All people must die'. Saying, 'Everyone must die' would simply be '**tolvys morghūlis**'. But the greeting phrase, for some unfathomable reason, refers only to the inevitable death of the male portion of the population.

High Valyrian is not as well developed as Dothraki. It does have a complex, advanced system of grammar, but so far only around 2,000 words. Peterson hasn't spent as much time on it as he has on Dothraki, and there has been no reason to expand the High Valyrian vocabulary beyond the lines needed in the TV series. Peterson has said that he is aiming for a 10,000-word-strong glossary of High Valyrian eventually, but not any time soon.

Peterson personally initiated the work of developing a course in High Valyrian on language app Duolingo, which has helped develop the language a little bit in itself. But, more importantly, this has given many fans around the world the opportunity to easily learn High Valyrian for free. When the final season of *Game of Thrones* aired in 2019, there were 989,000 High Valyrian students active on Duolingo!

Here is an example of how the exiled queen, Daenerys Targaryen, the character who speaks the most languages, introduces herself in High Valyrian in the third season of *Game of Thrones*:

> **'Nyke Daenerys Jelmāzmo hen Targārio Lentrot, hen Valyrio Uēpo ānogār iksan. Valyrio muño ēngos ñuhys issa.'**

'I am Daenerys Stormborn of the House Targaryen, of the blood of Old Valyria. Valyrian is my mother tongue.'

A few useful words and phrases:

> **issa** – yes
> **daour** – no
> **rytsas** – hello
> **'Udrizi Valyrio ydrā?'** – 'Do you speak Valyrian?'

In the TV series, Valyrian is represented by a variety of versions and dialects, but we mainly hear Astapori Valyrian, a creole language in a region that spoke Ghiscari thousands of years ago. A couple of phrases can also be heard in Meereenese Valyrian, an even broader dialect with more Ghiscari words. From what we have heard so far, it is a dialect full of profanity and insults, such as this borrowed retort from *Monty Python and the Holy Grail*:

> **'Byjan vavi demble eva o, trezy eme verdje espo jimi! Oa mysa iles me nýnyghi, si oa kiba tuziles espo tomistos!'**

'I fart in your general direction, son of a window-dresser! Your mother was a hamster, and your father smelt of elderberries!'

Thanks to its case system, High Valyrian has a relatively flexible word order, like Latin. But Astapori Valyrian does not have this feature, so its sentence structure is more familiar: subject-verb-object, as in English. High Valyrian has four genders (lunar, solar, terrestrial and aquatic), whereas Astapori Valyrian has only two genders (celestial and terrestrial). Another difference between the languages is that all long vowels (marked with a dash above the vowel) have disappeared from Astapori Valyrian, along with most of the diphthongs:

High Valyrian: **Dovaogēdy**
Astapori Valyrian: **Dovoghedhy**
Meereenese Valyrian: **Thowoá**
English: 'The Unsullied' (Daenerys' eunuch soldiers)

High Valyrian: '**Mittys iksā. Āeksia tolī kostōbi issi.**'
Astapori Valyrian: '**Ska me gurp. P'aeske si kotovi uvuve.**'
Meereenese Valyrian: '**Shka ma khurf. P'ashkesh she kraj waov.**'
English: 'You are a fool. The masters are too strong.'

David J. Peterson first translated what was needed for the TV series into High Valyrian, and then applied the grammatical and sound changes undergone by the different Valyrian variants in order to create the sentences.

In the free cities, several other Valyrian dialects are spoken that are not influenced by Ghiscari. Each city-state has its own dialect, but sometimes they are known by a collective name: Low Valyrian.

Peterson didn't participate in the actual filming of the television series during its decade-long production. Lines were sent to him and he would send back the translation, an audio file, and a literal back-translation to English from Dothraki or Valyrian. Peterson would then have no idea what happened with his translations until he saw them on television. Usually, he would be pleased with the end result, as can be seen in the various comments on Peterson's blog. But sometimes, the end of a sentence would be cut off prematurely or a line would be slightly altered from the original. However, thanks to his continuous involvement and up-to-date comments on the spoken language in the TV series, these errors didn't become a big deal. Peterson could simply point out the mistake so it could be corrected before fans had time to learn it, wrongly believing it to be accurate.

One such example, oddly enough, caused Valyrian to acquire a loanword from Dothraki: '**valahd**!' – 'fly!' This is said by Daenerys Targaryen when urging her dragon to fly, but the scene was originally filmed in English and when the director later realised that this line should be in Valyrian, the actress' lip movements didn't match the High Valyrian '**sōvēs**!' So instead, they came up with **valahd**, which has a meaning closer to 'jump', from the extensive vocabulary of Dothraki. Funnily enough, this is not all that far-fetched, seeing as the character Daenerys Targaryen speaks Dothraki too.

And last but not least – we have a Valyrian sentence that proves that the geek world has well and truly embraced the language. David J. Peterson helped a fan of both universes translate the motto from *Star Trek*, the famous bedrock of TV geekdom, into Valyrian for a tattoo:

'**Skoriot daorys gō istas nēdenkirī jagon**.'
'To boldly go where no man has gone before.'

Mag Nuk

Several more languages are implied and hinted at in George R.R. Martin's world, mostly through names and individual words, but these never took shape in the books or the television series. But David J. Peterson has sketched out some fragments of a couple of other languages, such as Asshai'i and the White Walkers' planned language, Skroth, although they didn't end up being used – the White Walkers were deemed to be more menacing without speech. Gerna Moussha, the speech of the Children of the Forest, was developed for the sixth season but was also never used, and all the lines Peterson wrote were recorded in English instead.

Peterson also sketched out the Old Tongue, as spoken by the First Men, in order to produce a single line for the Giants. The Giants, who are said to have limited brain capacity, are described as speaking a very simplified variant of the Old Tongue. When the Giant Wun Weg Wun Dar Wun became a recurring character in the series it seemed appropriate that he say something in his own language, Mag Nuk – 'the Great Tongue'. Peterson imagined it would sound like this:

'**Lokh doys bar thol kif rukh**?'
'What the hell are you looking at?'

Which is a simplification of how the sentence would sound in the language of the First Men:

'**Lokh doysen bar thol kifos rukh**?'

But when David J. Peterson heard the line on the TV series, he was delighted to find that it had been shortened to something even more giant-sounding: '**Lokh kif rukh**?' From the books, we also know that the Giants call the Children of the Forest **woh dak nag gram** – 'the little squirrel people'. The Old Tongue is still spoken by some of the wildlings on the other side of the Wall, probably in several different dialects, as there are seven different languages spoken north of the Wall. At least we know the Thenns speak the Old Tongue.

Five spin-off series set in George R.R. Martin's detailed universe have been considered for production: a couple were scrapped; a couple put on hold; and one has gone on to film a pilot. So, there is plenty of time for the Old Tongue, Gerna Moussha and High Valyrian to continue being developed in years to come. In interviews, David J. Peterson has said he would be very happy to expand the languages in the *Game of Thrones* world, but his contract forbids him from saying any more. And let us not forget that beyond the TV series, George R.R. Martin is still chipping away at the last two books in the series – and now he has Peterson to help with the languages.

Tolkien's Secret Vice

A WORLD BUILT ON LANGUAGES

Quenya, Edhellen, Telerin, Doriathrin, Falathrin, Sindarin, Khuzdul

In the beginning was the language. No Hobbits. No rings. No Sauron. Only the language. And Tolkien saw that it was good, and he created Middle-earth.

If it hadn't been for J.R.R. Tolkien's passion for language, we would never have got *The Hobbit*, *The Lord of the Rings*, or *The Silmarillion*. Language was his first love; mythology and storytelling came second.

Tolkien was a professor of Old English at Oxford University, but even as a child he was fascinated by foreign languages. He had learned to read by the age of 4, and when he was 5 his mother began teaching him French, German and Latin. When he was 8, the young Tolkien discovered Welsh, a language that was to beguile him for years to come. Then he moved, along with his mother and brother, into a house behind a train station in Birmingham where railcars transporting coal would pass by. They had curious names such as *Nantygol*, *Senghenydd* and *Tredegar*, sparking the already wild imagination of the young Tolkien.

At 11 years old he began studying classical Greek and medieval English, and the focus of his linguistic interest moved to the structure of and relationship between languages. Over the coming years, Tolkien acquired some dusty old books on German philology, studied Spanish and the extinct languages of Gothic and Anglo-Saxon, and deepened his studies in medieval English.

It was also at this age that Tolkien began to construct his own languages. His younger cousins invented Animalic and they all collaborated on Nevbosh ('new nonsense'), both of which were fairly simple code languages. But Tolkien also worked on his own language, Naffarin, which was strongly inspired by Spanish. However, he soon put Naffarin to one side in order to create a variant of Gothic that he also developed 'backwards' into his own proto-Gothic.

It is worth mentioning that the study of classical languages had a completely different status in the early twentieth century than it does today. Tolkien was able to impress his school mates by switching into Greek, Gothic or Anglo-Saxon during school debates, which were delivered in Latin. When Tolkien was 18, he received a scholarship in classical languages to Exeter College in Oxford, where he was able to immerse himself fully in the study of language structures.

Tolkien fell in love with Old Norse fairy tales and the Finnish epic *Kalevala*. Naturally, he taught himself both Finnish and Old Icelandic in order to read the works in the original languages. (He also knew enough Swedish to declare his disapproval of the first Swedish translation of *The Lord of the Rings* by Åke Ohlmarks and went on to write an explanation of how his works should be translated.) Tolkien had a special affinity with the Finnish language, which he considered extremely beautiful. He later wrote, 'It was like discovering a *wine-cellar* filled with bottles of amazing *wine* of a kind and flavour never tasted before. It quite intoxicated me.'

He only learned enough Finnish to be able to pick his way through *Kalevala*, but it went on to have a decisive influence on his fictional languages. He developed a conlang inspired by Finnish – the language that would eventually emerge in his stories as Quenya or High Elven. Three years later, Tolkien took the first steps towards creating his own mythology by writing *The Song of Eärendil*, about a sailor whose ship leaps into the sky and becomes a star, in his newly developed language:

Ai lintulinda Lasselanta
Pilingeve suyer nalla ganta
Kulvi ya karnevalinar
V 'ematte singi Eldamar.

If you read it aloud, the Finnish inspiration can be clearly heard. There is no translation of this early version of Quenya, but the first line apparently means, 'Oh, sing swiftly of leaf-fall [autumn]'. **Karnevalinar** directly translates to 'red fire of power' and **Eldamar** is the 'elvenhome' in the west.

Tolkien began to wonder what beings might speak this beautiful language and, over the years, his curiosity grew. He came to realise that language needs a historical background, its own myths and, above all, someone to speak it. In 1915, it all fell into place when it dawned on Tolkien that the Elves encountered by the sailor Eärendil on his travels must be the speakers of the language. And the rest, as they say, is literary history.

Tolkien was interested in these languages and their developments on their own merits, as opposed to as mere accessories to his fictional world. So, his actual writing career started as a sort of excuse to devote himself to what he called his 'secret vice' – language construction, or conlanging, as we call it today. 'Nobody believes me when I say that my long book is an attempt to create a world in which a form of language agreeable to my personal aesthetic might seem real. But it is true.'

He described his language creation as an artform and likened it to writing poetry. Writing poetry is something that goes against any sense of conscience and duty. Poetry takes time away from more 'important' things, such as studying useful topics or working for a living. A vice, therefore.

Tolkien worked on his languages throughout his writing career and was constantly making corrections, changing spelling rules, grammar or internal language history. It was his hobby and passion, and the languages were never finished. Readers of *The Hobbit* and *The Lord of the Rings* trilogy might not take much notice of the languages. There are a few examples, but it is difficult to imagine their true linguistic complexity. Appendices provide us with a little background on pronunciation and the exquisite Elven script of Tengwar, where Tolkien opens the door just a crack into his fascinating language world.

Tolkien didn't publish any comprehensive work on his languages during his lifetime; it was only long after his death that the true complexity and advanced development of his languages became clear. Research on his languages is ongoing and new findings are published periodically.

Given Tolkien's lifelong passion for language, his 'secret vice' and career choice, it is hardly surprising that the complexity of the internal language history he developed is on a par with that of natural languages. Tolkien describes the evolution of his languages over thousands of years, with numerous names, concepts, languages and dialects. So, before you embark on the history of the Elvish languages, bear in mind that this was Tolkien's true passion.

The History of the Elvish Languages

The Elves, or Quendi as they call themselves, awoke in the far east of Middle-earth in a place called Cuiviénen. It seems the Elves all initially spoke the same innate tongue, but when they divided into three clans, **Minyar** – 'the first', **Tatyar** – 'the second', and **Nelyar** – 'the third', the language gradually evolved into three dialects.

One group of Elves heeded a divine summons to migrate westward and became known as the **Eldar** – 'people of the stars', while the Elves that remained were called the **Avari** – 'the unwilling'. To distinguish themselves from the Avari, the three clans took on new names: **Vanyar** – 'the fair', **Noldor** – 'the wise', and **Lindar** – 'the singers'. During their long westward journey, they travelled in clans. The Nelyar/Lindar clan was the largest and consisted of half of the entire Elf population. Their vast numbers meant that they set off later and travelled more slowly than the other two clans, so they came to be known as the **Teleri** – 'the last'. During their 250-year walk to Valinor, the Teleri developed their own distinctive dialect.

When the Teleri arrived to cross the Misty Mountains, a large number turned back. They came to be called the **Nandor** – 'the ones who returned'. The Vanyar and Noldor did arrive in the holy land of Valinor eventually. It is around this time that **Quenya** – 'High Elven' – is believed to have evolved from Eldarin. The two dialects, Vanyarin and Noldorin, differed somewhat but were mutually comprehensible. There was a quotidian version of Quenya, **Tarquesta**, and the more formal version, **Parmaquesta** (**parma** – 'book', **questa** – 'language'), which was used ceremonially.

After the arrival of the Elves at the sacred land of Valinor, Quenya also came to be used by the Valar and Maiar – two forms of angelic or godlike spirit in Tolkien's mythology. The Vanyar lived closer to the Valar than the Noldor, and in time came to incorporate words from the Valar language, Valarin, into their variant of Quenya. The Noldor left Valinor for Middle-earth a few thousand years later. Their variant of Quenya is sometimes called Exilic Quenya. This variant has no loanwords from the language of the gods, but later incorporated some Sindarin vocabulary.

The Grey Elves and Sindarin

The Teleri clan eventually arrived at Valinor but lost many along the way. One group never crossed the sea to Valinor and stayed in the region known as Beleriand. The group that remained eventually became known as the Sindar, or 'Grey Elves', who went on to develop the language Sindarin. In Valinor, Telerin continued to be spoken and retained many features of the Eldarin language. Some believe that Telerin was a language of its own alongside Quenya, while others consider it a dialect.

The famous Quenya greeting phrase used by Frodo in *The Lord of the Rings* – 'A star shines on the hour of our meeting' – serves as an example of the close relationship between Quenya and Telerin:

Quenya: '**Elen síla lúmenn' omentielvo.**'
Telerin: '**Él síla lúmena vomentienguo.**'
Sindarin: '**Êl síla ned lû e-govaded vín.**'

In their basic forms, many words are similar in Sindarin and Quenya, but they are inflected differently:

Sindarin	Quenya	English
ithil	isil	Moon
narwain	narvinye	January
aglar	alcar	Honour
alpha	alqua	Swan
cor	corma	Ring

The Sindar Elves did not call their language Sindarin at first. During the millennia in which they were the only Elves in Middle-earth, they called themselves the **Eledhrim** – 'the Elves', and their language simply **Edhellen** – 'Elvish'. It was only when Elves of the Noldor clan returned to Middle-earth from Valinor after 3,000 years that the Noldor began to call them Sindar – 'the Grey'.

There is not much Sindarin in *The Lord of the Rings*, only a few verses and phrases. Perhaps the most famous is a poem about the Star Queen, which begins as follows:

A Elbereth Gilthoniel,	O Elbereth Starkindler,
silivren penna míriel	white-glittering, slanting down sparkling like a jewel
o menel aglar elenath!	the glory of the starry host!

Peter Jackson's films introduced a larger audience to Sindarin for the first time when Elven Princess Arwen comes to the aid of the injured Frodo:

'**Frodo. Im Arwen. Telin le thaed. Lasto beth nin. Tolo dan nan galad.**'

'Frodo. I am Arwen. I have come to help you. Hear my voice. Come back to the light.'

The Ban on Quenya

The Noldor left Valinor in a rebellion against the Valar spirits, and when they returned across the sea to Middle-earth so much time had passed that they no longer understood the dialect that had developed there. When news reached Thingol, Lord of the Sindar, that the Noldor had killed Teleri during the uprising in Valinor, he forbade his subjects to speak Quenya, which meant that the Noldor had to use Sindarin in their communication with the Sindar. Quenya lived on as a ceremonial language and for singing and poetry, sort of like a Latin for the Elves of Middle-earth.

Then, some of the Nandor Elves (you know, the ones who turned back at the Misty Mountains) appeared and settled in eastern Beleriand. They came to be known as the Green-Elves and had their own language too. Sindarin came to be a lingua franca among different Elf clans and when they came into contact with Men and Dwarves.

Of course, Sindarin developed several different dialects. North Sindarin, or Mithrim, was the dialect developed among the Noldor on their return. The dialect changed rapidly due to influences from Quenya. North Sindarin is also believed to be partly based on another language called Ilkorin, which Tolkien developed but never used in his writing.

Doriathrin, spoken in Doriath, retained many ancient features and was not affected by Quenya influences. Falathrin was spoken in Falas, the coastal region of Beleriand, and was the only dialect that survived, forming the basis of the Sindarin spoken in the Third Age when *The Lord of the Rings* takes place. So these days, when we refer to Sindarin, it is usually Falathrin that we mean.

Then the High Men of the island of Numenór came to adopt Sindarin and develop their own version of the language, a variant of which lived on in the kingdom of Gondor. To cut a long story short …

As you can see, Tolkien's writings are a goldmine for anyone who shares his fascination with language history. By reading his books, you can put together a linguistic-historical puzzle. All the Elven languages are related to each other and ultimately derived from Quendian, the primitive Elvish language, but have developed in divergent directions, as we have seen. It came naturally to language professor and conlanger Tolkien to develop the languages along different paths, with real languages as examples. Quenya is inspired by Finnish, Latin and a little Greek, Telerin took some features from Italian, and Sindarin has borrowed elements from Welsh and the Scandinavian languages.

Quenya – Elf Latin

As previously mentioned, Quenya was Tolkien's first Elven language, which he worked on throughout his life. The language has gone through many forms and stages, not just within Tolkien's fantasy world but in the real world too, where he continuously polished it and added new ideas retrospectively. So, people tend to refer to 'fully developed Quenya' and '*Lord of the Rings* Quenya' or 'Qenya' (without the 'u') when they mean an early version of the language. The different versions may look alike at first glance, but the grammatical rules are completely different.

The breakthrough for the study of Quenya and Tolkien's other languages came with the publication of *The Lost Road* in 1987, fifteen years after Tolkien's death. From 1977 onwards, his son Christopher Tolkien published seventeen books of Middle-earth material that he had edited from the manuscripts his father had left behind. Thanks to this, we now know a lot more about Tolkien's languages than we ever did during his lifetime. Tolkien never published any lexicon or glossary; most of the information is scattered in various texts, notes and appendices.

After Christopher Tolkien published the seventeen volumes of his father's edited manuscripts, there remained swathes of unpublished material that touched upon Tolkien's languages in one way or another. Christopher Tolkien donated copies of these documents to the Elvish Linguistic Fellowship (ELF) for further study and publication in their journals *Vinyar Tengwar* ('*News Letters*') and *Parma Eldalamberon* ('*The Book of Elven Tongues*'). This shows how the study of Quenya is ongoing and new information is continually coming to light.

As previously mentioned, Tolkien was inspired by several languages in his development of Quenya. The influence of Finnish is obvious, but not in terms of vocabulary. Approximately 1 per cent of the known words in High Elvish are direct loans from Finnish. In fact, Tolkien seems to have drawn inspiration from Latin for some of his 'Elf Latin' words.

Quenya	English	Latin
lambë	tongue	*lambere* – lick
ma	hand	*manus*
ure	heat	*uro* – burn
aurë	daylight	*aurora* – 'Goddess of the Dawn'
orco	orc	*orcus* – 'God of Death'/'Kingdom of Death'
carnë	red	*carne* – meat

In early versions of Quenya (Qenya), the influence of other languages is more evident. Tolkien played with the idea that the similarity between European languages might be because ancient Europeans encountered Elves before the last of them travelled west, resulting in Elvish loanwords in Western languages.

However, Quenya is not a complete language, and remains unfinished. If we wanted to translate it into a Shakespearean play, for example, there would be too many gaps. And although in the long term some of these gaps will be filled, it will never be a fully developed language that can be used for everyday speech. At least, not if you adhere strictly to what came directly from Tolkien's pen.

Nonetheless, new words can be constructed. Since the Elvish languages are all related, and Tolkien described in detail the development of the various languages, such as how a certain sound evolved over time, it is possible to construct a missing word in Quenya based on its Sindarin equivalent. This is similar to the way language historians have reconstructed Indo-European from what they know about the evolution of related languages.

This method was used for Peter Jackson's dramatisation of *The Lord of the Rings* to create credible new dialogue, as well as the verses contained in the books. It is mostly Sindarin that you hear in the films, but there are some phrases in Quenya too. The lines were designed and partially reconstructed by one of the world's foremost Elvish experts – David Salo.

Some hardcore Tolkien fans disapprove of this because it is not authentic Elvish from the books, but many accept the language in the films as 'genuine' nevertheless. The phrases' inclusion in the films has given them a sort of official status, so in practice they are generally recognised by fans as true Elvish.

Unsurprisingly, the Quenya in the films is used mainly in ritual contexts, such as when Saruman casts a magic spell:

> **'Cuiva nwalca Carnirassë! Nai yar vaxëa rasselya taltuva ñotto-carinnar!'**
> 'Wake up cruel Redhorn! May your blood-stained horn fall upon the enemy-heads!'

Redhorn is the name of the rock that the Fellowship of the Ring ascends, which we know to be called **Caradhras** in Sindarin, which is why Salo came to translate it as **Carnirassë** in Quenya. **Yarvaxëa** ('blood-stained') is not a word Tolkien mentioned, but Salo constructed it from **yar** – 'blood', and **vaxëa** – 'to colour' or 'douse'.

David Salo is not the only one who has mastered the Elvish languages. There is a large group of Elvish linguists who study, explore and aim to master Quenya. The original texts written in Quenya are mainly poetry and songs. Elvish expert Maciej Garbowski, from Poland, is responsible for translating the 'Ring Verse', which is central to *The Lord of the Rings* trilogy, and which Tolkien himself never translated into Elvish. So, thanks to Garbowski, we now know how the 'Ring Verse' may have sounded in Elf Latin:

Quenya	English
Neldë Cormar Eldaron Aranen nu I vilya,	Three Rings for the Elven-kings under the sky,
Otso Heruin Naucoron ondeva mardentassen,	Seven for the Dwarf-lords in their halls of stone,
Nertë Firimë Nérin yar I Nuron martyar,	Nine for Mortal Men doomed to die,
Minë I Morë Herun morma-halmar yassë	One for the Dark Lord on his dark throne
Mornórëo Nóressë yassë I Fuini caitar	In the Land of Mordor where the Shadows lie.
Minë Corma turië të ilyë, Minë Corma hirië të,	One Ring to rule them all, One Ring to find them,
Minë Corma hostië të ilyë ar mordossë nutië të	One Ring to bring them all, and in the darkness bind them,
Mornórëo Nóressë yassë I Fuini caitar.	In the Land of Mordor where the Shadows lie.

Khuzdul

David Salo's Tolkien expertise has also been used to extrapolate other less-developed languages mentioned in the books. For example, Salo created lines and lyrics in the Dwarves' language Khuzdul, which he calls 'Neo-Khuzdul' because it was not just a case of reconstructing the language but also creating entirely new words, albeit with a great deal of knowledge behind him. From Tolkien's books, we mainly have the battle cry: '**Baruk Khazâd! Khazâd ai-mênu!**' – 'Axes of Dwarves! The Dwarves are upon you!' We also have this inscription in the runic alphabet, Cirth: '**Balin Fundinul uzbad Khazad-dûmu.**' – 'Balin son of Fundin Lord of Moria'.

Other than that, a little vocabulary is known, including:

tarâg – beard
aglâb – language
kibil – silver (probably borrowed from Sindarin, **celeb**)
rukhs – Orc
shathûr – cloud
kheled – glass (loaned to Sindarin as **heledh**)

Salo went to great lengths to expand Khuzdul into Neo-Khuzdul, finding roots for new words from Tolkien's other languages and protolanguages. For example, the word for 'fire' is **urus**, which is a direct loan from the Valarin, the language of the gods. This is plausible, as the language of the Dwarves was created by Aulë of the Valar. He taught the language to the seven fathers of the Dwarves before being laid to rest until the time came for their awakening (after the Elves awoke).

Salo took the word for 'old', **gamil**, from early Scandinavian – easily compared to the modern Swedish, *gammal*. This was an educated guess based on Tolkien's one-time mention of a Dwarf named Gamil Zirak, or Zirak the Old. In Tolkien's world, Adûnaic is spoken by Men and includes loanwords from Khuzdul, so to make **taburrudi** ('to be heavy'), Salo started from **burôda**, the Adûnaic word for 'heavy' in Adunai, and returned the loan, so to speak:

gagin – again (proto-German – **gagina*; German – *gegen*)
tur – through (from Quenya – *ter-*; as well as Old English – *þurh*)
ku – who (from Indo-European root – $\sqrt{kwo}$-)
kalil – cold (proto-German – **kalda*; compare with Swedish – *kall*)
kâmin – earth (Quenya – *cemen*)

Tolkien also used Semitic languages as inspiration for Khuzdul, so Salo based its grammar on the features that Semitic languages have in common, mainly what is known as three-letter roots. All Semitic languages exhibit a unique pattern of consonant roots that normally consist of three consonants. Nouns, adjectives and verbs are formed by adding a prefix, suffix or infix to these roots. So kh-z-d ('kh' is one letter in the Dwarvish language) is the three-letter root behind **Khazâd**, **Khuzd**, **Khuzdul** – 'Dwarves', 'Dwarf', 'Dwarvish'. However, Salo did not use many words from Hebrew, Arabic or any other Semitic language to expand the Neo-Khuzdul vocabulary, because the language would risk becoming a variant of a Semitic language, instead of simply displaying some Semitic features.

The huge success of the *Lord of the Rings* and *Hobbit* films probably means that (Neo-)Khuzdul has a future as a language. Even if David Salo doesn't continue to expand the language after the films, there is more than enough interesting material for fans to build upon. Attempts have also been made in the past to expand the Dwarves' languages, and the linguist fans who construct these languages look closely at Salo's Dwarvish and incorporate most of his ideas into their language development. Tolkien is the ultimate authority, but the impact of the films means that Salo's version also carries weight.

8

Klingon

FROM PROP TO PUBLIC PROPERTY

---

tlhIngan Hol, paramount Hol, Klingonaase

Did you ever hear that more people speak Klingon than Esperanto and Navajo put together? This isn't true, of course, but urban legends such as this are exactly the kind of wider cultural impact that makes Klingon special. Klingon, more than any other conlang before it, has transformed from a world-building prop to living language, to pop-culture public property. In the United States, where *Star Trek* is much bigger than in my home country of Sweden, virtually all Americans know of Klingons. They recognise the alien race, they know that Klingon is a language, and they know that nerdy *Star Trek* fans speak it.

Klingon has become an almost universally recognised reference, thanks to the fact that the artlang has been mentioned and featured on other TV shows, talk shows and films that have nothing to do with *Star Trek*, including *The Simpsons*, *Frasier*, *ER*, *NCIS* and *The Big Bang Theory*, to name but a few. And the reason Klingon is able to appear in these popular TV shows is precisely because Americans get the reference.

Not even Tolkien's languages can compete with this level of notoriety. Tolkien's works are well known, of course, but few know about his languages or the people who study and speak them. Hardcore Tolkien fans are more likely to be cosplayers than linguists, wearing Elf ears and play-fighting with swords.

In contrast, the hardcore nerdy *Star Trek* fans, known as Trekkers or Trekkies, have long been a stereotype, recognised by many in the United States and beyond. Speaking a fictional extraterrestrial language is a badge of ultimate geekiness. There are even Trekkies who like to cosplay as Klingons who still think that fans who have learned Klingon have gone too far and 'give Trekkies a bad reputation'.

During my own Klingon studies, I discovered that Klingonists actually don't generally consider themselves Trekkies. They are first and foremost interested in linguistics. Some came into contact with Klingon via their interest in language and others via *Star Trek*. Some of the people I interviewed considered themselves Trekkies once, but as their interest in Klingon grew, their interest in *Star Trek* waned.

My studies also revealed that those who speak Klingon fluently – at least as fluently as possible for an earthling – differ somewhat from the average Trekkie. Many I spoke to hold a PhD, or a double Masters degree, and all except one had academic qualifications or studies under their belt.

So, when the Klingonists got together and organised themselves, it wasn't to form a traditional fan club, but the Klingon Language Institute (KLI), which publishes a peer-reviewed journal indexed by the Modern Language Library in Washington and awards scholarships to linguistics students. This serious and academic approach to the study of Klingon has certainly contributed to the success of the language.

The translation work done by the KLI – including *Hamlet*, *Much Ado About Nothing*, *The Epic of Gilgamesh* and *Tao Te Ching* – has also influenced the language's reputation among a wider audience. A language that can reproduce the classics of world literature is taken much more seriously than one that appears only on TV and in films.

The Language History of Klingon

Let us start from the beginning. Klingon was developed in earnest for the third *Star Trek* movie, *The Search for Spock* (1984), in which Klingons play an important role. Klingons first appeared in the television series in the 1960s, but we never heard their language spoken. In 1984, the producers thought it would be cool if the Klingons spoke a foreign language that could be subtitled in the film, particularly as subtitles were an exotic concept in and of themselves to an American audience.

Apparently, one of the inspirations for this idea was the West German film *Das Boot* (1981), about a submarine crew during the Second World War, which had enjoyed success in the USA. The characters' lives aboard the dark, narrow submarine was an influence on the *Star Trek* filmmakers' depiction of life aboard a Klingon spaceship. They wanted to capture a similar feeling and mood. So the German film may have been crucial to the making of the language. *Das Boot* has made at least one lasting impression on Klingon – the word for 'boot' is **DaS**!

Producer Harve Bennett engaged American linguist Dr Marc Okrand, who has a PhD in the Native American language Mutsun, to develop a language as a world-building prop. Okrand pointed out that Klingon already existed as a language because there were a few phrases in the first *Star Trek* movie from 1979. They were just a couple of lines of gibberish invented by James Doohan (Scotty in *Star Trek*) and spoken by Mark Lenard in the film. Based on these phrases, Okrand got a basic idea of the sound, broke the sentences down into words and grammatical elements according to the subtitles, and expanded the language from there. Okrand did a thorough job and created more Klingon than necessary for the lines in the script. Slowly, a working language emerged. He called it **tlhIngan Hol**.

They came up with the idea of publishing Okrand's work in *The Klingon Dictionary*, and the rest is linguistic history. Okrand never thought anyone would study Klingon seriously, but might buy the dictionary for fun to have as a coffee-table book. So, he was rather taken aback when people started speaking to him in the language and sending him letters that he couldn't understand. Not even Okrand was fluent in Klingon at first, and he had to get studying to keep up with the Klingonists.

In 1992, the scattered Klingonists joined forces to form the KLI and began to explore and promote the language more seriously. Marc Okrand has always maintained regular contact with the Klingonists and continued to develop the language, spurred on by the KLI and the analytical articles published in KLI's journal, *HolQeD* (**Hol** – 'language', **QeD** – 'science').

One thing that has contributed to Klingon's success and made it a source of fascination for linguists is that, as a language, it doesn't feel artificial. Invented languages are often overly regular and straightforward in their grammar. This is all too easy when a language emerges at someone's desk rather than evolving naturally over millennia. But little irregularities have crept into Klingon in a way that makes its development feel somewhat organic.

Marc Okrand designed Klingon based on Doohan's deft gibberish and made every effort to create a truly extraterrestrial language. His starting point was that it must differ greatly from English, but also be possible for the actors to learn and speak. So, Okrand chose unusual grammatical devices and sound combinations for Klingon. Of course, they are all linguistic features that do exist in earthly languages, but the combinations are rare, to say the least.

Klingon word order is object-verb-subject, which is unusual in itself. Only about 1 per cent of all human languages use this sentence structure and it is the exact reverse of what is most commonly found in English. Languages that have the sound 'v' usually have the sound 'f' as well. But Klingon lacks an 'f' sound, even though it does have a 'v' sound. The sounds 'd' and 't' also usually go together in earthly languages. The pronunciation of both is either dental (with the tongue in front of the teeth) or retroflex (with the tongue against the palate). In Klingon, 'd' is retroflex as standard while 't' is dental. Extraterrestrial.

Language Development in the Cutting Room

The language had already begun taking on a life of its own during film production. Sometimes actors misspoke and couldn't do a second take, so Okrand incorporated their errors into Klingon and made it correct. New words were added, the grammar changed, and irregularities were formed.

It was intended that *The Klingon Dictionary* would be released at the same time as the film, but the book was delayed. This proved to be a blessing in disguise because a lot changed in the language during post-production. Some scenes filmed in English suddenly needed to be in Klingon and Okrand had to write Klingon sentences to sync with the English lip movements. The English word for 'animal', for example, became **Ha'DibaH** (meaning both 'animal' and 'meat'), which, when properly pronounced, matches the lip movements of English. In another scene, the subtitles were changed, so **'qama'pu' jonta' neH**!', originally translated as 'I told you – only the engines!', was suddenly supposed to mean, 'I wanted to capture prisoners!' This isn't as strange as it sounds, given that the scene is of a spaceship gunner getting told off by his captain for destroying an enemy vessel instead of just damaging it.

This shift obviously affected both the vocabulary and grammar. The previous word for 'prisoner', **yaS**, was already included in the dictionary and used in a number of sample sentences, but now **qama'** had to mean 'prisoner'. Okrand kept **yaS** in the examples but changed its meaning to 'officer'. However, he forgot to delete the previous word for 'officer' – **'utlh**. Okrand only explained the distinction between the terms a decade later: **'utlh** means 'officer emeritus'. Also, the word for 'prisoners' was obviously plural, so **-pu'** had to become a plural suffix.

The problem was that Okrand had already used the plural suffix -**mey** in several places. So another 'extraterrestrial' grammatical detail was born: -**pu'**, as the plural suffix for beings with an ability for speech, and -**mey** as the plural suffix for anything else. Okrand liked the idea and subsequently introduced a third plural suffix, -**Du'** for body parts! To complicate the plural inflection situation even further, there are also words with an irregular plural, such as 'torpedo' – **peng**, for which the plural is **cha**, while 'one plate' is **jengva'**, and 'several plates' is **ngop**. 'Ancestor' and 'ancestors' are **qempa'** and **no'**, respectively.

Jonta' ('engine') and **neH** ('only') had already been used elsewhere in the film, so Okrand had to introduce homophony, which is when two words are pronounced the same but have different meanings, as in 'there' and 'their'. 'To capture' became **jon** + suffix -**ta'**, which marks it as a conscious completed act; **neH** became a homonym meaning both 'only' and 'want'. The phrase '**qama'pu 'jonta' neH**' influenced the grammar in a number of other ways, but I think this will suffice as an example of how individual decisions, errors and film edits have affected the language.

Once *The Klingon Dictionary* was published, it became more difficult, although not impossible, for Marc Okrand to parry unexpected errors in the upcoming films and new TV series, *Star Trek: The Next Generation*. In 1992, a revised edition of the dictionary was published with an addendum containing new words and grammar from the next two films and TV series, and Okrand was able to legitimise some mistakes retrospectively.

Actor Christopher Plummer, who played Klingon General Chang, came to influence the language's development when he quoted Shakespeare's 'to be or not to be' in *Star Trek VI: The Undiscovered Country* (1991). Given that there is no verb for 'to be' in Klingon – an alien grammatical curiosity that Okrand had already made a big deal of in *The Klingon Dictionary* – this presented a problem. Okrand suggested the solution '**yIn pagh yInbe'**' – 'to live or not to live'. But Plummer thought this sounded clumsy and invented the more powerful '**taH pagh taHbe**'. So, Okrand was magnanimous enough to invent the verb **taH** – 'to continue'.

A few years later, a Klingon language course was released on cassette tape in which Okrand happened to make a mistake in recording. One unusual grammatical quirk of Klingon is, as previously mentioned, the construction of sentences in the order of object-verb-subject. While it is uncommon in natural terrestrial languages, it does still exist. One lesson in the language course teaches Klingon toasts, where Okrand made a mistake in the word order of the phrase 'May your blood scream', saying '**IwIIj jachjaj**' when it should have been '**jachjaj 'IwIIj**'. The retrospective explanation was that traditional toasts follow different grammatical rules, which is important to learn because Klingons do not take kindly to incorrect pronunciation of their ritual expressions.

After this, the language development in the cutting room took a break for thirty years until 2013 with *Star Trek into Darkness*, the twelfth *Star Trek* movie and the second J.J. Abrams reboot of the classic television series. In the film, Uhura, played by Zoë Saldaña, speaks Klingon with a Klingon warrior, so the producers asked Marc Okrand to translate the lines. Okrand didn't personally participate in the film shoot, but alien conlang expert Britton Watkins assisted the actors with the pronunciation.

When the film came out, the Klingon was completely impossible even for Klingonists to understand. The foremost Klingonists of the time transcribed the spoken Klingon and tried to make sense of it alongside the subtitles. But they could make neither head nor tail of it – even though they knew that Okrand had been involved!

The explanation was found in the cutting room. The lines the film team had received from Okrand had been edited in a different order from that of the script; some lines had been wholly or partially cut, and in one case even played backwards! To that end, the film team decided that the Klingon lines would need a different translation: it had become completely incomprehensible.

The filmmakers understood that this would not go unnoticed among the fans, so they contacted Marc Okrand to write new Klingon dialogue that suited the subtitles and could be dubbed over the existing lines. This was no easy task. When the Klingon was first changed in the cutting room in 1984, *The Klingon Dictionary* had not yet come out and Okrand could simply make changes to the language without anyone noticing. Thirty years later, with all the Klingonists who could speak and understand the language, it wasn't going to be as simple as just inventing new grammar. This meant Okrand had to write new Klingon dialogue that could be dubbed in to match the lip movements of actors already speaking Klingon!

Okrand's solution was to come up with about twenty fresh words for the new translations. So, it was on account of this new vocabulary that the Klingonists didn't understand the Klingon in the finished film. It was only later that Okrand explained what had happened and published the new words.

For example, Okrand had to come up with the Klingon verb **yI'** ('to speak in an honourable or respectful way'), as a complement to the usual verb 'to speak' – **jatlh**. To adhere to different lip movements, Okrand had to come up with two synonyms for 'compatriot', **vInDa'** and **chud**, which Okrand points out have a very similar meaning. Even with the new lines written and recorded, it turned out that one of the actors wrongly pronounced **Hegh** – 'to die' – making it sound more like 'Hey'. When Okrand heard the finished result, he simply invented the verb **Hey** – 'to fight against one's own' (as opposed to an enemy).

'toH, Hey Humanpu'. qatlh DISaH?'
'Why should I care about humans killing humans?'

Thus, the mispronounced sentence was saved, and the same general meaning preserved; Klingon was enriched with yet another unusual and culturally specific word.

Language Development on TV

After Klingon had been appearing regularly in the TV series for a few years, Okrand published the book *Klingon for the Galactic Traveller*, in which he continued to expand the Klingon vocabulary, while explaining some of the mistakes made in the TV series retrospectively. For instance, actors' poor pronunciation of certain Klingon sounds is explained by a variety of Klingon dialects. Phrases in the television series that scriptwriters have made up themselves and which aren't even close to correct tlhIngan Hol are explained by the fact that they are speaking **no' Hol** – 'the language of the ancestors'. In other words, old-fashioned phrases that have become idiomatic and, although understandable, make no literal sense in modern Klingon.

The very un-Klingon phrase '**maj ram**' – 'good night' (literally, **maj** – 'good', **ram** – 'night'), written by a random scriptwriter who didn't know that these sorts of courtesy phrases don't exist in Klingon, also got an explanation. It is not wishing someone else a good night, which would be very un-Klingon; rather it is a statement – 'Good, now it is night time'. It is a contraction of two other terms:

> '**maj, ngaj ram**.' – 'Good, the night is short.'
> '**maj, nI'ram**.' – 'Good, the night is long.'

But Marc Okrand hasn't been able to explain or justify all the Klingon in the TV series. It can't all be **no' Hol** – the language of the ancestors. Klingonists have analysed the Klingon phrases until they are blue in the face but have not always been able to make sense of them. Some sentences contained words that could be Klingon but are highly illogical in the context. These irregularities were named after the film company, Paramount – **paramount Hol**, as opposed to genuine Klingon – **tlhIngan Hol**.

Language Development Beyond *Star Trek*

Although *Star Trek*, the TV series, took a long break between 2005 and 2017, and there was only a limited amount of Klingon in J.J. Abrams' new films, Marc Okrand continues slowly but surely to expand the language. Up until 2004, he did so in the journal *HolQeD* and, to this day, he continues to receive wishlists of suggested new words from Klingonists at the annual 'qep'a'' conference.

The backstory for this is that Okrand keeps a Klingon officer called Maltz prisoner in his basement (Maltz was a supporting character in *The Search for Spock* and is thanked as a source in *The Klingon Dictionary*) and simply asks him for words and expressions. Maltz responds in his own way and doesn't necessarily always answer the exact question but will always say something relevant. The KLI used to have an honorary award called **matlh jupna'** – 'friend of Maltz', where the honoured new friend of Maltz could ask for a single word that they didn't yet know. Often the reply was complicated and resulted in the addition of several new words to the Klingon vocabulary.

Klingon is usually written in Roman script but with a mix of uppercase and lowercase letters. This is a system that Okrand invented to help the actors. The letters written in uppercase are pronounced differently from English, although some difficult Klingon sounds and letters are written in lower case, such as **tlh** (place the tongue as if to pronounce the letter 't' and then squeeze out air between the tongue and teeth) and **gh** (like a French gargled 'r'). This way of mixing uppercase and lowercase letters gives Klingon an extraterrestrial flavour and is therefore used by Klingonists too.

There is also a Klingon written language called **pIqaD**, but Marc Okrand didn't describe it in *The Klingon Dictionary*. However, pIqaD is sometimes used in the films and TV show, and an anonymous source from the film company leaked a guide to the KLI, who then began to use pIqaD, or as it was sometimes called, **pIqaDqoq** – 'so-called pIqaD'. But in retrospect, this system has been recognised as the real written language of the Klingons and many Klingonists now also read and write in this alien alphabet. At first, many people were disappointed precisely because it is an alphabet and not at all as unique and exotic as the rest of the language.

This journey came full circle when **pIqaDqoq** was used comprehensibly in the TV series *Star Trek: Discovery* (2017). So, the written language used by fans since 1989 is now also used by the Klingons in the TV series, which means that wary Klingonists can finally do away with the suffix -**qoq**.

The main impetus behind the language's development in recent years has been its popularity and impact *beyond* the world of Klingons and *Star Trek*. In 2010, a Dutch ensemble performed a Klingon opera: *'u'* – '*Universe*', based on a book which was also published at the same time, *paq'batlh* (**paq'** – 'book', **batlh** – 'honour'). This book is mentioned in an episode of *Star Trek: Voyager* and is akin to a Klingon bible, about the life of Klingon Emperor Kahless. Klingons come to revere Kahless and his ideas of honour to an almost religious degree. According to the backstory of *paq'batlh: The Klingon Epic*, by Floris Schönfeld and Marc Okrand, it was reconstructed from several fragmentary historical sources. However, the book also brings together Klingon myths and stories that appeared previously in *Star Trek*.

In the book, Okrand provides a few sentences in **no' Hol** (the language of the ancestors), which give the Klingonists some clues about how Klingon has evolved over time. Since we have already mentioned plural inflections, one good example is that old Klingon had only one plural suffix: -**maa** (-**mey**). So **teqmaa** ('hearts') and **'qinmaa** ('gods') have the same plural suffix. In modern Klingon, the corresponding words would be inflected with different suffixes: **tIqDu'** and **Qunpu'**.

The opera performance *'u'* was staged in the Netherlands, Croatia and Germany, and received a lot of media attention. The ensemble prepared for several years, constructing 'alien' instruments and experimenting with unique soundscapes and singing styles. A performance of *'u'* was filmed and can be watched online. There is also a documentary, *The **QIH** Act*, about the creation of the opera.

No actual Klingons were present at the premiere, despite Marc Okrand recording an invitation in Klingon and it being transmitted by CAMRAS, the Dwingeloo radio telescope in the Netherlands, to the co-ordinates where the Klingon home planet **Qo'noS** should be. That said, it's hardly surprising that no Klingons accepted the invitation, seeing as **Qo'noS** is thirty-six light years away.

A Klingon version of 'Monopoly' came out in in 2010, giving examples of new and unexpected uses of the language. Eurotalk, which publishes interactive language courses in 130 languages, added Klingon to its range of courses that year. The courses are standardised, with all the same words and phrases translated in all languages, so a lot of new words and adaptations to Earth customs were required. Klingonists were rather sceptical of this, as it removed a certain amount of its alien appeal.

Eurotalk doesn't take cultural context into account, like the fact that Klingon lacks greeting phrases, but the form of the course required the creation of these terms in Klingon. I previously mentioned the example of 'good night', **maj ram**, for which Okrand eventually managed to give a moderately reasonable explanation. Eurotalk hit us with 'good morning', 'good day' and 'good evening' all in a row: **maj po, maj pov, maj choS**. And this time there was no reasonable explanation – a Klingon would simply never say 'good morning'. The closest thing they have to a greeting phrase is '**nuqneH**?' – 'What do you want'?

Even though real Klingons would never use these phrases, or even understand the concept, plenty of useful words were created to expand the vocabulary for Klingonists on Earth. For instance, examples were given of how to transcribe various earthly names into Klingon. Eurotalk mentions several countries by name, so Okrand had to address the question of what these countries would be called in Klingon. Most countries get their Klingon name from what they call themselves in their own language, for example **'Inglan** ('England'), **DoyIchlan** ('Germany') and **vIraS** ('France'). Others get a Klingon description, such as the United Kingdom – **tuqjIjQa'** (**tuq** – 'tribe', **jIj** – 'co-operative', **Qa'** – 'union') and the United States of America – **'amerI'qa' SepjIjQa'** (**Sep** – 'region', **jIj** – 'co-operative', **Qa'** – 'union').

The fact that Klingon has been used outside of Klingonist and Trekkie circles means that the language has gradually transformed from pure alienese to an extraterrestrial language adapted to terrestrial conditions – Klingon integration, plain and simple. When the Korean pop hit 'Gangnam Style' spread across the globe like wildfire, female-driven comedy collective Comediva made a version called 'Klingon Style' with 5 million views on YouTube; successful PC game *Minecraft* has a Klingon language setting and Nokia produced its own typeface of the Klingon alphabet **pIqaD** for its phones. The Eton Institute in Dubai has started offering courses in Klingon; a local politician in North Carolina wrote his resignation letter in Klingon; and Klingon beer and Klingon (blood)wine are available for purchase. You can switch Google's search function to Klingon and Microsoft's search engine, Bing, now offers, among forty-five other languages, translation into Klingon, both in regular letters and in **pIqaD** – you can now translate everything from Swedish to Urdu directly into tlhIngan Hol.

So, Klingon really has become mainstream, reaching far beyond *Star Trek* circles. Klingonist culture has partially adapted to this development. Some have accepted that Klingon has become an earthly language used for earthly matters. One group has even been working on translating Facebook features, which obviously entailed a few stretches and guesses. This Facebook translation led to debate, and often votes were cast on which expression seemed most suitable for each function.

The hardest fight was over the days of the week. Rather than use names for each day, Klingons number them: 'the first day', 'the second day', and so on. There was one example from Okrand, **jaj wa'** ('day one'), but this was a tough nut to crack since most Klingonists are from the USA where Sunday is counted as day one, while European Klingonists consider Monday the logical start to the week. Both the Bible and the international standard ISO 8601 have been used as fodder in this controversy.

The debate raged for two years before Okrand stepped in and solved the problem in a very neat way. It turns out the Klingons have a six-day week:

DaSjaj – Monday
povjaj – Tuesday
ghItlhjaj – Wednesday
loghjaj – Thursday
buqjaj – Friday
lojmItjaj or **ghInjaj** – Saturday (**lojmItjaj** is used on more formal occasions, but otherwise the two names are used interchangeably)

To describe systems that have weeks of more than six days, the Klingons add one, two, three, etc., to the days in addition to the six-day week … so Earth's Sunday becomes **jaj wa'**. So, now the Klingon version of Facebook is ready to go.

qun tlhegh – timeline
nuv De' – profile
naD – like
yup ru cher wI' – friend request
vay 'parmaqqay ghaH – 'in a relationship'

The only question remaining is whether a Klingon would understand how Facebook works, or be utterly baffled by the concept.

A New Level of Language Development

The TV series *Star Trek: Enterprise* came to an end in 2005, and for a long time it looked like there wouldn't be any more, not even when J.J. Abrams relaunched *Star Trek* for the silver screen in 2009. But finally, a new series came: *Star Trek: Discovery*. Klingonists were looking forward to the TV series, of course, but were not particularly optimistic about the use of genuine Klingon, due to past experience.

To the *great* surprise of Klingonists the world over, promotions for the new series in summer 2017 displayed correct Klingon! And using the Klingon writing system, **pIqaD**, no less. So, expectations were very high for the premiere. It turned out that the first episode alone contained at least as much Klingon as all the previous TV series and movies put together! And correct, high-quality Klingon, at that. Instead of using Klingon words and phrases as an exotic garnish, the Klingon characters actually spoke to each other exclusively in Klingon, rather than just switching to English after an introductory phrase.

The Klingon spaceship décor featured text written in **pIqaD**. Klingonists zoomed in on these characters to find that it was indeed the **pIqaD** that had emerged among fans, outside of *Star Trek*, so to speak, and was fully understandable. So the writing was not being used as mere decoration – it was all real Klingon!

It was both a fantastic and inevitable development. Klingon has been around for such a long time and is so well known, even outside of *Star Trek*, that overlooking it in a new TV series or film simply wasn't an option, especially considering the rapid development of other fictional languages in films like *Avatar* or TV series such as *Game of Thrones*. If these film and TV producers can manage proper dialogue in Na'vi, Valyrian and Dothraki, it would be unforgivable if *Star Trek* failed to do so.

Another sign of how established and mature the language has become is the fact that they didn't hire the original creator to translate the Klingon dialogue, but a Klingonist, and a pre-eminent one at that: Robyn Stewart from Canada. She is the closest thing to a fluent Klingon speaker you can find on Earth, and one of the people behind the Klingon translation function for the search engine Bing.

The fact that it was a Klingonist and not Marc Okrand who translated the dialogue messes with the strict Klingonist criteria for what counts as the official Klingon canon – in other words, what is considered genuine Klingon. Technically the official canon can only come from Marc Okrand and since he was not directly involved in the translation of the dialogue in *Discovery*, the Klingon featured in the TV series is not considered strictly canonical, except for a few new words that came about after Robyn Stewart asked Okrand for advice. But the dialogue *is* part of the *Star Trek* canon. Seeing as it has appeared in a *Star Trek* series, it is officially the way the Klingons speak, and seeing as the translations are accurate and high quality, it must be true Klingon.

Already there was more spoken Klingon in the show than ever before, but on top of this amazing development, Netflix came up with the marketing gimmick of making Klingon subtitles available for the entire first season. This task was assigned to German Klingonist Lieven Litaer, who, like Robyn Stewart, is one of the foremost experts in Klingon (on Earth), having translated, among other things, *The Little Prince* into Klingon – **ta'puq mach**. Lieven Litaer translated the script from English and subtitled the Klingon lines too, so you can watch the entire first season with Klingon subtitles. Although not considered strictly canonical from a Klingonist perspective, this resulted in a handful of new words that Litaer had to ask Marc Okrand about.

Some examples of words from the new TV series that expanded the Klingon vocabulary:

jem'IH – fortress
DuHmor – palace
SanmIr – spore

loy' – to have a personality
nev'aQ – everyday sarcophagus
nebeyll' – a more ornate, ritual sarcophagus
pel'aQ – coffin or eggshell
jItuj'ep – mummy

Perhaps the most important aspect of these language developments is that the **pIqaD** alphabet has finally, after almost thirty years, become official and now is the true written language used by the Klingons in *Star Trek*.

Klingonaase

In addition to Marc Okrand's tlhIngan Hol, the dialects, and the older language variants he describes, there is another independent Klingon language: Klingonaase. It is roughly the same age as Okrand's Klingon and is also based on the original phrases invented by James Doohan, as heard in the first *Star Trek* movie. But it is a different interpretation of the first Klingon lines, and has led to a completely different language.

The language was created by John M. Ford for the 1984 book *The Final Reflection*, probably the most highly respected book about Klingons among Trekkies. The language was then expanded thanks to one of Ford's later books, as well as in a *Star Trek* role-playing game. Although the language is not as elaborate as tlhIngan Hol and inevitably took a back seat to the more successful language, there are still some fans who adamantly claim that Klingonaase is far more interesting and nuanced.

klinzhai – home planet of the Klingons
klin zha – Klingon game
hum zha – human game (chess)
Kahlesste kaase – Khaless' hand
komerex – growing structure

komerex Klingon – the Klingon Empire
'**komerex tel khesterex**.' – 'What does not grow must die.'

Klingonaase has appeared in a lot of fanfiction and a few terms are used by some *Star Trek* fanclubs, often in combination with tlhIngan Hol. In particular, Klingonaase has a system of honorifics that have influenced Klingonists and Klingon role players who will often use Klingonaase honorary titles even if they use tlhIngan Hol the rest of the time. Perhaps they could be considered loanwords from one Klingon language to another. From lowest rank to highest:

tai
vestai
sutai
zantai
epetai

In 2014, Marc Okrand made role players' lives a lot easier by providing instructions on how to spell these words in tlhIngan Hol:

tay
veStay
Sutay
Santay
'Iptay

Okrand also shares his Klingon informant's explanations of the etymology of these titles, relating them to words in Okrand's version of Klingon. **veStay**, for example, has to do with the word **veS** – 'warfare'; **Santay** has similarities with the word for 'a thousand' – **SanID**; and **'Iptay** clearly originated from **'Ip** – 'oath'. So, the loanwords from Klingonaase are firmly rooted in tlhIngan Hol, and we can now suppose that the two languages are related to each other.

In *The Final Reflection*, the readers follow Vrenn, who starts from humble beginnings but rises through the ranks of the **komerex Klingon** – 'the Klingon Empire'. This is marked by a name change: first he gets a name beginning with 'K', then later can add new titles to his name. So, Vrenn becomes Krenn tai-Rustazh when he is promoted to spaceship captain, then vestai-Rustzh, and so on, as he rises in status and climbs the hierarchical ladder.

'K' is an important letter in Klingonaase and a striking number of words in the known vocabulary begin with this letter. Funnily enough, there is no 'k' in tlhIngan Hol. Marc Okrand decided to do away with the letter because he deemed it too prevalent in fictional space languages. The 'k' sound in Klingon is indicated by 'q', while 'Q' is like the sound of trying to cough up a piece of food that has gone down the wrong way.

Klingon is a language that has grown away from its fictional origin and truly taken on a life of its own.

Klingonists have long doubted whether Klingon would survive without new *Star Trek* TV seasons coming out to interest new generations of speakers. Yet the language has flourished. And when *Star Trek* did finally return as a TV series after a twelve-year break, it contained more and better Klingon than ever. *Star Trek: Discovery* has inspired a new generation of the Klingon-curious to start studying the language, who are now exploring a fully matured language with a wealth of experienced speakers to help and teach them, with plenty of readymade study materials and translated books available. In 2018, the language study app Duolingo even released a free course in Klingon, with Swedish Klingonist Felix Malmbeck as the driving force. A year later, more than 493,000 earthlings were studying this out-of-this-world language.

9

The Language of Fanfiction

WHEN THE LANGUAGE OUTGROWS ITS CONTEXT

Vulcan, Parseltongue, the Divine Language, R'lyehian, Gallifreyan, Kryptonian, Black Speech, Orkish, Nunihongo, Toki Pona, Kēlen, Aeo

---

What happens to a novel's characters after the last page of the book? Or after the last episode in the series? The story doesn't stop dead; we are left with some idea of what happens next. But, not content with merely wondering what happens next to Frodo Baggins or Anna Karenina, more and more fans are choosing to write their own continuations and publish them either online or through self-publishing. This is called apocryphal fiction, better known as fanfiction.

The phenomenon of printing stories in fanzines first became widespread in the 1970s; before that, it was more or less exclusive to *Star Trek* fans. Of course, the internet has made it easier for writers to publish and distribute their work at no cost, sparking an explosion in fanfiction. *Harry Potter* is currently the biggest inspiration for fanfiction – there are over 200,000 alternative *Harry Potter* stories on Archive of Our Own (AO3) alone, many of which are novel length or longer.

The fanfiction phenomenon has also gained momentum with the success of writer Snowqueen's *Icedragon* and her fanfiction about *Twilight* characters Bella Swan and Edward Cullen – better known as *Fifty Shades of Grey* by E.L. James. Her fanfiction was so popular it was turned into an original work that turned out to be a bestseller. The success of E.L. James and other fanfiction writers in wider circles has, of course, contributed to increased interest in fanfiction and recognition of the genre.

Bengt Ohlsson certainly wasn't thinking in terms of fanfiction when he wrote *Gregorius*, with characters from Hjalmar Söderberg's classic *Doctor Glas*, nor was David Lagercrantz when he expanded on Stieg Larsson's world with Mikael Blomkvist and Lisbeth Salander. However, it is partly the same fanfiction mechanism driving the two authors. They are curious about what happens next to the characters of an existing work and want to continue these characters' trains of thought and action to see how it all plays out. The characters become too large to be contained by their original works.

Star Trek fanfiction is an old and well-established genre, and even has its own sub-genres like 'Kirk/Spock slash', in which fans explicitly explore the homoerotic tension between Kirk and Spock. Other fans use their own characters in their fanfiction but place their stories in the same universe, benefiting from the detailed history that has been built up in *Star Trek* since the 1960s.

Fanfiction is not limited to the written word and there are dozens of fan-produced TV series on the web that play out in the *Star Trek* universe, as well as some feature films. In 2015, *Star Trek: Axanar* raised over $800,000 through crowdfunding for its fan production with a professional film team, special effects and actors. Some of the actors that took part appeared previously in the actual *Star Trek*, reprising their roles in the film as their canonical characters.

The pilot that was used to raise the money is presented as a documentary, in which the protagonists are interviewed about what really happened in the four-year war during which the film is set. Naturally, the film team contacted Klingonists to help get the Klingon lines just right …

Fanfiction is a testament to our need for storytelling, our commitment to fictional characters, and our passion for the worlds in which they live. Tolkien's world has been shamelessly drawn upon by generations of fantasy writers. What would fantasy be without Elves, Dwarves and Orcs? Yet Tolkien, for his part, was inspired by and borrowed from fairy tales and myths. It is hardly surprising that fans choose to spin their yarns in this same world. For many young wannabe writers, it is easier to tell a story in a familiar world than to construct the plot, characters and entire universe from scratch. Writing 'Bredo was a young Hobbit' is enough to immediately give readers a great deal of understanding about the character, his background and habitat, and an expectation of what is about to unfold.

Fanfiction has engendered a culture of collaboration, and prompt feedback is often provided in the comment threads of fan forums online. Writers get tips, criticism and encouragement from readers and fellow writers, which inspires and spurs on further writing. This co-creative culture means that writing can be a collective process, where new works are developed via comments, based more on existing fanfiction than on the original work itself.

Just as fans feel they have the 'right' to tell new stories about their most beloved film and literary characters and develop them further, some may also feel the same way about artificial languages. For many, conlang phrases read in books or heard in films arouse huge curiosity. Alien or Elvish writing script is irresistible and simply begging to be deciphered. Does it really mean anything? Can it be genuinely used for communication? How might the full writing system work?

You might see a vocabulary list of individual words and wonder how to say this or that in the language. Then maybe you go on to discover the connection between individual words and get a sense of the grammar behind them, or maybe you figure out the logic of how to make new words … and before you know it, you've started developing the language yourself.

In the books about John Carter on Mars, the Barsoom language doesn't feature much, other than in the names of characters, plants, military titles, units of measurement and places on Mars. But it was enough to get fans interested in the language. John Flint Roy went through all eleven books, compiling the vocabulary and produced a glossary of over 400 words in *A Guide to Barsoom*. There are enough words to be able to see patterns and perhaps derive new words for something basic like cardinal numbers, for example. The books list only one, four, seven, eight and ten, but it is possible to make educated guesses based on what is mentioned. The domestic name for the planet Mars is **Barsoom**, which we know to mean 'the eighth planet', so **bar** is very likely to mean 'eight'. Therefore, we can suppose that **-soom** means something like 'planet' or 'celestial body' (which also includes the sun and moons). The books mention five other planets in the solar system by name, all ending in **-soom**, so it seems likely that the names of the planets are simply ordered in relation to the sun. From **Rasoom** – 'Mercury', **Cosoom** – 'Venus' and **Jasoom** – 'Earth', we get the numbers **ra** – 'two', **co** – 'three' and **ja** – 'five'.

Many fans find this method of seeing connections between words and deriving the meaning behind them absolutely fascinating. Much can be reconstructed, reasoned and guessed from 400 words. When Paul Frommer was commissioned to create a language for the movie *John Carter*, he used the same method but with the added bonus of a hundred years' worth of fan-led exploration and study of Barsoom. Out of respect for the original language, Frommer created only what was needed for the few Barsoom lines spoken in the film. Now, a century after its creation, the language has acquired grammar and a handful of sentences. Who knows how fans might build on this over the next century?

These types of fans are sometimes described as 'fan scholars', which is to say fans who use academic methodology and theory in exploration of their interests. The Elvish Linguistic Fellowship (ELF) and the Klingon Language Institute (KLI) are typical examples of this. These sorts of organisations tend to be made up of people who hold an academic degree and explore the language as they would a subject at university. They publish academic articles, hold conferences, organise training courses and peer review each other's research. Dr Lawrence M. Schoen, chairman of the KLI, has said that many fans, Trekkers, and Trekkies, are disappointed when they get in contact with the KLI hoping to find a regular fan club, and instead are met by dusty academics in a linguistic society. Most truly advanced Klingon speakers do not describe themselves as Trekkies, but as language nerds.

ELF and KLI hold a special position because they are prominent academic organisations and can come under criticism from other fans who wish to use Elvish and Klingon more freely, making up their own new words as and when. But ELF and KLI are very restrictive and cautious in their creation of new words, defining the languages through their own investigations and use. Above all, they control and standardise the use of the languages, acting as a kind of *Oxford English Dictionary* for their respective conlang by determining which words are acceptable.

In the case of Na'vi and Láadan, the conlangers started out with the intention that their languages would take on lives of their own beyond their work and prepared as necessary. Na'vi creator Paul Frommer urges fans to submit suggestions for new words, which he then approves (or rejects). Fans have been invited to participate in this type of fanfiction from the outset as the co-creators of Na'vi – but under regulation. Suzette Haden Elgin proceeded in a similar way because Láadan was intended partly as a feature of her trilogy and partly as a ten-year experiment to see if there was any interest or call for a women's language. So, Elgin worked officially with other people who were interested in Láadan, gradually expanding the vocabulary in collaboration with the speakers/fans.

The extent to which publishers and film companies will tolerate fanfiction usually depends on whether they intend to make money from developing the work further. There is a limit where fanfiction borders on brand parasitism. In the 1990s, the book *Secret Fighting Arts of the Warrior Race* came out as a kind of fanfiction. It was a manual on how to fight with the Klingon weapon **betleH** and contained pictures of people dressed up as Klingons demonstrating how to perform the movements, with phrases in Klingon. The film company that owns the rights to *Star Trek* and Klingon threatened legal action and made sure that the book was quickly withdrawn. This event revealed that the film company also considered themselves to own the Klingon language, and the KLI had to negotiate for a licence approving their use of it.

The idea is that an artificial language can be protected under copyright because it has an author, unlike natural languages such as English. But, if there are grammar books and textbooks teaching the language, and people start to genuinely write and speak it, can a company really own it? Can they own everything written and spoken?

This was in the 1990s when the internet was in its infancy. Fanfiction and the use of artificial languages have exploded since then, especially Klingon, which has become an established part of popular culture like no other extraterrestrial language before it. These days, it would probably be difficult for the film company to claim that it still holds the copyright to the Klingon language.

Languages as Props

There are fans of Klingon, Dothraki, *Lord of the Rings* and Na'vi who are not primarily interested in language but are intrigued by the character traits of fantastical beings and their cultures.

They love recreating costumes, gadgets, jewellery, art and artefacts belonging to fictional races. This is an important part of fan culture: dressing up, also known as cosplay, which is part of going to meetings and conventions. Cosplay is a form of fancy dress or performance in which the cosplayer dresses up as a character from science fiction, fantasy films, computer games or manga. When the word 'cosplay', short for costume play, was coined in Japan it was mainly associated with dressing up as characters from anime and manga. Nowadays, it is a much more diverse phenomenon.

Many cosplayers might be content with having a name inspired by the language and some greeting phrases to use when they are 'in character'. Maybe they want to know enough of the written language to be able to write or inscribe something on an object. The language simply becomes one of their world-building props, which is used to tell a richer story.

It is also not uncommon to use artificial languages for communication during role play and cosplay. Live-action role play, or LARP, is a kind of collective improvisation where players assume roles and identities for a weekend or so and fully immerse themselves in their character and scenario. Tolkien-esque worlds are popular, where people role play as Dwarves, Hobbits, Orcs or Elves. So, taking Elves as an example, these LARP games have led to the development of a number of Elvish dialects that originate from Tolkien's Elvish languages and can be used to lend credibility to the game. Some role players memorise phrases from books or films such as greetings, '**Mae govannen**' ('Well met') or '**Namárië**' ('Farewell'), while others use whatever vocabulary they know as more of a pidgin language. They may also use Elvish words but with the grammar of their own language, garnished perhaps with their own self-developed vocabulary. They only use the elements of the language they feel they need. Sometimes the languages are expanded and become their own dialect, used by a particular LARP Elf clan, while another clan speaks a similar but slightly different dialect. The languages and dialects of the Orcs are largely fanfiction and have their own section below.

Then there are the fans who have gone and become 'official'. David Salo, one of the world's foremost experts in Tolkien's artlangs, was hired as a consultant for the *Lord of the Rings* and the *Hobbit* films. Not only did Salo help the filmmakers get Tolkien's languages right, but he also developed and created words and languages to cover all the lines required by the films' scripts. So, what status can we ascribe to the language that appears in these films? They are not derived directly from Tolkien's works, but they are official in that they are spoken in the films, yet are only the interpretation of an individual fan scholar …

A great deal, if not all, of the languages that arise in popular culture and spread beyond the scope of their original work are influenced by the fans, to a greater or lesser degree. Often, there is an official version, and at least one extended fan version. Sometimes people are careful to keep the versions separate, and sometimes the expanded versions are seen as a part of the original. The culture of co-creation can enable rapid language development. Competing versions can collaborate or become mortal enemies.

In many languages, the grammatical rules are defined through fans' efforts to analyse the existing fragments and extrapolate patterns. Fans may try their hand at creating new words through neologisms (forming new words from existing ones) or broadening the vocabulary by finding words in another language that might have served as a model for the artlang. For example, fans have made new words for Huttese from *Star Wars*, based on the South American language of Quechua.

Attitudes to newly created words and personal initiatives vary according to which fan subculture you subscribe to. Fan scholars study what is available and are unwilling to draw hasty conclusions or let the language develop aimlessly, whereas the average layperson wants easy-to-use language for limited communication to use as an accessory in LARP and cosplay.

Let us take a closer look at some languages that have developed in different ways. The Vulcan language from *Star Trek* has been a broth with many cooks since the 1960s and is on its way to a fan-led official version. The Divine Language from the cult film *The Fifth Element* hasn't spread particularly widely, but one individual fan has developed it into a full new artlang. In *Harry Potter* circles, Parseltongue, the magic language of serpents, has been designed by fans as a kind of elaborate homage. We have not been told much about Gallifreyan from *Doctor Who*, but this just makes it all the more intriguing to fans.

Interestingly, it is mainly the written language that fans have adopted. Kryptonian, the language spoken on Superman's home planet, Krypton, has been represented in writing since the 1950s but was never linked to a full language. It was only when fans started to associate the characters with sounds and develop a Kryptonian grammar and vocabulary that the language came into existence. Finally, we have Orkish, which was only ever outlined by Tolkien himself but has since been expanded via a number of interesting routes, mainly in LARP circles.

Vulcan

Star Trek's Mr Spock is arguably the most famous alien in the world. For forty-five years, actor Leonard Nimoy portrayed the iconic extraterrestrial with nothing but pointed ears, painted eyebrows and a bowl haircut as his props. Even in the modern day, the notoriety of Mr Spock as an alien being is not thanks to a rubber mask, advanced make-up or realistic computer animation – his extraterrestrial identity is not so superficial. Spock is half-human (on his mother's side) and is constantly wrestling his Vulcan upbringing, which taught him not to feel or show emotions. Spock's strict logic and unflappable calm become a sounding board for the heated, impulsive Captain Kirk, and for all that is human.

From the very beginning, when the TV series *Star Trek* first aired in the 1960s, fans were fascinated by Mr Spock's alien language. It didn't take long for them to piece together the few pieces of Vulcan they heard in the TV series and make their own versions of the language. In the episode *Amok Time*, the television audience was introduced to strange cultural customs from the planet Vulcan as well as the names of other Vulcans, T'Pau, T'Pring and Stonn, plus a few words:

plomeek – a type of soup
pon farr – mating time
kah-if-farr – begin
koon-ut-kal-if-fee – wedding or challenge(!)
'**kroykah!**' – 'Stop! Enough!'
lirpa – traditional weapon
ahn woon – another traditional weapon

The fans took the names as a model on which to base the creation of further Vulcan names. They also began to write fanfiction and add more words in the same style as those revealed in the TV series. Certain words and phrases that appeared in the fan-driven versions stuck and spread. The greeting phrase 'Live long and prosper' came to be '**Pastak v'edora lashe**' (more variants of this phrase later), and **Pastaklan Vesla** (meaning 'Peaceful Thoughts') was the name of an early fanzine.

The most elaborate and widespread Vulcan language of the 1960s was developed by linguist Dorothy Jones Heydt for use in her own fanfiction. The language, or at least some of the words from her story, were taken up by other fans and fanfiction writers. Perhaps the most interesting word Heydt invented is **ni var** ('two form'), which denotes a Vulcan art form in which an object is compared from two different points of view or where two aspects of an object are juxtaposed. **Ni var** was adopted by other fanfiction writers and **ni var** poetry and art appeared in the *Spockanalia* fanzine in the 1970s.

'Ni var' was also the name of a fan novel by Claire Gabriel, which was later condensed into a short story and published in the *Star Trek* anthology, *The New Voyages* in 1976. Mr Spock himself (Leonard Nimoy) wrote an introduction to the novel explaining that **ni var** was a Vulcan term referring to the duality of things: 'Two who are one, two diversities that are a unity, two halves that come together to make a whole'. From this short story, the authors of a later TV series, *Star Trek: Enterprise*, picked up the term as a tribute and named a spaceship from the planet Vulcan *Ni'Var*. Finally, in *Star Trek: Discovery*, it shows up again: when the Vulcans and Romulans unite, they change the planet's name to **Ni'var**. So, this word that was invented in fan circles in the 1960s became a true Vulcan word in the television series of the 1990s, and replaced the name of the Vulcan homeworld itself in 2020!

The Vulcan language has a colourful history. In 1977 a small six-sided booklet was published, *The Vulcan Language Guide: Starfleet Academy Training Manual*, where we are told that there are over 100 dialects on the planet Vulcan, but the main dialect spoken by 75 per cent of Vulcans is called Anakana. Other major dialects include Nikana (10 per cent) and Noyokana (5 per cent). Another 5 per cent speak a ceremonial language called Senurakana, and 3 per cent apparently speak Taiyakana, which is described as the ancient language. The explanation of dialects was probably a way to account for the differences that existed between the guide's version of Vulcan, the Vulcan invented by various fans, and, most importantly, the official Vulcan heard in the TV series, as Anakana differs a great deal from the Vulcan spoken by one Mr Spock. It sounds like made-up Japanese, or at least a language heavily inspired by Japanese:

'**Wanimo woku ra yako itisha ta?**' – 'Where is the hotel?'
'**Yana ra Yakana ro futisha ta?**' – 'Do you speak Vulcan?'
'**Ha, wani ra Yakana ro futisha.**' – 'Yes, I speak Vulcan.'

Thanks to the small booklet describing the language in a fairly systematic way, explaining simple grammar and including a glossary, this version of Vulcan became more widespread. In recent years, Anakana has made a comeback via the web, as it is a relatively easy language to learn and many fans think that a few A4 pages' worth of language notes is quite enough, thank you.

The Vulcan Language Guide is probably quite correct about the plethora of languages on the planet Vulcan and it is a logical way to explain why Vulcan can sound and look very different in different contexts. The first *Star Trek* feature film from 1979 includes not only Klingon, but a few lines of Vulcan as well and, just as with the first Klingon sentences, it was actor James Doohan (Scotty) who made up the nonsense phrases. In the case of Vulcan, he invented sentences to match the lip movements of pre-recorded dialogue in English. For example:

> **'Dakh orfikkel aushfamaluhr shaukaush fi'aifa mazhiv.'**
> 'Our ancestors cast out their animal passions on these very sands.' (!)

Or the iconic Vulcan greeting phrase:

> **'Dif-tor heh smusma.'** – 'Live long and prosper.'

This is the phrase in Anakana: **'Tai nasha no karosha'**. The Klingon, in case you were wondering, is **'yIn nI' yISIQ 'ej yIchep'**.

It started off as gibberish invented by a linguistically minded actor. But for the second *Star Trek* movie, linguist Marc Okrand was hired to create the Vulcan dialogue. Just as in the first film, it was a question of developing Vulcan to match the actors' English lip movements. Okrand's contribution was a short conversation between two Vulcans, Spock and Saavik:

'**Wakli ak'wikman – ot-lan?**' – 'What surprises you, lieutenant?'
'**Ish-veh ni … komihn.**' – 'He is so … human.'

Marc Okrand returned for the third *Star Trek* movie and created more Vulcan, and again for an episode of *Star Trek: Enterprise* and the re-launch of *Star Trek* in 2009. In *Star Trek: Discovery* (2018), the occasional new phrase appeared along with a few new Vulcan words.

Alas, no official Vulcan dictionary came out as it did for Klingon. It was *The Klingon Dictionary* that really set that particular *Star Trek* language on its incredible journey. However, fans continued to develop Vulcan regardless, embarking on an ambitious project to produce a Vulcan dictionary.

Trekkie and language enthusiast Mark R. Gardner was dumbfounded when he heard the Kolinahr master speak Vulcan in the first *Star Trek* movie and became utterly obsessed with the language. More Vulcan was spoken in the two subsequent films and Mark R. Gardner realised that there was now enough material to analyse and learn more about the language. He was in a good position for such analysis because not only had he studied Russian, Turkish, French, Greek, Latin, Icelandic and American Sign Language, but also worked as a language analyst in the military and so was experienced in transcription.

Gardner played the scenes where Vulcan is spoken over and over on his Betamax video player and analysed the sentences in detail. When he read the actors' lips, he discovered to his great surprise that they were speaking English with exaggerated mouth movements (which was also later confirmed by the film company). To be sure of his results, he took a recording of the Vulcan dialogue to an acquaintance who worked as a speech therapist and asked them to analyse the tape. Their perceptions of the words and sounds spoken differed on only three words.

Gardner then performed a mechanical analysis of the words until he finally felt satisfied that he had arrived at a full Vulcan soundscape.

Gardner then began his investigations into Vulcan grammar: which words were verbs, how sentences were constructed and, of course, which words meant what. He looked for patterns and saw that the verbs almost always come first in the sentence and that the words are composed of short root words.

He began to use the words that featured in the old TV series from the 1960s and searched through *Star Trek* novels. In time, more words appeared in the new TV series, films and short stories. But Gardner and his fan-scholar colleagues at the Vulcan Language Institute were also constructing new words based on what they had already learned about Vulcan, in which known root words were combined to form new words.

Eventually, they had a language with a well-developed grammar and a dictionary of thousands of words. They called their language Golic Vulcan, explaining that it consisted of two distinct but very closely related tongues: traditional Golic Vulcan – the formal language spoken by ancient Vulcan philosopher Surak and used as a ceremonial language all over the planet – and modern Golic Vulcan, a more informal language used regionally and by certain clans in the present day (by which I mean, of course, the future).

Gardner's version of the language was disseminated across the internet courtesy of his Vulcan Language Institute, and later via the printed version of *The Vulcan Dictionary*. It is, without a doubt, the most elaborate Vulcan language to date, incorporating all the Vulcan words and phrases that have appeared in the *Star Trek* films, series and books so far, while laying out a coherent grammar. Other fans have since built on this language and new words are added every now and then.

Then there are the fans who have tried to get to grips with the written Vulcan that can be seen in the TV series and films.

Briht'uhn, the Vulcan enthusiast behind the website korsaya. org has got the furthest with this and has built several beautiful and fascinating writing systems from the few characters and writing samples available. This, in turn, has inspired even more fans to start learning Vulcan, because interesting and well-developed writing systems are not common among languages that have emerged from TV. Usually, film and television production companies are content with writing that plays a primarily ornamental role, so it looks good on screen but has no real relationship with the language. Either this, or else it is a simple alphabet where the characters correspond directly to English letters. So for a writing language to become genuinely interesting and extraterrestrial, it needs fans!

Perhaps the circle will finally be closed with the TV show, *Star Trek: Picard* (2020) – and in a fascinating and peculiar way. For *Picard*'s first season, the conlanger Trent Pehrson was hired to develop Romulan dialogue. Pehrson was instructed to use pre-existing fragments of the Romulan language from earlier *Star Trek* shows and films (see the section on Romulan in Chapter 4). But he was also asked to consider some canonical Vulcan dialogue. The thinking was that Vulcans and Romulans are related to each other, and so their languages should be, too. Pehrson found the Vulcan fragments useful for fleshing out the linguistic history of Romulan.

As it happens, Trent Pehrson is also an expert in the fan-developed Vulcan language and has even developed a few Vulcan and Romulan writing systems. So it seems quite likely that the fan-developed Vulcan language will eventually find its way into *Star Trek* canon in coming seasons of *Picard*. As long as Pehrson continues to be engaged as a language consultant for the show, and as long as we get to meet Vulcan characters, we will most likley get a canon Vulcan language that will be familiar to the Vulcan languages fans.

Parseltongue

A multitude of beings and beasts feature in the universe of *Harry Potter*, but little is known about the languages they speak. Only three are mentioned: Gobbledegook, spoken by the Goblins; Mermish, spoken by the Merpeople; and Parseltongue, spoken by serpents and mainly dark wizards.

The Goblins are mysterious magical creatures that we mostly know from Gringotts Wizarding Bank, and the *Harry Potter* books only give us one example of their language Gobbledegook: **bladvak**, meaning 'pickaxe'.

The Merpeople are classified as beasts, having refused the offer of being reclassified as beings. They are half-human with a fish-like lower body and speak a magical language that sounds like nothing more than high-pitched screaming on land but is comprehensible to humans underwater. Harry Potter discovers this during the contest for the Goblet of Fire when a clue has to be heard underwater to be understood.

The language of the serpents, Parseltongue, is the most frequently mentioned in Harry Potter's world. Those who can speak it are known as Parselmouths, which J.K. Rowling says was inspired by an Old English word for someone with a deformed mouth such as a cleft lip. Presumably, this is a reference to the forked tongue of a snake.

Parseltongue is a magical language used mainly by Voldemort and Harry Potter in the books and films. Knowledge of the language and the ability to speak it seem to be largely innate. A Parselmouth understands and speaks Parseltongue fluently and automatically without the need to study vocabulary or grammar. Harry isn't even aware that he is speaking a different language when he first communicates with a snake.

The books describe the serpent language as a whispering and hissing, so the films required a sound effect to match. But the producers went one step further and hired Francis Nolan, professor of phonetics at the University of Cambridge, to construct credible snake speech. It was only a handful of lines, but this was enough to require Nolan to sketch out a language.

Parseltongue is an ergative language with geminate consonants and verb-subject-object word order. It has a high frequency of pharyngeal fricatives to acoustically mimic the physique of a snake. And because snakes do not have flexible lips, the language has no rounded vowels or labial consonants. It all sounds a bit like a phonetic magic formula, on the basis of which Francis Nolan conjured up a number of lines for the films:

> '**Sayha gassi hëf, haśéa gassa śig**!' – 'Leave him alone, go away!'
> '**Aiśa gassi sëzz**!' – 'Excuse me, Lord!'

A couple of additional lines that Francis Nolan translated didn't make it into the films but were revealed to *Harry Potter* fans later:

> '**Sa ŋagala's nësjä lëhä sëzz**.' – 'There's a Muggle outside the door, Lord.'

Harry Potter has given rise to a rich fan culture, mainly in fanfiction where countless stories are written about Harry and other characters in this magical universe. The *Harry Potter* cosplay and LARP community is also strong. For example, there are two magical wizardry schools in Sweden, Bifrost and Yggdrasil, where young people and adults have been performing live-action role play of pupils and teachers twice a year since 2012. Fans have adapted the magic sport of Quidditch to worldly conditions and dubbed it Muggle Quidditch. So, it is not all that surprising that fans have extrapolated and expanded Parseltongue into a more complex language as well.

There are a couple of different fan versions of the language. One is called Stilio and builds on Nolan's ideas, while also borrowing features from Bantu and the Dravidian languages. Far from a fully developed language, it is more a musing upon how the grammar might work – an extended sketch. Neither is the vocabulary particularly elaborate, which is not unusual for fan languages.

Another version, with a completely different interpretation of the serpent language's grammar, is called Parseltongue-inspired and is also mostly a hypothetical but thorough reflection on how the language might be structured. It has been used to translate lines from the books that are written in English but supposed to represent Parseltongue:

> 'Psā!' – 'Stop!'
> 'Efe iska?' – 'Do you speak it?'
> 'Sā, skæ. Hút fis Marvolo?' – 'Yes, I speak it. Where is Marvolo?'
> 'Tæn. Suōs tænas, au?' – 'Dead. Died years ago, didn't he?'
> 'Simī hí fú?' – 'Who are you, then?'

Another fan language that has its own website, complete with lessons, exercises and tests, is Parseltongue 101. This version has taken inspiration from Parseltongue-inspired and supplemented it with an expanded vocabulary with contributions from several fans. Their interpretation of Parseltongue seems to include a significant number of English loanwords:

> **ou** – you
> **iangsteur** – youngster
> **aposlogahs** – sorry (apologies)
> **apsle** – apple
> **kups** – cup

In another fan project, they have simply invented letter combinations to replace English letters, so that you can 'convert' your name or other words in your own language into something that looks like Parseltongue:

haa – A
ethaa – B
hass – C
ssaah – D

Harry Potter enthusiasts, whether engaging in live-action role play or writing fanfiction, don't seem particularly fussed about conversing in a fully developed language. They are happy with just a smidgen more than what has been provided in the book, or a system for producing languages as cinematic sound effects. The foundations for an advanced Parseltongue have been laid, but there hasn't been any need to expand it into a full language, or at least, not yet.

The Divine Language

In 1997 French director Luc Besson realised a teenage dream when he made *The Fifth Element*. The script emerged back when Besson was at school and the film went on to become a cult sci-fi masterpiece, with costumes by Jean-Paul Gaultier.

The film's protagonist, Leeloominaï Lekatariba Lamina Tchaï Ekbat De Sebat, is a perfect being, the Fifth Element, brought to Earth by an extraterrestrial race called the Mondoshawan to prevent a sphere of pure evil from destroying the entire planet. Apparently, evil spheres are a recurring problem and need to be combatted every 5,000 years or so. At the beginning of the film, we see an archaeological expedition in 1919 taking place in an ancient Egyptian temple, which discovers information on this phenomenon. However, most of the film's action takes place in the twenty-third century.

The Fifth Element, nicknamed Leeloo, speaks the Divine Language used 'throughout the Universe before time was time', which is a kind of protolanguage for the universe itself. There is at least one person on Earth who speaks the language, Father

Vito Cornelius. He is the last in a long line of priests with knowledge of the recurring Great Evil and the Mondoshawan aliens, and knows through prophecy that the Fifth Element will appear.

The other four elements are represented by stones featuring the elements' signs, to be placed in the Egyptian temple to stop the Great Evil. A curious titbit in this context is that **Leeloo** means 'stone' in the Divine Language and her full first name, **Leeloominaï**, means 'gemstone'. Director Luc Besson, who also created the language, has said that Leeloominaï Lekatariba Lamina Tchaï Ekbat De Sebat's second name is her surname, the third is her dynasty and the last one means she is the seventeenth in her lineage. But this statement from Besson has never sat well with the fans, who have their own speculations about what her name *really* means. World expert in the Divine Language, T. Leah Fehr-Thompson, has made an educated guess at the true meaning of the name through Arabic, English and Hebrew etymological studies: 'Precious Gem of the Earth and Honourable Defender of Light and Life'.

T. Leah Fehr-Thompson is a typical fan scholar who fell in love with the Divine Language. Her study of the language is probably the most detailed in the world, other than the 150 words published in *The Story of the Fifth Element*, which contains the only official published lexicon. Not all that much of the language then, but enough for fan scholars to sink their teeth into.

Fehr-Thompson's interest in the language and desire to make it coherent as a working language has led to a fanfiction conlang that she calls Divinian, extrapolated into a reasonably functional language with grammar and a lexicon of 1,300 words. Milla Jovovich, who played Leeloo and developed the language with Besson, has said that the language consisted of 800 words when she got it from Besson, but other than the few words in the film and the 150 in the lexicon, there wasn't much to build on.

Fehr-Thompson has hoovered up everything there is to know about the language and has created new words based on existing ones, as well as totally new ones from Romanian, Polish, Czech, Portuguese and Hebrew roots. This is partially justified by Milla Jovovich's statement in an interview that the Divine Language was partly based on earthly languages to make it sound natural.

Here are three phrases from the film:

'**apipoulai**' – 'greetings'
'**akta gamat**' – 'never without my permission'
'**domo danko**' – 'thank you very much'

And three phrases from the fan-developed language:

'**Sän mechtaba on domo kala.**' – 'This book is very good.'
'**Me o y'am chimmäs.**' – 'I am a mother.'
'**Kan chämas on domo assinou.**' – 'That woman is very friendly.'

Another Divine Language: R'lyehian

In the 1920s and 1930s, author Howard Phillips Lovecraft wrote short stories known as 'pulp fiction' for various inexpensive adventure and fantasy publications. These magazines, like *Weird Tales* and *Amazing Stories*, were called 'pulps' because of the poor quality of the paper they were printed on. H.P. Lovecraft was not particularly famous, widely read or successful during his lifetime, and when he died of cancer in 1937 it was in poverty and solitude.

Lovecraft never claimed to be anything other than a skilled craftsman, but his cult status as an author first emerged during the second half of the twentieth century. Since then, he has come to be regarded as a pioneer in modern horror literature, a successor to Edgar Allan Poe, and the creator of a mythology so original that it could stand side by side with that of Tolkien or George R.R. Martin.

Dormant gods and powers await their violent and chaotic return, alongside an intricate pantheon of ancient deities, cosmic powers, terrifying forgotten civilisations and monstrous sunken cities. They are tales of creeping, crawling, pestilent creatures waiting in the deep, and unthinkable demonic horrors.

The mythology that emerged in Lovecraft's short stories is often referred to as the Cthulhu Mythos, but this also includes later works by other writers who have emulated the universe and literary style that made Lovecraft a cult phenomenon. It was author August Derleth, a friend of Lovecraft, who coined the term 'Cthulhu Mythos'. He also wrote for *Weird Tales* and joined in with Lovecraft's pseudo-mythology, introducing more gods, linking different creatures to the four elements, and developing it into more of a battle between good and evil. Derleth was also the person who managed Lovecraft's writing after his death.

The sleeping god, Cthulhu, lies 'dead but dreaming' in the sunken city of R'lyeh, somewhere below the depths of the Pacific Ocean. When the stars align, the monster will awaken, and forces of chaos will plague the Earth. This gigantic creature is the high priest of even more powerful godlike beings, the Great Old Ones, whose return will bring about chaos, madness, devastation and finally, the destruction of the world.

H.P. Lovecraft also pondered non-human language. He believed that most attempts at alien languages and names of alien races in science fiction were thinly veiled expressions of the creators' native language. His names Cthulhu and R'lyeh, on the other hand, are only approximations of sounds utterly unpronounceable by humans. Indeed, R'lyehian is more or less unspeakable with the respiratory system and speech organs of a human, and difficult for our limited consciousness to grasp conceptually. The word Cthulhu is usually pronounced 'katulu' or 'kutulu', although the role-play game *Call of Cthulhu* states that it is pronounced 'kuh-THOOL-hoo', whereas Lovecraft apparently said that the closest a human can get is 'khlûl'-hloo'.

The first syllable requires thick, guttural articulation. In a letter, Lovecraft wrote:

> The best approximation one can make is to grunt, bark, or cough the imperfectly formed syllables Cluh-Luh with the tip of the tongue firmly affixed to the roof of the mouth. That is, if one is a human being. Directions for other entities are naturally different.

There are fragments of this extraterrestrial language in Lovecraft's novels, although he never developed it in more detail. Lovecraft borrowed one word, or sound rather, from Edgar Allan Poe: '**Tekeli-li! Tekeli-li!**', a bizarre, eerie sound emitted by creatures called shoggoths. Otherwise, the best-known example is a sentence that has also appeared in several other writers' works since Lovecraft's death:

> '**Ph-nglui mglw'nafh Cthulhu R'lyeh wgah'nagl fhtagn.**'
> 'In his house at R'lyeh, dead Cthulhu waits dreaming.'

Naturally, fans have carefully analysed this sentence and other fragments. Someone supposed that **fhtagn** means 'sleep' or 'wait', **mglw'nafh** – 'dreaming', and **wgah'nagl** – '(its) home', and then proceeded to unpick other phrases. What might be a prefix or suffix? How might the grammar work?

People also began looking at phrases and fragments from other writers who wrote in Cthulhus' mythological universe, such as this sentence from August Derleth:

> '**Iä Hastur cf'ayak'vulgtmm, vugtlagln vulgtmm!**'
> 'Glory to Hastur! We send you prayers, answer our prayers!'

The glossary that fans seem to have agreed on covers around ninety words and is most commonly used in role-playing circles, because much of the Cthulhu Mythos has been continued through role play since 1981 so it is used to create props or clues in various games. Then came the first of seven editions of the role-playing game *Call of Cthulhu*. The game's rule books and various quests have functioned as a kind of standardisation of the mythology, compiling and systematising the fragments mentioned in various books. As well as *Call of Cthulhu*, there are plenty of other popular board, card and computer games that explore the mythology. These games have given rise to different written characters and typographies, inspiring fans to develop several fonts and hieroglyphic systems to write in R'lyehian. The written languages seem mainly to be used as props.

There is another kind of fanfiction, or whatever you want to call it, created by satanists and chaos magicians who invoke Lovecraft's fictional gods in a kind of religious role play, which just goes to show how well constructed the mythology is. Are unthinkable fictional gods really any more incomprehensible than any other type of god?

Lovecraft's stories often mention fictional ancient texts that refer to the Cthulhu Mythos. These books tell of the return of the Elder and the Outer Gods, as well as how to expel them. More often than not, these books are written by people who have lost their mind as a result of this knowledge. One of the most famous and important of these is eerie occult text the *Necronomicon*, which is said to have been written around 720 BCE by Abdul Alhazred, also known as 'the Mad Arab'.

Its original Arabic title is said to have been *Kitab al-Azif*. The *Necronomicon* has taken on a life of its own life, far beyond Lovecraft's world and mythology. It is used by many other authors and is becoming a common reference in popular culture. The fact that the book is fictional seems to have been lost on some people. Even during his lifetime, Lovecraft had to make a statement declaring that the book was his invention and did not actually exist, but this did nothing to prevent several versions of varying quality of the horrific book coming into existence after Lovecraft's death. Some were written by honest fans, but perhaps more were written by people wishing to leech off the phenomenon.

There are a lot of very beautiful pages from the *Necronomicon*, where fans have used exotic scripts and hieroglyphs along with occult diagrams and drawings to give artful form to their vision of the legendary book. Whether these really are in R'lyehian, I wouldn't like to speculate. In any case, it is safest not to read too much into the book …

The 'crazy' and 'unthinkable' nature of Lovecraft's mythology is his way of highlighting that myths are only human interpretations of the greater fundamental truths of the universe – truths that lie beyond human grasp. In the books, any human encounter with an unthinkable cosmic horror becomes vague and incoherent in its details. The interpretation must don the costume of human language for it to be comprehensible. Otherwise, gaining insight into or knowledge of these truths leads to madness and ultimately suicide. From the dizzying perspective of the cosmos, human beings are insignificant, and our perception of time is meaningless. We are subservient to immense powers and forces that are indifferent to humanity.

Similarly, R'lyehian is incomprehensible to the human mind and trying to delve deeper into its mysteries also supposedly leads to madness. This is not a million miles from the basic premise of *Native Tongue*, which is described in Chapter 5 of this book, where extraterrestrial and human brains are so different that it is highly dangerous for humans to penetrate alien languages and ways of thinking.

So far, fans don't seem particularly interested in developing R'lyehian for communicative purposes, seemingly satisfied with a language that remains as difficult to grasp as the rest of Lovecraft's world. Interestingly, the fans don't seem too concerned about what counts as 'original' and what has been added later – there is a general acceptance of the extended Cthulhu Mythos and R'lyehian language to which other writers have contributed. So, it's possible that a future writer may endow R'lyehian, or Cthuvian, as fans sometimes call it, with more structure and a greater vocabulary. But for now, we make do with what we have:

'Iä, Iä! Cthulhu Fhtagn!'

Gallifreyan

The British TV classic *Doctor Who* holds the Guinness World Record as the world's longest-running sci-fi television series. It ran for twenty-six seasons between 1963 and 1989 and was successfully revived in 2005. The series, about an extraterrestrial time traveller, the Doctor, has had a huge impact on British popular culture and has a cult following around the world.

The Doctor looks human but comes from the planet Gallifrey and belongs to a species known as the Time Lords, who have the technology to travel through time – but only to observe, not intervene. However, the Doctor is a renegade, fleeing from other Time Lords because of his tendency to interfere in the events of various epochs. Luckily for us, the Doctor has a fondness for Earth and humans, and has saved humanity from annihilation a number of times – not least from the extraterrestrial cyborg mutants, the Daleks.

Like all Time Lords, the Doctor can travel through time and space in a ship that grows as a partially organic entity called the TARDIS (Time And Relative Dimension In Space), which is larger on the inside than the outside due to its 'dimensional transcendence'. Usually, a TARDIS can take whatever form necessary to blend in with whatever environment and era it finds itself in, but the Doctor's TARDIS always looks like a British police box from the 1960s because it has a faulty 'chameleon circuit' and is therefore stuck in this camouflage position.

The Time Lords of the planet Gallifrey live much longer than humans, and the Doctor is said to be around 1,000 years old. He has lived to this rather respectable age thanks to the Time Lords' ability to regenerate. This method allows Time Lords to postpone their death by replacing every cell in their body, which leads to a whole new look and slightly different personality, while retaining the same memories and identity. This is a pretty handy concept for such a long-running TV show because the leading actors can change on a regular basis. We are currently following the thirteenth incarnation of the Doctor.

Although the Doctor speaks British English fluently, his native language is Gallifreyan. However, neither Gallifreyan nor any other extraterrestrial languages encountered by the Doctor are heard in the television series. The TARDIS translates everything into English. Or rather, almost everything – snippets of written Gallifreyan slip through every now and then. As a result, there have been glimpses of different writing systems over the years. There is one that looks like a mixture of Greek letters and mathematical symbols, and another that looks like intricate circles and geometric shapes.

Since the language is only hinted at in the TV series and not explained in more depth, it has obviously aroused the interest of the fans – the Whovians. Unfortunately, there isn't much to go on. The only known words in Gallifreyan are **Valeyard** – 'learned court prosecutor', and **Mi'en Kalarash** – 'blue fire'. The closest thing to a clue we have to the written language is that $\partial^3\Sigma x^2$ signifies the Doctor's name.

So, the Whovians have a lot of leeway when it comes to interpreting Gallifreyan, which has led to the creation of several fan-developed languages and writing systems. Whovians collaborate online through the Gallifreyan Conlang Project, started by a student of linguistics who took the initiative to develop a Gallifreyan language, inviting everyone who wanted to be involved to join in. A significant number of people have worked together to develop a large vocabulary and grammar. They use two written languages: Linear Gallifreyan and Circular Gallifreyan. The linear form is based on the written language that appears in the TV series and seems to be a mixture of Greek letters and mathematical symbols. Circular Gallifreyan has borrowed from another ambitious fan project: Sherman's Gallifreyan.

This visually stunning and ingeniously designed written language is based on symbols, which only began to appear on the TARDIS in the 2005 TV series. It features circles, semicircles and dots of various sizes and forms. The inspiration is said to have come from the cogs inside old pocket watches. The symbols in the TV series were designed not as a language, but merely as decoration, yet it struck a chord with many fans who began to think about how it might work as a written language. Various fans experimented with its construction and several versions appeared.

In the summer of 2011, American teenager Whovian Loren Sherman wanted to write something in Bettenbender's Galifreyan, created by their friend Catherine Bettenbender, but didn't have access to a guide. Sherman tried to recreate the alphabet and rewrite the rules from memory, but instead their efforts led to the development of what is now known as Sherman's Gallifreyan, which has become the dominant version of the circular written language. Sherman has developed it in stages, taking breaks when they were too busy at college and later at the university of MIT, and the written language has periodically been expanded into an ingenious and fairly comprehensive system. They have even devised systems for representing music and mathematical calculations.

Successful fan projects, as we have sometimes seen, can return to their roots and be embraced by the original work, and Sherman's Gallifreyan has indeed been taken up by the BBC. Although it is yet to be featured in the TV series, images have appeared on the official *Doctor Who* website and in promotional videos for various *Doctor Who*-related things.

Much to the fans' disappointment, it remained mostly poor Gallifreyan that lacked clear meaning. In some cases, it has at least been possible to guess the meaning; for example, there were circles reading **tattis thtating**, which is probably an attempt to write 'TARDIS crashing'. The BBC eventually succeeded in formulating a correct sentence in Sherman's Gallifreyan on the cover of a comic book about the Eleventh Doctor. What's more, it was a Sherlock Holmes quote: 'When you have eliminated the impossible, whatever remains, however improbable, must be the truth.'

Another fan-developed written language, Doctor's Cot Gallifreyan, has made an appearance in more official contexts. Doctor's Cot was developed by a designer in the United States, Brittany Goodman. She was fascinated by Sherman's Gallifreyan, but saw a clear image of written Gallifreyan on the Doctor's old cot in an episode of *Doctor Who* from 2011 and noticed that the characters differed from the symbols in Sherman's system. Goodman then developed her own version that was closer to the symbols in this particular episode. She took inspiration from her favourite language, Hebrew, and created not an alphabet, but an abjad – a consonant-only writing system.

This language wormed its way into an official context on a *Doctor Who* poster, where an accurate Cot Gallifreyan phrase appears discreetly in the background, translating to 'Bow ties are cool'. The only fly in the ointment is that the artist obviously just image-searched Gallifreyan and came upon symbols from another context.

A fourth version of a circular Gallifreyan writing system was produced by Nicola Fahey in 2013: Clockwork Gallifreyan. This language was designed to return to its roots, more closely emulating the original form, inspired by the clockwork in pocket watches. So far, this language has not been used in any official capacity, but it is certainly the version that comes closest to what is seen on the television series.

Of course, Whovians all over the world are eagerly waiting for the world's longest-running sci-fi series to display some readable Gallifreyan on screen, and maybe even hear it spoken. Who knows? The 2017 regeneration is certainly showing forward-thinking and fresh ideas anyway, because for the first time in thirteen incarnations, the Doctor is a woman.

Kryptonian

Just before the planet Krypton exploded, newborn baby Kal-El was sent away by his parents, Jor-El and Lara, in a spacecraft, after they foresaw the destruction of their planet through their research. The vessel carrying little Kal-El eventually landed on Earth, in a field where he was taken in by a farmer couple. Krypton's strong gravitational field and the resulting differences between the physiology of humans and Kryptonians, as well as the fact that Krypton orbited a red star (Rao), gives Kal-El superhuman powers. With these superpowers, Kal-El, or Clark Kent as his adoptive parents call him, grows up to become the mighty Superman.

Jerry Siegel and Joe Shuster are the creators of this DC Comics classic featuring Superman and the planet Krypton. Superman's home planet was first mentioned in 1938, but we've never found much out about it since. We know little about the written languages used, for example.

Since Superman's main medium has always been comic books, extraterrestrial languages can easily be symbolised using exotic writing characters in the speech bubbles, which is how Kryptonian speech was always represented. From the mid 1950s until 1986, when the series got a reboot, Kryptonian was represented by more or less random curves in speech bubbles.

Naturally, these titbits have aroused curiosity. Some fans have tried to decipher the speech bubbles while others have pondered how this Kryptonian language came about. To ensure continuity and internal logic throughout the various Superman stories, editor and screenwriter E. Nelson Bridwell had the editorial task of keeping track of all details about the planet Krypton. He was also responsible for answering readers' letters and received a number of enquiries from fans wondering whether they might ever create a readable Kryptonian alphabet with twenty-six squiggly letters, some of whom also provided their own suggestions. DC Comics were asked to publish the Kryptonian alphabet so often that Bridwell eventually replied, mainly to try to put an end to the recurring letters: 'That would be difficult, since the Kryptonian alphabet has 118 letters, and most of the words are longer than "supercalifragilisticexpialidocious".'

Of course, this just piqued fans' curiosity all the more. Now that they knew that Kryptonian had an alphabet with 118 letters, they inevitably began to wonder what these letters were, and what sounds they represented. Even Bridwell himself became curious and started going back and compiling all the fragments of Kryptonian that had appeared in the speech bubbles over the years, eventually putting together an alphabet with 118 characters!

Bridwell's creation wasn't well known during his lifetime. Superman super-fan Al Turniansky got to know Bridwell and was one of the people who cleared out his apartment when he passed away in 1987. Among Bridwell's papers on Kryptonian history, Turniansky found his compilation of the 118 characters that appeared in the series and the sounds associated with each one.

Thus, Al Turniansky saw himself as the guardian of the Kryptonian language and began developing a grammar and vocabulary for it. He intended to publish his work on the internet, but only managed to produce a simple bitmap font before his death. Unfortunately, his work on Kryptonian grammar and vocabulary was lost.

Later, American Kryptonian expert Darren Doyle created a neat and useful font of the classic 118 characters as a tribute to Bridwell and Turniansky.

When Superman made a comeback in 1986, his background and parts of the history of his home planet were also revised. Kryptonian was revived and now written with various geometric characters. But these letters were still only used randomly in the speech bubbles to mark the fact that they were now speaking Kryptonian.

It wasn't until 2000 that the Kryptonian symbols actually started to mean something. DC Comics created a typeface with the Kryptonian letters, designed by Georg Brewer, similar to the ones used in the series since 1986. But only the characters themselves were extraterrestrial – in fact, they corresponded directly to English letters and an only slightly altered form of English was used in the speech bubbles to represent Kryptonian. All speech in the language of Superman's home planet could now be read by anyone who could crack the code.

Darren Doyle grew up with this form of Kryptonian in comic books. The TV series *Smallville* (2001–11), about the young Clark Kent/Superman, also used this Kryptonian font, and Darren Doyle's fascination grew. He began to wonder what sounds the characters would represent if they were really writing in Kryptonian instead of English. He also mused on how numbers and mathematics might work on Krypton. So, in 2003, the foundation of a Kryptonian language began to emerge, although Doyle was not yet intending to develop it into a full conlang.

It wasn't until 2006, when Doyle took a course in constructed languages at the University of Texas, that he returned to this project and began expanding it. In his development of the language, Doyle tried to be faithful to the Superman canon and incorporate as much as possible from what is known about the planet Krypton – despite all the contradictions over the years – to make the language appropriate to the cultural conditions in which it would have come about. It has become an impressive fan language and Doyle's site, kryptonian.info, has become the centre for the study of the different languages on the planet Krypton.

However, not all of the examples of Kryptonian that have appeared over the years were incorporated into this language. For instance, the Kryptonian heard in the animated film *Superman/Batman: Apocalypse* (2010), which is used in a dialogue between Superman and his cousin, Supergirl, turned out to be essentially Esperanto(!) with a few made-up words.

Of the Kryptonian words that have appeared in the comic series over the years, it was primarily the names of people and places that gave Doyle an idea of Kryptonian phonology, such as Kal-El, Jor-El, Zor-El, Zod, Lara and the shrunken and stolen city of Kandor. But there were also a few Kryptonian words mentioned that gave Doyle something to work with:

drygur – elected leader
bythgur – queen
bethgar – king
tanth – sir
thrib – Kryptonian second
dendar – Kryptonian minute
wol – Kryptonian hour
zetyar – Kryptonian day

Also, Doyle knew that Kryptonian had a verb-subject-object word order, like Celtic languages for example, and the plural is formed with the suffix 'o'. In the TV series *Smallville*, logograms were eventually added to the simple code alphabet used in the comics.

Based on this, and his sound knowledge of the culture and history of Krypton, a Kryptonian language was developed. Doyle assigned sounds to the Kryptonian alphabet and meanings to the logograms. Most importantly, Doyle's Kryptonian is written with its extraterrestrial writing system; when Kryptonian is transcribed into Latin letters it is called 'Kryptonese':

'**.kaogahv skilorodh zhehd zw kehpes shokh**' – 'Let the person who knows the truth speak.'
(**.kaogahv** – 'allow', **skilorodh** – 'speak', **kehpes** – 'have', **shokh** – 'truth')
'**.rroshodh khuhp w rurrelahs bim**' – 'I am going home.'
(**.rroshodh** – 'go', **rurrelahs** – 'home', **bim** – 'to')

A new TV series in the Superman canon, *Supergirl*, began airing in 2015. It is about Kal-El's (Superman's) cousin, Kara Zor-El (Supergirl), who also ended up on Earth. In this TV series, the audience gets to hear Kryptonian spoken for the first time (not counting the Esperanto Kryptonian), based on Doyle's version of the language. The first line is:

'**ehl fidh I ehrosh :divi – ehl kypzrhig I raogrhys**' – 'Star, make my journey light. Star, build my power.'

At least, that was the idea. In reality, one of the screenwriters had just glanced at Doyle's language and tried to put a sentence together themselves, resulting in a phrase that was not grammatically correct. So Doyle reformulated the sentence in correct Kryptonian:

'**.,rao, sokaofidh nahn w khuhp I ehrosh ni :divi – .,rao, sokaokypzrhiges w khuhp raogrhys**'

For example, he changed **ehl** ('star') to **.,rao** (the star of the Krypton solar system).

Doyle even wrote on his blog that he was offering his services to help with future translations into Kryptonian in the TV series, but despite the number of Kryptonian lines featured in *Supergirl*, no one jumped at the chance to have real expert consultation, so the Kryptonian remained poor quality.

In 2013, a completely new and advanced Kryptonian written language appeared. Before production started on *Man of Steel* (2013), the film team decided they wanted to feature Kryptonian. They hired Dr Christine Schreyer, who teaches anthropological linguistics at the University of British Columbia in Canada, to develop a new and unique writing and speaking language for Krypton, distinct from previous versions of Kryptonian. Together with graphic designer Kirsten Franson, she designed a beautiful and complex written language that took inspiration from the syllabic writing of the Cree people. It is not an alphabet but an abugida, or alphasyllabary, in which symbols represent consonants with an accompanying built-in vowel. There are 153 character combinations to represent sounds – even more than the 118 characters of the classic Kryptonian alphabet.

The Kryptonian written language is richly represented in the film, but none of the lines recorded in Schreyer's Kryptonian made it on to screen. Schreyer has said that she created around 300 Kryptonian words for the film. She teaches a course on artificial languages such as Klingon and Na'vi and has recently been able to add her own artlang to the course syllabus.

Since the Kryptonian script is actually Schreyer's Kryptonian language, as opposed to mere atmospheric decoration, it is possible to interpret the writing in the film:

'mutɛ sã́odɪn guɹæn nika' – 'you are not alone'
'kæl ɛl mæ lum.ɹæ ju.dʒɛk.sɪɛ' – 'creates Kal-El's language'

The new Kryptonian writing language has also appeared in two subsequent films, but it is unclear whether it is used only as decoration, or if it is grammatically correct Kryptonian.

So, there are films with written but no spoken Kryptonian, and a TV show with another form of Kryptonian writing and a little bit of spoken, grammatically incorrect, fan-created Kryptonian!

Black Speech and Orkish

Black Speech, or the Dark Tongue of Mordor, as it is also known, is a constructed language, even in Tolkien's world. Its creator is the Dark Lord himself, Sauron, who needs an Esperanto of evil to facilitate communication among all the creatures of darkness. Much like in the case of Esperanto, however, Sauron's attempt to create a common lingua franca is unsuccessful and only the nine Nazgûl fully embrace the language.

There are very few examples of Black Speech, and the best known is of course the ring inscription:

ash nazg durbatulûk, ash nazg gimbatul, ash nazg thrakatulûk agh burzum-ishi krimpatul

'One Ring to rule them all, One Ring to find them, One Ring to bring them all and in the darkness bind them.'

ash – one
nazg – ring
durb-at-tu-lûk – 'to rule them all'
gim-ba-tul – 'to find them'
thraka-tu-lûk – 'to bring them all'
agh – and
burzum-ishi – 'in the darkness'
krim-pa-tul – 'to bind them'

Apart from the above, there are a few individual words and names and one sentence in Orkish, which is believed to be closely related to Black Speech – but that's all. Over the years, many skilled Tolkien linguists have interpreted and examined the little that exists of the Dark Tongue. Russian historian Alexander Nemirovski has pointed out its similarities to the extinct Hurrian language that was spoken in an area that stretched from present-day Eastern Turkey to present-day northern Iraq 3,000 years ago.

In the films, Peter Jackson needed more Black Speech and Orkish than was known at the time, so Elvish consultant David Salo worked on these languages too. Salo managed to find enough Black Speech to translate the entire 'Ring Verse'. The introductory line in his Neo-Black Speech reads:

shre nazg golugranu kilmi-nudu

We can recognise the word for 'ring' – **nazg** – which, by the way, seems to stem from **naškad** in the divine Valarin, Sauron's mother tongue. **Golugranu** consists of the word for 'Elf', **golug**, which comes from Sindarin **golodh**, meaning 'Noldor Elf', and **ran**, which probably shares its root with the Sindarin word for 'king' – **aran**, plus **u** meaning 'to/for', which makes sense in the context of what is known about the Black Speech. Salo invented these three words: **shre** – 'three'; **kilmi** – 'sky'; and **nudu** – 'under'. There may be an Elvish root word behind **nudu**, thus: 'Three rings for the Elven-kings under the sky.'

The second line, 'Seven for the Dwarf-lords in their halls of stone' becomes:

ombi kuzddurbagu gundum-ishi

for which Salo has borrowed two words from the Dwarves' language, Khuzdul: **kuzd** – 'Dwarf'; **-dum** – 'halls' (from Khazad-dûm – the Dwarves' subterranean halls).

He found the rest of the words in Black Speech, Elvish or his imagination:

durbagu – ruler (from the ring inscription, **durb** – 'rule')
ombi – seven (Salo's own invention)
gun – stone (possibly from an Elvish root word)
-ishi – in (from the ring inscription, **burzum-ishi** – 'in the darkness')

Just like his work with Dwarf language, Neo-Khuzdul, David Salo created a new, carefully considered and well-researched expansion of the language, rooted in Tolkien's other linguistic creations. How close Salo's constructions come to Tolkien's ideas is impossible to say, but he certainly didn't create them out of thin air.

David Salo also created various Orkish dialects for the films. The Orcs from Mordor, Moria and Isengard, as well as the Orcs in the Misty Mountains in the *Hobbit* films, all speak different but related dialects. The dialect of the Mordor Orcs is heavily influenced by the Black Speech while the Orcs from the Misty Mountains have the fewest Black Speech loanwords.

David Salo received instructions from the scriptwriters about the general feeling they wanted to convey through the dialects of the various Orcs. The language of the Mordor Orcs should be stiff and guttural and the Moria Orcs more secretive, whispering and hissing, while the Uruk-hai from Isengard should be more aggressive, hateful and disciplined.

Salo first created proto-Orkish root words and then developed the different dialects by applying rules for how the sounds changed over time. For example:

English	Proto-Orkish	Mordor	Isengard	Moria
war	*kutmu	kutum	Kūm	ūm
come	*lutu-	lutu-	ludu-	ruzu-
sun	*ūru	ūr	Ūr	ū3
flesh	*marna	marn	Mān	mān

(The Proto-Orkish words are marked with an asterisk to mark that it is a protolanguage not in use at the time in Middle-earth.)

For the later films, based on the adventures of the Hobbit Bilbo, Salo created even more Orkish dialects that differ from the three examples above. It is entirely in the spirit of Tolkien that the Orcs would speak different dialects, which are often a variant on the local language. Sauron's attempt to launch the Dark Tongue of Mordor as a lingua franca didn't work, but some loanwords from the Black Speech have stuck in the vocabulary of various forms of Orkish.

Black Speech Dialects in Live-Action Role Play

David Salo is not the only person who has put time and thought into the Black Speech and Orkish. Some people actually want to speak Orkish on the weekends. Many of the popular live-action role-play (LARP) games are set in a Tolkien-esque world, where players can choose to play as Elves, Dwarves, Hobbits or Orcs. Some players spend a lot of time learning LARP's version of a conlang, usually Elvish or Orkish. When it comes to the various Elvish languages, players tend to just memorise words and phrases that are only loosely based on Quenya or Sindarin – they are usually individual words joined together and inflected with a simplified grammar.

As for the language of the Orcs, there isn't much to go on, as previously mentioned. In the 1990s, a role-playing game appeared called *Middle-earth Role Playing*, which came with a glossary containing some new words. Based on this, and the words that have come out of Swedish LARP culture, Mikael 'Adragoor' Bynke in the late 1990s constructed and systematised the language Uruk Gîjab, or *Svartiska* in Swedish, which might translate literally as 'Blackese'.

The language achieved great success in LARP circles and spread far beyond Sweden. And while Black Speech words are most often used with Swedish grammar, there is also a complex grammar and thought behind the language. It borrowed vocabulary from another fan variant of the Black Speech, Mugbûrz, so different Orc clans came to speak different dialects depending on which words they used and how close to Black Speech their grammar was. LARPer Pierre Fröberg published two books in his *Blackblood Series*, in which Orcs were the protagonists and their dialogue was printed in the author's own variant of 'Blackese', based on the vocabulary of Uruk Gîjab.

In 2011–12, a LARP group called 'Utumno' made an ambitious attempt to create a new Black Speech – which was almost as ambitious as Tolkien himself. Accepting Alexander Nemirovski's theory that Tolkien's Black Speech was based on the long-extinct Hurrian language, the group felt this was an appropriate starting point. They also acknowledged and respected Bynke's Uruk Gîjab, which was the leading LARP language at the time, but saw this more as a variant of Orkish than as a true dark lingua franca. Utumno's resulting dialect was a mixture of Black Speech and Hurrian. For the most part, they used Uruk Gîjab vocabulary but tried to recreate the Black Speech with Hurrian grammar. An impressive grammar and introduction to Utumno's variant of the Black Speech was compiled, but it is unclear how widespread this version actually became.

Part of the great success achieved by Bynke's Black Speech dialect was because it had a vast vocabulary of over 3,000 words. This meant that other versions of fan-constructed Black Speech borrowed words that they were missing from their own lexicons. One of the major international variants, Shadowlandian Black Speech, has incorporated Uruk Gîjab into its language as well as other language variants such as Mugbûrz and Horngoth.

A few examples from *Svartiska*/Blackese:

'**Laug ti za-bagronk-ishi.**' – 'Laug is in the cesspit.'
bagronk – latrine

-ishi – in
'**gur ti latob durub.**' – 'I am your ruler.'
durub – ruler (derived from the **durbatulûk** – 'to rule
them')
gur krimp-at-ul – 'I shackled'
krimp-at-ul – shackled/bound (verb in imperfect tense,
from the Ring Verse's **krimpatul** – 'bind them', but with
-ul interpreted as an imperfect suffix)

As fans analyse the lines in the *Hobbit* trilogy and David Salo
publishes more of his work on the Black Speech and Orkish
dialects on his blog, Salo's thoughts and vocabulary will likely
be incorporated into the major fan languages, in keeping with
the collaborative tradition that has characterised the fan culture
around Black Speech dialects thus far.

Conlanging as an Art Form

Finally, a few words about another group of fans who could
be described as language artists. Conlang is an abbreviation of
'constructed languages', and fans who create their own invented
languages are often called conlangers. They build languages for
their own sake, with no intention of their personal language
projects becoming new world languages or having any other
practical benefit.

Conlanging is often described as an art form – language
art. By this logic, Esperanto creator, Zamenhof or Klingon
creator Okrand, cannot be considered typical conlangers,
even though they have created some of the most successful
artificial languages of all time – but Tolkien can. He was a
typical conlanger, or language artist, in that he created his
own languages throughout his life purely as an art form.
Tolkien had no intention for his languages other than his own
immense pleasure.

The internet has facilitated an explosion in conlanging as a hobby. It suddenly became easy to show off homemade languages to a wider circle. In fact, the internet has been the real driving force in the development of the fan culture around conlangs. Prior to 1991, conlangers were solitary types, usually creating and refining their conlangs in their bedrooms. Most never showed their creations to anyone else. But in 1991 an email list called the Conlang Listserv was set up and, slowly but surely, conlangers began to make contact with each other. The Conlang Listserv also coined the term 'conlang', taking the first syllables from 'constructed' and 'language', simply because they needed a short name for the list server. Pretty soon the list splintered into various factions of conlangers with differing views on conlang's true purpose. Just as with fanfiction, there is now a widespread co-creation culture. If a conlanger gets stuck there is prompt feedback and help available.

The languages often accompany fictitious worlds. There is a closely related fan culture called conworlding; that is, people creating fantasy worlds for fun.

It is not uncommon for conlangers to have several different conlangs published on the internet, which they update occasionally. Most of these conlangs probably exist only in written form, and it is impossible to say how many are spoken by anyone other than their creators. Getting people to speak their language is certainly not a goal in itself for most conlangers; it is more about having an outlet for their creative urges or exploring linguistic concepts.

For example, there is a Swedish conlang project that explores whether it is possible to build a common language for modern pagans, called *Heden Tunge* – 'heathen tongue'. In this case, the conlanger looks at the form of a word in a range of languages – English, German, Dutch, Norwegian, Danish and Swedish – notices the similarities, and creates a mishmash version. It is a sort of pagan auxiliary language.

Heden tunge er en helpe tunge for heden folker. Kanna du grijpa?

How would a half-Japanese, half-English language look? It might look something like artlang Nunihongo. Or what about a language that is only for expressing positive thoughts, perhaps something like minimalist language Toki Pona, with only 125 words, based on Taoist philosophy. Or imagine a language without verbs, like Kēlen, or one that consists only of vowels, like Aeo:

ae – I
aoao – water
oaeoeoeaoe – the sun

All imaginable variants of possible and impossible languages have been dreamt up and tried out by conlangers, constructing their languages bit by bit. It might be a quick sketch or a project that spans decades. Creating your own language often means learning about linguistics and understanding how languages work, and many conlangers become linguists if they aren't already, or at least fan scholars.

Naturally, there is a society for conlangers, the Language Creation Society, which collects literature and holds talks and conferences. Unsurprisingly, their symbol is the Tower of Babel set against a backdrop of the rising sun. They also have a small employment agency, where writers or directors can advertise if they need a language for their book or television series, for example.

With the growing thirst for artlangs in literature and film, a niche labour market has opened up. As previously mentioned, David J. Peterson, who developed the languages for *Game of Thrones*, was chairman of the Language Creation Society and had been involved in conlanging for many years before winning the contest to develop Dothraki for the television series. Now, Peterson is the only person in the world making a full-time living out of conlanging, primarily for film and TV. His hobby became a profession.

Unlike most linguists hired to invent languages for television series, Peterson had built several complex conlangs before getting his first paid job. He already knew how to make a conlang seem 'natural'. When journalists and other curious types ask him about the languages that inspired Dothraki and Valyrian, Peterson referred to his earlier creations. He is inspired by his own conlangs rather than real languages! In his book, *The Art of Language Invention* (2015), he guides the reader through the basics of linguistics necessary for creating a conlang, and the examples of grammatical features come from real languages as well as his own.

In the decade since he created Dothraki, Peterson has been hired to create more than twenty different languages for a number of TV series and a few films. For the science-fiction series *Defiance* (2013), which ran for three seasons, Peterson created three languages. First, he was commissioned to create two extraterrestrial languages for the most prevalent aliens in the series, the Castithans and Irathients, for which his only instructions were that the difference between the languages be obvious. Naturally, this set Peterson's conlanging imagination in motion and he decided to create two languages that were each other's opposites; one would place the head word first in the sentence and the other last, one would be spoken quickly and the other slowly, etc. The series also asked Peterson, much to his delight, to create written languages, which is his greatest passion. Dothraki is not a written language and the only trace of Valyrian writing in the television series uses Latin letters (whereas Peterson imagines a Valyrian writing system reminiscent of hieroglyphs).

A recurring feature of the languages Peterson constructs is that he sneaks in tributes to his wife, Erin Allegra Peterson:

High Valyrian	**erinagon**	to win
Dothraki	**erin**	friendly
	alegra	duck
Castithan	**erino**	tea
Irathient	**erin**	knitting needle
Indojisnen	**erin**	water
Shiväisith	**erin**	tree
Sondiv	**eren**	balance

Peterson has also held contests on his blog – for example for the best haiku in Dothraki or Valyrian – where sometimes the prize is the chance to become a word in one of his languages. That is, Peterson would adapt the winner's given name to fit into the language.

Of course, for many conlangers, creating languages for TV and film is the dream. And although the market for such languages has exploded in recent years, it is still very small. But Peterson reminds us that there are plenty of science-fiction and fantasy writers, like George R.R. Martin, who are not conlangers themselves, but need languages for their books. Connecting authors with conlangers would be fruitful for everyone.

Conlanging often goes hand in hand with an interest in artlangs of popular culture. Most conlangers draw inspiration from the plethora of worlds and alien civilisations in books, films and TV series, and build on them in much the same way as those who write fanfiction.

So, curiosity about an artificial language in popular culture is not all that different from curiosity about what happens to the characters after the book or series ends. If you are passionate about a story or a world and want to know more (or even, everything) about it, a language can give profound insight into the literary or cinematic works from whence it came. Or you could have a go at making the language yourself.

Bibliography

Adams, Michael (ed.), *From Elvish to Klingon: Exploring Invented Languages* (Oxford: Oxford University Press, 2011).

Besson, Luc, and Andrew Wildman, *The Story of the Fifth Element* (London: Titan Books, 1997).

Burtt, Ben, *Galactic Phrase Book & Travel Guide* (New York: Del Rey, 2001).

Conely, Tim, and Stephen Cain, *Encyclopedia of Fictional and Fantastic Languages* (Westport, CT: Greenwood Press, 2006).

Elgin, Suzette Haden, *A First Dictionary and Grammar of Laadan* (Society for the Furtherance and Study of Fantasy and Science Fiction Inc., 1985).

Gardner, Mark R., *The Vulcan Language* (Raleigh, NC: Lulu Publishing, 2011).

McNelly, Willis (ed.), *The Dune Encyclopedia: The Complete, Authorized Guide and Companion to Frank Herbert's Masterpiece of the Imagination* (New York: Berkley Books, 1984).

Meyer, Walter E., *Aliens and Linguists, Language Study and Science Fiction* (Athens, GA: University of Georgia Press, 1980).

Okrand, Marc, *The Klingon Dictionary* (New York: Pocket Books, 1985).

Okrand, Marc, *The Klingon Way* (New York: Pocket Books, 1996).

Okrand, Marc, *Klingon for the Galactic Traveler* (New York: Pocket Books, 1997).

Okrent, Arika, *In the Land of Invented Languages: Adventures in Linguistic Creativity, Madness, and Genius* (New York: Spiegel & Grau, 2009).

Peterson, David J., *Living Language Dothraki: A Conversational Language Course* (Living Language, 2014).

Peterson, David J., *The Art of Language Invention: From Horse-Lords to Dark Elves, the Words Behind World-Building* (New York: Penguin Books, 2015).

Salo, David, *A Gateway to Sindarin: A Grammar of an Elvish Language from J.R.R. Tolkien's* Lord of the Rings (Salt Lake City, UT: University of Utah Press, 2004).

Smith, Wu Kee, *How to Speak Wookiee: A Manual for Intergalactic Communication* (San Francisco, CA: Chronicle Books, 2011).

Rogers, Stephen D., *A Dictionary of Made-Up Languages* (Avon, MA: Adams Media, 2011).

Rosenfelder, Mark, *The Language Construction Kit* (Chicago, IL: Yonagu Books, 2010).

Roy, John Flint, *A Guide to Barsoom* (New York: Ballantine Books, 1976).

Wahlgren, Yens, *Klingon as Linguistic Capital: A Sociologic Study of Nineteen Advanced Klingonists* [Hol Sup 'oH tlhIngan Hol'e' wa'maH Hut tlhIngan Hol po'wI' nughQeD] (Lund: Lund University, 2004).

Index of Languages